Joseph S. Park

AS/400 Security in a Client/Server Environment

John Wiley & Sons, Inc.
New York • Chichester • Brisbane • Toronto • Singapore

Associate Publisher: Katherine Schowalter
Editor: Theresa Hudson
Managing Editor: Mark Hayden
Text Design & Composition: SunCliff Graphic Productions

Designations used by companies to distinguish their products are often claimed as trademarks. In all instances where John Wiley & Sons, Inc. is aware of a claim, the product names appear in initial capital or all capital letters. Readers, however, should contact the appropriate companies for more complete information regarding trademarks and registration.

This text is printed on acid-free paper.

Copyright © 1995 by John Wiley & Sons, Inc.

All rights reserved. Published simultaneously in Canada.

This publication is designed to provide accurate and authoritative information in regard to the subject matter covered. It is sold with the understanding that the publisher is not engaged in rendering legal, accounting, or other professional service. If legal advice or other expert assistance is required, the services of a competent professional person should be sought.

Reproduction or translation of any part of this work beyond that permitted by section 107 or 108 of the 1976 United States Copyright Act without the permission of the copyright owner is unlawful. Requests for permission or further information should be addressed to the Permission Department, John Wiley & Sons, Inc.

Library of Congress Cataloging-in-Publication Data

Park, Joseph S., 1960–
    AS/400 security in a client/server environment / Joseph S. Park.
      p.   cm
    Includes index.
    ISBN 0-471-11683-1 (paper/disk)
    1. IBM AS/400 (Computer).   2. Computer security.   3. Client/server computing.
I. Title.
QA76.8.I25919P29   1995   95-4057
005.8—dc20   CIP

Printed in the United States of America
10 9 8 7 6 5 4 3 2 1

This book is dedicated to WooSoon Park, who instilled in her children her thirst for knowledge and devotion to education. Her sacrifice made it possible for her children to succeed. And to those who color my world bright with the joy of laughter and love—Cheryl, Joey, Jerrica, and Christopher.

J. Park
June 1995

Contents

Preface xi
Acknowledgments xiii

PART ONE Management 1

CHAPTER ONE The Assault 3

The FS Project 7
Layers and Layers 9
Objects and Files 11
Scope of Security 12
The Dream Team 13
Horses, Worms, and Viruses 14
The Objective 15

CHAPTER TWO System Values 17

Security Levels 17
Password Controls 23
Security Controls 25
Audit Controls 28

CHAPTER THREE User Profiles 33

Profiles and Portraits 34
Work Groups 35
Secret Passwords 37
Other Significant Threats 39

CHAPTER FOUR Object Management 43

Anatomy of an Object 43
Ownership Authority 45
Public Authority 46
Private Authority 46
Authorization Lists 47
Authority Holders 48
Authority Adoption 49
Primary Group Authority 52

CHAPTER FIVE Communication Management 55

Fundamental Concepts 57
User Exits 59
Client/Server Connections 60
Shared Folders 62
Integrated File System 63
PC Workstations 65
Data Encryption 66
Device Configuration 67

CONTENTS vii

CHAPTER SIX Client/Server Issues 69

Client/Server Concept 70
Client Platforms 72
C/S Role Topology 73
C/S Environment Security 74
Folder Object Security 75
Application Object Security 77
Dataset Object Security 79
Function Object Security 80
Function Option Security 80
Field Object Security 81
Data Security 83
Portable Clients 83

CHAPTER SEVEN Object States and Domains 87

Background 88
Program Compilation Process 90
The Road Less Traveled 91
MI Purpose 93
A for Effort 95
The Solution 98
In Practice 100

CHAPTER EIGHT Impact of Altered Objects 103

The Worst Enemy 110
Eminent Domain 112
Altered State 113

CHAPTER NINE Program Validation Values 117

CHAPTER TEN The Core War 127

PART TWO Implementation 129

CHAPTER ELEVEN Physical Security 131

Phone Phreaks 132
Local Switches 133
Protocol Analyzers 134
Encryption Devices 137
Conclusion 138

CHAPTER TWELVE System Values 139

Adjustments 139
Password Validation 142
Recommendations 143

CHAPTER THIRTEEN Designing Profiles 155

Work Groups 156
Application Groups 157
Group Profiles 157
User Profiles 158
Primary Groups 159

CONTENTS ix

Exception Management 163
Technical Profiles 165
Data Processing Operations 167
Application Development 168
Network Administration 170
Security Management 170
Customer Support 171

CHAPTER FOURTEEN   Authority Management   173

Objects 173
Libraries 175
Job Descriptions 176
Saved Objects 178
Restored Objects 178
System Objects 179

CHAPTER FIFTEEN   Backup and Recovery   183

Saving Security Data 183
Recovering Security Data 184
Restoring Objects 185
Restoring Programs 186

PART THREE   Auditing   189

CHAPTER SIXTEEN   System Values   191

Security Audit Journals 192
Resource Accounting Journals 193

CHAPTER SEVENTEEN   User Profiles   195

Indefinite Password Duration   195
Invalid Signon Attempts   196
System Profiles with Passwords   197
Privileged Users with Unlimited Access   198
Patched User Profiles   199
Group Profile Audit   199

CHAPTER EIGHTEEN   Resource Usage Audit   201

Establishing Security Journals   202
System Audit Journals   204
Program Failure Journals   206
Authority Adoption Audit   206

CHAPTER NINETEEN   Soul of a Hacker   209

Cold Calls   210
Curious Staff   211
Parlor Tricks   212
Gift Horses   213

APPENDIX   Sample Programs   223

Bibliography   279

Index   283

Preface

This book focuses on AS/400 security; in doing so it also discusses design, architecture, and the philosophy behind one of the most successful business computer systems on the market today. The book follows the evolution of the AS/400 from its earlier System/38 days, and looks ahead to the future and the Advanced Series.

Most AS/400 professionals are convinced that their AS/400s are secure from tampering, provided that they practice reasonable security measures outlined in the Security Management manual. The very idea that AS/400s are just as vulnerable as other computers to "attacks" by software developers or hackers is looked upon as blasphemous. Since the architecture of the AS/400 disallows creation of any low-level programs, all programs created must abide by the operating system rules, which, in turn, may be controlled by the system security officer; hence, no virus should conceivably go undetected or even be created...so the myth goes.

This book is for all those who believe in that myth. It is also for newcomers and seasoned veterans who would like to know more about how to secure their systems. But most of all, this book is for those who spread that myth—through their denial, they inadvertently pose the greatest risk. This book will challenge the most thorough security administrator's auditing procedures and provide a frightening wake-up call to the rest of the AS/400 community.

This book is also for managers. It recognizes the needs of business and acknowledges that there are as many forms of security as there are shades of gray. Risks and contingencies associated with too little security are discussed while bearing in mind business's need to run smoothly on a day-to-day basis. Although too much secutiry can hamper operations, there are areas that should never be compromised; this book will define those areas. Management's participation and endorsement is imperative for any security policy to succeed. Just as a technician has the responsibility to consider the business when making the case for or against a particular purchase, it is management's responsibility to understand the cost of intangible threats and benefits that often surround information technology. Without cooperation and support from management, the best security plan will suffer.

It seems quite apparent that the AS/400 is fast becoming the mid-range platform of choice. It is also apparent that more and more people are creating software on the AS/400 that will outperform, out-function, and simply "out-slick" older, more traditional software. These days the AS/400 is not only tasked to be user-friendly, like a PC, but also to provide solid mainframe security, stability, and reliability. IBM is advertising AS/400s as file servers, mid-range business computers, and, in some cases, low- to mid-sized mainframes. AS/400 is supporting the open systems concept, POSIX environment and C languages are supported, and TCP/IP communication protocols are offered as an alternative to the traditional SNA protocols. IBM is not just trying to establish the AS/400 as a business machine; they are committed to making the AS/400 the premier file server to client/server networks, the epitome of the mid-range business world, and the distributed database management solution for downsizing mainframe machines. In this highly lucrative, competitive, and fast-paced environment, everyone is trying to gain technical advantages—no matter what it takes. AS/400 is no longer looked upon as simply a follow-on to a "cult" machine.

Those who have been assured of the integrity of the AS/400 should not become complacent, but should prepare themselves for the same level of invasion by hackers previously experienced by those in the PC and mainframe worlds. Those clever systems programmers who once undermined the System/38 haven't disappeared. And as the AS/400 flowers into popularity, the best of hackers from all kinds of platforms will gather to cut their teeth on your machine—at your expense.

One of the primary goals of this book is to illustrate and recommend sound security guidelines established on theories and principles that govern the dissemination of information. Another is to fulfill a moral obligation to inform the public of the potential threat to security without fostering or proliferating that threat. In a perfect world, neither of these issues would need to be addressed. However, since we don't live in a perfect world, this book goes beyond reiterating variations on manufacturer's recommendations for security explore the improbables and the impossibles—no matter how unlikely they may appear to the average user.

Acknowledgments

I wish to acknowledge the contributions of Ronald J. Harvey and Steven P. Richardson for their insight and advice. I would also like to thank John Wiley & Sons, for providing their assistance and the opportunity to write this book. Most of all, I am grateful to my wife Cheryl, without whom this book would still be but a pile of technical gobbledygook.

PART ONE

Management

This section of the book is written specifically with a management staff in mind. Its function is to explain the security issues surrounding the various aspects of the AS/400 without drowning readers with technical terms and nitty-gritty details. It allows managers to visualize the threat and exposes the myths and misconceptions surrounding commonly held ideas about security. It also details the history of the AS/400, its purpose, and the reason for its successful growth; it is much easier to understand today's AS/400 if we view its development from its inception. In order to illustrate abstract concepts and make the technical information accessible to all readers, the management section utilizes many figures and tables. Specific technical recommendations and auditing procedures are not discussed in detail in this section, but rather are deferred until later chapters; however, the weaknesses of the AS/400's security system are discussed here in some detail. To that extent, the management issues outlined in this section address the complete picture of AS/400 security, from the traditional resource authorization models to today's client/server environments, and the details of the most secret and seldom discussed questions pertaining to the AS/400's system integrity—where viruses live. By reading this section alone, management personnel may gain a thorough, conceptual, and nontechnical view of what to consider when securing an AS/400.

CHAPTER ONE

The Assault

> Don enters the computer room and sits in his usual chair. Behind him looms an AS/400 F70 with five racks of assorted peripherals. The room is cluttered with cables, modems, and patch panels. In one corner behind the patch panels sits an impressive battery backup unit blinking "Ready" in its amber LCD window. Don stares at the console, trying to remember the security officer's password. The clock reads 8:30 A.M., Monday morning. Laser printers are still spitting out reports from jobs that were executed over the weekend. He strikes the Enter key a few times and turns his head to scan the 8mm tape unit, making sure it's in the unloaded position. The job scheduler he had purchased some time ago makes his life a lot simpler by automatically backing up all user information to a tape every night.
>
> The computer room is already heating up from the AS/400, affectionately named Miss Piggy. Don is the only one who really understands Miss Piggy; after all, he was the one who watched as she came to life four years ago. He takes a sip of coffee and refreshes the active jobs screen, watching as the first of the day's users sign on. Soon there will be over a hundred users, all demanding their reports at once. Through the computer room window, he can see the clerks and accountants gathering around the coffee pot. The usual morning ritual has begun.

4 MANAGEMENT

The little green processor light flickers now and then and the worn out disk drives are whining to life as the phone rings. Debbie from the Accounts Payable department is having a problem. She explains that the option she is using to list the reports she had created doesn't work—even though it seemed to be fine just a few minutes ago. "Jeez, Monday," Don thinks to himself. He'll humor her. Instead of asking her whether her CapsLock key is on, he asks for the name of the report so that he can print it for her himself. He enters the command to list all outstanding reports on the system. To his surprise, he finds himself looking at a list of submitted jobs. "Must be some kind of mistake," he mutters as he tries again. It happens again. He leans back into the chair staring dazedly at the screen. He takes another sip of coffee. "So help me, if Steve is pulling another one of his infantile pranks. . . ." He picks up the phone and dials. His irritation fades as he realizes that Steve is not the culprit. As he lowers the phone, Greg and Dave walk in, complaining that their jobs are dumping. The phone rings again; no one from the third floor can sign on. Miss Piggy's processor light glows brightly. Don refreshes his screen once again. This time, however, the console freezes up. He waits, not knowing what to do. Steve arrives with a few more annoyed users. The computer room is now filled with users watching Don watching the machine. Finally, the yellow system attention light comes on and the dreaded code 11 shows in Miss Piggy's LCD panel. It's going to be a long week. Don resignedly approaches the LCD panel. He focuses on the system reference code and begins to copy down the numbers on a scrap of paper. He can sense the bewilderment on people's faces and the silent blame directed at him from the crowd gathered behind him.

The IBM customer engineer arrives around noon and reboots the system. The SRC code says the problem is the operating system. The CE recommends reloading the operating system from the last system backup. Don locates the last system backup tapes while the CE proceeds to dump the main storage, to be sent to Rochester Labs. After several hours, the system comes back to life. Whatever the problem was, it's almost over.

Don signs on from the console, browses the active jobs list, and displays the output queues and the system status. Everything seems to run normally. With a sigh, he starts up the printers and enters a request to bring up the output queues again. Instead, a list of jobs fills his screen. It's happening again. The backup was no good. In a cold sweat, Don searches for the oldest system backup tapes. This is his last chance—the original operating system tapes have long been recycled. There are no archived system tapes, just non-system tapes. After all, there had never been a reason to keep the old system tapes. If these tapes don't work, Miss Piggy is going to be down for a while. Don reloads the operating system tapes long after everyone has gone home. The CE has determined that there is no hardware problem. Don is instructed to contact his systems engineer if he needs further assistance. Never in his career has he experienced this kind of a problem. Sure, he's had his share of HDA (Head and Disk Assembly) failures, but an operating system failure for no apparent reason? This was just too funky.

It takes nearly six hours to reload the operating system and recover from the previous crash. Don stares at the sign-on screen for a moment and quietly hopes that this nightmare is over. He takes a deep breath and signs on, then retraces the exact commands he had used some twelve hours ago. He watches the processor light flickering on and off intermittently with every command. Suddenly his heart sinks to the floor as he reads a message that says, all too simply, that the operating system program is dumping. In disbelief he watches the processor light race madly. Miss Piggy has died once again.

Steve has almost finished loading a brand new copy of the operating system from the local IBM branch office when Don arrives the next morning. The memo that Don had left the night before made it clear that there were no clean system tapes available on site. Steve asks why the backup tapes didn't work. Obviously the operating system was in working order when the backup ran. Could that mean the operating system is not really the problem, and something else is turning Miss Piggy into a vegetable? Could it be a virus? Neither of the two really believes such a thing, because everyone knows that viruses can't be created on AS/400s.

After another full day of unsuccessful reloads, IBM first-level support decides to take a look. The folks from the customer services lab dial in and take a snapshot of what they think is a SEPTWorm—a worm

> that attaches itself to the System Entry Point Table and propagates itself to another location within the spinal column of the AS/400 operating system every time someone uses an infected command. Once the system is infected, there is no way to fix the problem. The only thing to do is to reload the operating system.
>
> Apparently, the backup system tapes were either good tapes or contained a dormant virus; otherwise, the operating system from the backup tapes could not have reactivated Miss Piggy. On the other hand, if the system backup tapes didn't contain a dormant virus, the virus may still be on the system, lurking in one of the user libraries. But which library? What would the virus look like? Would they be able to identify it? They reach the inevitable conclusion that nothing on the system can be trusted. The SEPTWorm must be neutralized, but how? Where is it? What command triggers it? How did it get in the machine? How many times will they have to reload? If they can't disinfect it, what are their alternatives? An AS/400 is not a PC that a company can do without or easily replace. It often controls the very survival of a company. How will Don explain this? What could he have done to avoid the disaster? Just how much will this virus cost?

This scenario is just an example; the tools to create such a virus exist on every AS/400. A single programmer who can read IBM manuals has all the tools necessary to destroy an entire system like Don's. However, AS/400 professionals often have a difficult time believing that such a thing is possible—which is absurd, when you consider that the technical skills involved in creating such a virus are no more complicated than those used to create a mailing label program. The differentiating factor is *persistence*, not intelligence.

The probability of an intentionally created, harmful program grows every day. There were over 250,000 AS/400s worldwide as of May 1994. If we consider an average of four programmers for every AS/400, including consultants, there are approximately 1 million AS/400 programmers. If the brightest 10 percent of these programmers are at least familiar with the AS/400 Machine Interface language, and if we further assume that only 10 percent of those programmers have worked with the System

Entry Point Table, that still leaves as many as 10,000 programmers who are capable of creating a program that could disable a system like the one in the example. Think of it—10,000 tenacious, type A personalities. If we give all but 1 percent the benefit of the doubt, there remain at least 100 AS/400 programmers who have the wherewithal to introduce these kinds of vile creations, guaranteed to wreak havoc at any security level. What members of any IS department should be concerned about is not *whether* these kinds of viruses can be created, but rather *when* such a virus will manage to infiltrate their system.

The ramifications of the situation in the example are grim. Without the ability to locate and destroy the SEPTWorm, the operations manager has very little choice. He will have to save what data he can and reload every program from the original distribution tapes. Any software developed in-house will have to be recompiled, and data files will have to be repopulated from the backup. Still, there is the possibility that the virus occupies a purchased software package. Maybe it was even designed to activate one year from the time it was installed on the system. How will Don know next year which piece of software was the culprit? Perhaps he will think the virus has been reintroduced during the course of the year. In the meantime, business suffers. Poor Don may beg to be fired—at least he won't have to deal with this mess! The owners of this business, however, will not be able to escape so easily. They are in for the duration.

The FS Project

The basic architecture of the AS/400 was designed by a small team of specially selected individuals from IBM's key divisions. They were part of a new Advanced Systems Development Division (ASDD), which was personally created by Frank Cary in 1973, with Jack Bertrum as the president. The project was code-named the "Future Systems" project, its intention, to replace the current IBM mainframe systems. This team was tasked to create a new machine that would "leap frog" the existing hardware and software technology. Jack Bertrum had his pick of people from any of IBM's labs in technical and marketing divisions throughout the world. The idea of integrating applications that were traditionally purchased separately from third-party vendors originated from this group. However, one of the group's cardinal rules was that IBM would not break its promise to the System/370 community—customers would not have to suffer through another painful conversion to a new box as they had done converting from the System/360 machines.

The new machine's operating system was born of a totally new concept, called *object design*. When it was clear that the new operating system could not support the existing System/370 environment, the Advanced Systems Development Division abandoned the project. Some months later the General Systems Division inherited the prototype system and eventually completed it. The resulting machine, called the System/38, debuted in 1979. Though it initially suffered from much criticism, both deserved and undeserved, the System/38 matured, developing a cult of very loyal users (roughly 20,000 to 30,000 by the mid-1980s).

System/38 boasted an integrated relational database that rivaled the DB2 on the mainframe. However, no one noticed. What IBM did not advertise was the object-oriented architecture of the System/38. The traditional assembler interface, as it existed in System/370 BAL (Basic Assembly Language), was not allowed. Only high-level language compilers were available on this machine. This was not an oversight on IBM's part—the machine was purposely designed to isolate its lower depths from users and programmers alike. However, aspiring System/38 programmers requested and received much technical documentation from Rochester Labs (the birthplace of the System/38 and the AS/400). IBM was more than glad to provide any and all information about the System/38, since it was still struggling to establish itself as a mid-range business system. As time went by, the more adventurous System/38 programmers discovered the layers beneath the high-level languages and started to explore. Eventually, a few found their way into the resident operating system translator, called the Program Resolution Monitor.

When the AS/400 was announced on June 21, 1988, many System/36 and System/38 businesses chose to migrate to the new system. Those familiar with the System/38 had a much easier time, since the AS/400 was, in most senses, a System/38 with a new paint job. IBM never offered any real internal technical documentation on the AS/400. IBM's plan for the AS/400 seemed to be to make a slow transition from a fault-tolerant concept machine of the past to the strategic mid-range system of the future.

By the time version 1 release 3 of the operating system was shipped, there was clear indication that the AS/400 had system integrity problems. The Machine Interface layer was being exploited by system programmers and hackers who managed to gain authorities and access to restricted areas. So IBM introduced a concept similar to that of the Program Status Word originally used to ensure the integrity of the System/370 machines. Although the implementation was necessarily different than on the System/370, the concept was the same: system and user state processing based on program status flags. Version 1 release 3 of the OS/400 operating system introduced a program validation value to ensure the integrity of executable objects, and a "user vs. system" domain to ensure that all non-executable objects could not be directly accessed by user-written programs without the operating system's assistance. After release 3 of the operating system, IBM discontinued version 1 of the operating system and released version 2 release 1. Version 3 was introduced in 1994; it's rumored that the version 3 operating system will also cease to exist and the AS/400 models with 128-bit RISC chips running version 4 of OS/400 will succeed it.

Layers and Layers

In order to discuss various aspects of the AS/400's security, one has to understand some of its most basic design issues. The AS/400's operating system employs a layered architecture, which means, in lay terms, that there exist logical divisions of duties performed by different sections of the operating system. For example, the portion of the operating system that interacts directly with its users, from clerks to programmers, is known as the OS/400 layer. OS/400 programs are designed to enforce certain rules and regulations, resulting in a standardized interface to the lower layer of system programs, much the way a waiter or waitress takes an order from a customer and translates the request into cook's shorthand for processing in the kitchen. Because of this type of division of duties, the user has no way to directly interact with the "cook."

When System/38 was created, it left behind the traditional Monolithic Operating System model (Figure 1.1) and established a new Layered Operating System concept (Figure 1.2), which limited each layer to access

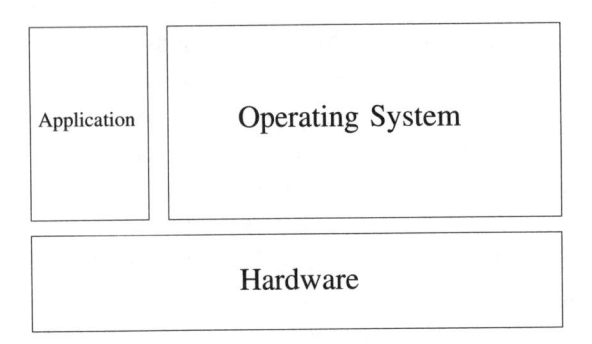

Figure 1.1 Monolithic operating system design.

the layer immediately below itself. This meant that no one program could harness the power of the lowest level hardware controls and the highest level user interfaces. Instead, lower level programs served the higher level programs in completing a desired task. It also meant that each layer could be created, debugged, or replaced independently without interrupting the other layers. By using this layered design, the OS/400 is able to protect the integrity of objects that it creates by providing specific methods by which they are created. This process is known as *object encapsulation*.

Among the various encapsulation procedures, the program compilation procedure is often used to illustrate the separation of layers. In the program compilation process, each program's source codes (RPG, COBOL, PL/I, etc.) are first compiled into common intermediate texts by individual compilers. Then an OS/400 service program known as the Program Resolution Monitor (PRM) assembles the intermediate text into a stream of binary codes that represents the intermediate text. This binary

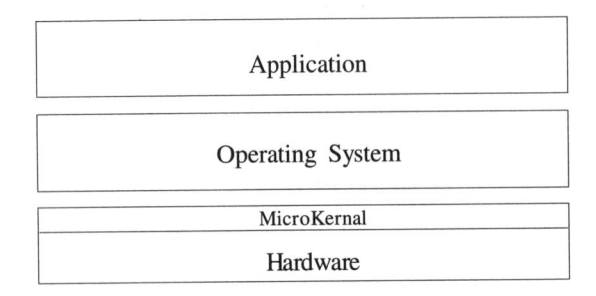

Figure 1.2 Layered operating system design.

stream is called a Machine Interface (MI) template. The MI template is further translated into executable instructions by an assembler module and packaged along with other attributes of the program in a structure defined as encapsulated object architecture. The OS/400 does not allow users to intervene in the object creation process, thereby completely isolating high-level requests from lower level services. This design has a fundamental impact on the implementation of security on the AS/400.

Objects and Files

One of the most distinctive aspects of the AS/400 is that it utilizes an "object" approach in its operating system design rather than a "file" approach. Traditionally, data kept in a file determines what actions may be taken with or against that file. For example, a file that contains processor executable instructions is generally called a program and is used by the CPU to perform a task. A file that contains data, text, or images, on the other hand, is usually manipulated by a program to exist in a particular state. File-driven operating systems must be told what the correct use of a file is. A file-driven operating system could be instructed to execute a non-executable file, and, conceivably, the operating system wouldn't know any better—it would try to execute the file, causing unpredictable results.

AS/400's object-oriented approach provides the operating system with reliability and consistency in its operation, since the operating system is, in a sense, aware of the fact that an object that is to be executed by the CPU must have certain predetermined attributes. These predetermined attributes are assigned by the OS/400 during the object's creation and are forever associated with the object for the life of that object. For instance, when a program is created, an internal type, a subtype, and a name are associated with the object. Type/subtype designations are used, internally, in conjunction with the program name when a user executes the program. By the same token, when a data file is created, different type and subtype designations are assigned. When a user tries to execute the data file as if it were a program, the operating system searches for the requested name preceded by a type and subtype designation that identifies a program. When it doesn't find a match, it reports a failure.

The AS/400's layered design also creates objects, based on their intended function. A Command object's internal layout is very different than that of a Message File object. By enforcing such a "black box" mechanism, the operating system has complete control over what to create, how to create, who can use, how to use, and what's required before it can be used.

The object-oriented approach used in the AS/400 extends to the authority management of objects. Each object, when it is created, is owned by its creator, who is generally given implicit authority. The object created is also associated with a default authority under which anyone else may use it. This authority is called "Public" authority. At this point, any other association of authority to the object must be explicitly designated by a user who has authority to the object. The AS/400 operating system, in its simplest form, allows a user to obtain authority to an object by default authority, by explicit authority, or by the owner's authority. If a user is not allowed to use commands that create objects, then that user should not be able to own any objects by creation. The design of the AS/400's operating system security seems simple and logical. However, implementation does not always reflect intent.

Scope of Security

Security means different things to different people. A user may be concerned with how to safeguard his or her laptop from theft. An application programmer may be concerned with implementing security at every level from field level to menu level within a user application. Operating system developers are probably concerned with providing enough flexibility in system security controls so that security administrators may select correct settings according to their needs.

In the case of the laptop user, an exercise in common sense may be sufficient to attain the needed security. The application programmer must, however, provide the means to secure and/or subset database records so that the data administrator may control who has the authority to access specific information through the security functions provided within the application. Such application security controls may be as limited as employing user-specific menus or as comprehensive as using mandatory data encryption at the field level.

Operating system developers are faced with two major issues: management of authorities and system configurations, and protection against and detection of system integrity violations. One could argue that issues of security are separate and distinct from those of integrity, but since the end result of an exploitation of either of these weaknesses could be potentially devastating, the two concepts are often addressed as one. However the security measures are provided on a given system, the most difficult job lies with the security administrator. It is the security administrator who must set the goal and balance the implementation of security guidelines, whether they encompass the tough C2 level government-rated security setting[1] or require more lenient security levels on the AS/400. The security administrator must also consider any restrictions imposed by a too-severe security plan that would affect a business just as adversely as infiltration from the outside.

The Dream Team

Ideally, management should accept the responsibility to educate and enforce security policies without exception. An effective security auditing department should be independent of the development, production, and quality assurance departments. Systems auditing personnel should be insulated from the influences of the organization's mid-management personnel. If an accurate, impartial audit of procedures, policies, and systems is to be performed, organizational politics should be minimized and any fear of management repercussion should be eliminated. A business-oriented, not necessarily technical, senior management–level person is often the best person to head such a department. If any real impact is to be achieved, the person in charge of this department must be of significant influence within the top management. Only in this way can there be a resounding change from the status quo to a more business-dependent, structured, and security-conscious entity. One of the primary

---

1. Department of Defense Trusted Computer Evaluation Criteria, DoD 5200.28-STD, December 1985.

responsibilities of the internal security management department is to identify those practices and policies that can easily be compromised. If these efforts are complicated by internal politics, or if the department is seen as insignificant, the members of the security department will lose enthusiasm and become ineffective. Although most organizations assume that security consciousness is an elective option, the fact is that there exists a federal government regulation that dictates the utmost care in securing corporate information assets for any company that deals with foreign countries (Foreign Corrupt Practices Act of 1977 [FCPA]).[2] By allowing the possibility of infiltration, the company not only endangers its own organizational assets, but violates this federal regulation.

Horses, Worms, and Viruses

In the AS/400 environment, operating system security mainly deals with system values, user profiles, communication settings, and object authorities. Other aspects of security on the AS/400 that are not as immediately recognizable include implementing product security, both for IBM software (i.e., the operating system) and for vendor-supplied software, ensuring system integrity, detection and correction of security weaknesses, and most importantly, knowledgeability as to how systems may be compromised. By studying the methods used to gain access to restricted areas, security administrators can better understand how to prevent similar attacks in the future. A sound understanding of the internals of AS/400 security is the most vital weapon against Trojan horses, worms, viruses, and other intentional time bombs that may find their way to your AS/400 in the future.

Although Trojan horses, worms, and viruses are not always harmful, for the purposes of this book they will be categorized as programs created with malicious intent to harm other computer systems.

A *Trojan horse* can be thought of as a disguised, apparently insignificant program that when activated properly can cause damage or allow damage to result. For example, one type of Trojan horse is a program that

---

2. Foreign Corrupt Practices Act of 1977 amendment to SEC Act of 1934, Public Law 95-213 (S.305), 15USC 78a, December 1977.

adopts a security officer's authority and activates the command entry screen if a user presents correct parameters. A *worm* is a program that hunts down and destroys all occurrences of a given variable and its associated variables in a network. Worms, which have the ability to replicate themselves so that their offspring will continue a destructive process, generally have a particular scope of search or a specific task in mind. For example, a worm may be created to destroy any occurrence of John Doe's credit history and all of its related information. The worm will hunt for the variable "John Doe"; upon finding its target, it creates a copy of itself that will destroy all data relating to the ABC Collection Agency that was associated with John Doe's data. There may or may not be predetermined limits on the worm's self-replication capabilities, although it is generally easier to create worms that do not have any predefined limits.

The term *virus* is used to describe just about any type of invasive program, but for the purposes of this book, it will be used to mean a program that when executed attacks another program and either replicates itself into or rewrites the host's instructions for a nefarious purpose. When an infected program is used, it proliferates the infection to other programs. Some viruses are complex and highly sophisticated; others are simple but deadly. For instance, the much publicized case of Robert Tappan Morris, the Cornell student who created and released a virus that infiltrated and proliferated throughout the Internet, crippling several thousands of systems in a matter of hours, involved a relatively simple program that went out of control.

The Objective

At this point, readers should consider their own reasons for learning more about security. Who should be secured? What information should be secured? Who or what represents the greatest threat to your system? In order to establish a long-standing security plan, these questions should be revisited on a regular basis. Unfortunately, the issues surrounding sound security measures can be thought of as non–user-friendly. Some security administrators are overly aggressive in their approach—usually in the wrong areas. Others are too lenient.

It is important to realize that the vast majority of the clerks who use their terminals from 9 A.M. to 5 P.M. couldn't care less about the system. That is not to say that they represent no threat, but that an overly aggressive approach may actually hinder their work efforts without any measurable security benefits. On the other hand, security administrators are generally less restrictive with the technical staff—perhaps because most security administrators are themselves senior technicians who have climbed the corporate ladder through the ranks of the programming staff, and they identify strongly with other developers. Unlike a clerk, however, who may develop a motive to harm the system but wouldn't have the technical skills, a programmer has not only the opportunity, but also the knowledge to seriously damage a system. In fact, ironically, security administrators themselves can pose the greatest threat to their own systems—and never be detected until years after they have left the company! To put a less technical person in charge of security, however, presents an equally unattractive alternative. For example, an operations manager, who knows the hardware configurations intimately but seldom possesses a wealth of programming skills, would probably construct a security system straight out of the IBM manuals—which, as we will see, can tend to be woefully lacking in their exploration of detection mechanisms. All the authority in the world won't help security administrators who don't have the means to verify whether or not their own security measures are being compromised.

The ideal internal auditing department combines management clout armed with technically strong security management and enforcement tools, as well as anti-virus utilities. Otherwise, a skilled programmer's inquisitiveness may ultimately be restrained only by the conscience of that programmer.

CHAPTER TWO

System Values

There are a variety of software and hardware settings that control security within OS/400. These range from the system value settings to network configurations and performance adjustment values. The primary purpose of these values is to provide defaults and standards by which the operating system is to execute. The system configuration values discussed in this chapter should be reviewed periodically, particularly when the system environment changes, such as after an installation of a new application or configuration of a new communications network. Some of these changes take effect immediately and others take effect only after the next IPL (Initial Program Load–boot-up).

This part of the book addresses some of the management issues surrounding the various options and techniques that may be used to form organizational security policies. More specific technical steps are presented in the Implementation chapters.

Security Levels

System values determine the characteristics of the AS/400 throughout the system. They set the tone under which the machine will function. There are several security-related values that should be considered. Among these, the security level (QSECURITY) parameter in the system values table is one of the most important. System security level values of 10, 20, 30, 40, and 50 determine the intended seriousness of the security implementation on the AS/400. Security level 10 is the level at which all new AS/400s are shipped from the factory. This level represents, in effect, no security at all. Anyone can sign on to the system—even destroy it at will. Security level 20 enforces password security, but not object security. Users are required to enter their profile and their password to gain access to the system; once signed on, however, a user has all authorities to all objects on the system, since the system grants all object authorities to every profile created under security level 20 and below. One could manually adjust the profiles that the system has created, but that kind of work becomes pointless considering the higher security levels that are already available on the system.

Most AS/400s are configured to execute under security level 30. This level ensures that each profile belongs to a valid user and that each user has the necessary authority to manipulate the object before it is made available. This setting is largely a reflection of the old System/38 configuration, safeguarding the system from unauthorized entry and unauthorized use of objects in the system; but it does nothing to prevent system integrity violations. If asked, it does log the violations, but that's like asking for the boarding ticket from a passenger who is obviously carrying a machine gun. One of the main reasons this security level exists today is so that those software vendors who had used lower level interfaces in creating applications on System/38s and AS/400s, with or without IBM's blessings, can still market their software. It was a compromise on IBM's part to address the known system integrity problems within the operating system and allow continued use of applications from third-party vendors that may solve customer's business issues. The problem is that as long as this security level is regarded as the de facto standard, system integrity problems will continue to proliferate. Furthermore, in some cases, utility vendors may be forced to use unsupported operating system interfaces so that they may compete with each other, especially where performance is the critical issue (i.e., PC Support, client/server, and LAN-server environments).

To understand the reasoning behind the need for security level 40, one has to travel back in time to the System/38 days. Although there was a great deal of fanfare surrounding the announcement of the AS/400 back in 1988, the architecture of the new box was actually indistinguishable from that of the System/38. As a matter of fact, aside from the name change of the CPF to OS/400, there weren't a great many changes in the layers below the operating system.

Even today's AS/400s are not so different from yesterday's System/38s, provided that the comparison is made on a relatively large scale and minor details are ignored. There is, however, one significant, albeit minor, difference between the System/38 and the AS/400 from a "techie's" point of view: the absence of almost half of the Machine Interface (MI) instructions from the MI instruction table. This omission is significant, since many System/38 professionals have learned how to take advantage of the System/38's common operating system compiler, which all high-level languages produce as output. Furthermore, because the underlying MI compiler is exempt from operating system rules, programmers skilled at working with MI are sometimes able to perform miracles, a few of which had to do with "stealing" authorities from the operating system through the use of resolved pointers. Among the most widely abused was the QSYS user profile pointer, which in every sense of the word was almighty as far as the machine was concerned. That meant trouble for System/38 developers; the System/38's whole realm of security was based solely on the object authority validation scheme, which would be rendered obsolete by any mechanism that could be devised to work around it. Acknowledging this weakness on System/38s, the initial OS/400 developers removed all MI instructions that they thought were dangerous—for our own good, of course. The early OS/400 developers must have thought that the removal of the restricted MI instructions, coupled with the requirement to essentially re-create (re-encapsulate, to be exact) all programs, would substantially lessen the chances of unsupported MI programs migrating over to the AS/400.

Unfortunately, the only thing this tactic accomplished was to force the more clever hackers to dig deeper into the microcode. Eventually, the necessary objects were brought from the System/38 over to the AS/400 as Job Description and Message File objects. Subsequently, the resident AS/400 root compiler program (QPRROOTP) was altered to use the migrated instruction tables from the System/38, thus defeating the IBM's best laid plans to contain the wicked. By the time version 1 release 2 of OS/400 was released, there existed a sufficient number of individuals who knew about the existence of the security loopholes to stir up interest in the trade press. Championing the cause to enlighten IBMers was Paul Conte, the senior technical editor for *NEWS 3X/400* magazine. Conte, armed to the teeth with program codes that violate every AS/400 rule known to humanity (to which I myself contributed a small part), faced off with IBM.

The subsequent release of the OS/400 introduced a new security level value of 40, which enforced the concept of *object state and domain*. This move was touted as the definitive means to secure that which could not be secured before. The object domain rule disallowed all user-created programs from accessing any object without the assistance of the operating system programs, with very few exceptions. The object state rule ensured that users could only invoke programs that were created by another user or allowed by the operating system through the use of authorized Application Program Interfaces (APIs). What's more, to ensure that no programs could be modified and restored, each program's executable instructions were added to, subtracted from, skipped, and shifted in mysterious ways to form a value known as the program validation value.

Although AS/400 professionals may think the state and domain concept is indigenous to the AS/400, the truth is that it had been in use even before the System/38 era, by the System/370 architecture machines. The concept was not an absolute success in the System/370 world. The introduction of security level 40 did, however, eliminate many security weaknesses. Some software vendors were outraged by this sudden restriction on undocumented operating system features. Many software products could not be executed under the new security level 40 standards. Although IBM had made noble attempts to deliver as many call-level APIs as possible, to replace those programs the software vendors could no longer use, not all that was requested was converted into APIs, nor did everyone ask for their programs to be converted. There are still many well-known software companies that use the unsupported, operating–system blocked instructions in their products. Some of these vendors require their customers to use the security level value of 30; others have found a way to change their programs to execute in the system state. There are even those who have altered the target objects to be contained in the user domain so that user-created programs may access them freely.

For these reasons, security level 40 should be the minimum standard under which all AS/400s run. Customers who purchase and utilize software that will not function at security level 40 should realize that they are at the mercy of the software vendors. IBM has made it clear that anyone with legitimate system interface requirements may request assistance directly from IBM.[1]

Security level 30 is at best adequate in its management of users and resources, but falls dangerously short at protecting intentional intrusions. That is not to say that all intentional intrusions are malicious, but even the beneficial applications are considered to be "subverting the integrity mechanism"[2] as far as IBM is concerned. Many software vendors and systems programmers may argue that point with IBM. One thing is for certain, however—there are inherent operating system weaknesses under security level 30 that do not exist at higher levels. It is possible, for instance, to gain access to an AS/400 running at security level 30 without specifying a profile and a password; it is not possible to sign on without a profile and a password under security level 40 and above. Other less obvious loopholes are eliminated at security level 40 or 50.

Security level 50, introduced with version 2 release 3 of the OS/400 operating system, was created to satisfy government C2 security requirements, offering the benefits of business opportunities associated with such certification. The difference between levels 40 and 50 may appear insignificant at first glance; however, in reality there is a great deal of difference, both technically and philosophically, for those required to abide by the C2 security guidelines. The intent behind security level 50 is to enable customers to adhere to the C2 guidelines set forth by the United States Department of Defense outlined in the Trusted Computer Evaluation Criteria standards. However, do not equate security level 50 with C2 certification. One cannot simply "turn on" C2 specifications; rather, they must be adopted and practiced religiously. Every piece of software and hardware must be certified individually to meet C2 specifications. For instance, all AS/400 models prior to the E model do not meet the C2 requirements, even with the security level 50 designation. Attaching a PC, using the IBM OfficeVision/400 licensed program, or most HLL compilers available on an Advanced Series AS/400 is forbidden if C2 security is

---

1. Ron Fess, Openness APIs: An Inside Look, *NEWS 3X/400*, March 1991.
2. Ibid.

Table 2.1 C2 Compliant AS/400 IBM Software as of Version 3 Release 1

Product ID	Product Description
5738-PW1	Source Entry Utility
5738-QU1	Query/400
5738-ST1	SAA Structured Query Language/400
5738-FNT	Advanced Function Printing Fonts/400
5738-FN1	Advanced Function Printing DBCS Fonts/400
5799-FBR	Common Cryptographic Architecture Services/400
5733-055	SAA ImagePlus Workfolder Application Facility/400
5733-119	SystemView ManageWare/400
5738-CX2	Integrated Language Environment C/400
5738-ES1	IBM OMEGAMON/400
5798-RYC	Facsmile Support/400
5798-RYD	KnowledgeTool Runtime/400
5798-RYE	KnowledgeTool Development/400
5798-RYT	Backup Recovery and Media Services/400
5799-EPJ	Ultimedia Video Delivery System/400
5738-SS1	OS/400 Operating System

to be maintained.[3] A list of C2 compliant AS/400 IBM software as of version 3 release 1 is provided in Table 2.1.

Security level 50, in addition to imposing the same restrictions found under level 40, verifies that all pointers passed by user programs to operating system interfaces, including pointers within messages, do not address any of the restricted system data areas. Under security level 50, authentication and validation rules will adversely affect system performance due to these additional verification processes. Also, under security 50, user spaces, indices, and queues are not allowed to reside in permanent libraries, but only in temporary libraries. These and other restrictions outlined in the use of security level 50 allow the AS/400 to run

---

3. Guide to Enabling C2 Security, IBM SC41-0103-00, November 1993.

according to C2 compliance—convenience and flexibility, however, get left in the dust.

In the average company running an AS/400, upgrading to security level 40 may significantly affect day-to-day processing. Some tools and applications may not function properly; however, such programs may have a hidden back door that no one knows about but the creator. It may be worth a onetime disruption of normal business to safeguard the company's assets against such a potential danger. Fortunately there is a way to quantify the potential disruption of security level 40 prior to its implementation; these are methods discussed in the Implementation chapters. In comparison, security level 50 provides very little additional protection for the general public. Unless an organization has the need to maintain C2 guidelines, it serves very little usefulness.

Password Controls

There are several system value parameters that control the formation of user passwords, ranging from the practical to the ridiculous. The fundamental intent of using these parameters is to make it difficult for an intruder to guess passwords, through the enforcement of stringent measures in creating and maintaining individual passwords. The paradox that presents itself to technicians is that the more difficult one makes it for users to come up with a new password, the more likely it is that users will keep notes as to what their password is, which in turn rewards anyone inclined to forage for passwords from the garbage. Unfortunately, it is the unlikeliest of attacks that managers must plan to thwart when planning security policies.

Passwords should not, however, be regarded as the most important security-related entities; the physical security of the AS/400 is just as important. An experienced hacker can acquire the necessary profile and a password in ways most people would never think of. For example, an unannounced internal security audit of one of the largest retail shopping center developers in New England has revealed that 80 percent of mall office workers readily gave out their profiles and passwords over the phone to a person who claimed to be a member of the Information Systems programming staff who was testing a new program that required their profiles and passwords. Incidents such as this suggest that password security entails much more than simply changing arbitrary characters frequently. Moreover, managers should bear in mind that the reason for password security is seldom for the prevention of invasion from the inside. The following paragraph explains and recommends uses of various parameters in the system values in an effort to establish an acceptable level of deterrence against possible internal and external intruders.

A password expiration interval of 30 days works well even in a large organization, provided the new password creation rules are not unreasonable. A minimum password length of six characters is suggested. Adjacent digits as in 123456 and consecutive repeating characters (i.e., AAAAAA) should not be allowed; requiring a numerical digit in a password would help further protect the password.

A password validation program has more potential problem areas than helpful ones. This kind of a program is one of the primary targets of hackers. Also, if the system has to be recovered from a crash and the Password validation program cannot be properly executed, no one will be able to use the system. Furthermore, the unencrypted passwords that are saved by password validation programs represent a significant internal and external security exposure. If the Password Validation Program user exit is to be used, categorize and manage the program in the same manner as the system start-up program discussed in the Implementation chapters.

There exists another parameter that validates any new password entered against the last 32 passwords that the individual has used. If a repeating password is found in this table, the new password is rejected. On the surface this seems like a good idea, but in practice, users inevitably choose passwords like MIKE1, MIKE2, and so on. Therefore, if other controls are activated to ensure that such a pattern cannot be used (i.e., cannot use some letter at the same location of previously used password), users often write down the passwords and complain about the frequency of password expiration intervals. Use of the feature which remembers the last 32 passwords is only recommended on systems that employ OS/400 version 3 release 1. In this release the number of passwords that the system can recall for comparison purposes is set between 0 and 32 and may be user selected. An ideal number of passwords to remember is four, allowing five rotating passwords, each of which would be valid for a period of 30 days.

Security Controls

In addition to password controls, the system values host several security-related parameters. These parameters are used to grant default authorities, limit sign-on abilities, and provide other general security-related system settings. Use of the system value QALWOBJRST is highly recommended. This will prevent restoration of system state programs and programs that adopt other users' authorities.

System value QALWUSRDMN which controls where user spaces, indices, and queues may be created, but it relates only to those sites where security level 50 is applicable. Most readers need not be concerned with this value. However, those who are required to uphold the C2 guidelines must specify the QTEMP library as the only library that may host these user objects.

The QCRTAUT system value controls the default authority given to anyone who does not explicitly have the authority to a particular object. All objects created on an AS/400 have default authority, and determination as to the power of that authority is governed by one of the attributes of the library in which that object is going to be a member. When a library object is created, the QCRTAUT system value is used to provide the public with default authority to the library. Furthermore, the same system value is designated to be the default authority of objects that may be created in that library in the future. It is recommended that the default public authority for each library and the default authority specified for new objects to be created in that library (CRTAUT) be reviewed and changed according to the purpose of the library. Figure 2.1 illustrates this authority propagation concept.

Although the AS/400 doesn't yet support an animated screen saver, it does have the capability to determine whether any activity has been associated with the workstation. The "activity" does not, however, mean an arbitrary keystroke or movement of a mouse as it does on a PC. It refers instead to a set of 32 function keys and an attention key recognized by the OS/400. If no action has been taken within the time interval specified in the QINACTITV system value, the job running at the workstation will be ended or disconnected, or a message will be sent to the message queue specified in the QINACTMSGQ system value.

26 MANAGEMENT

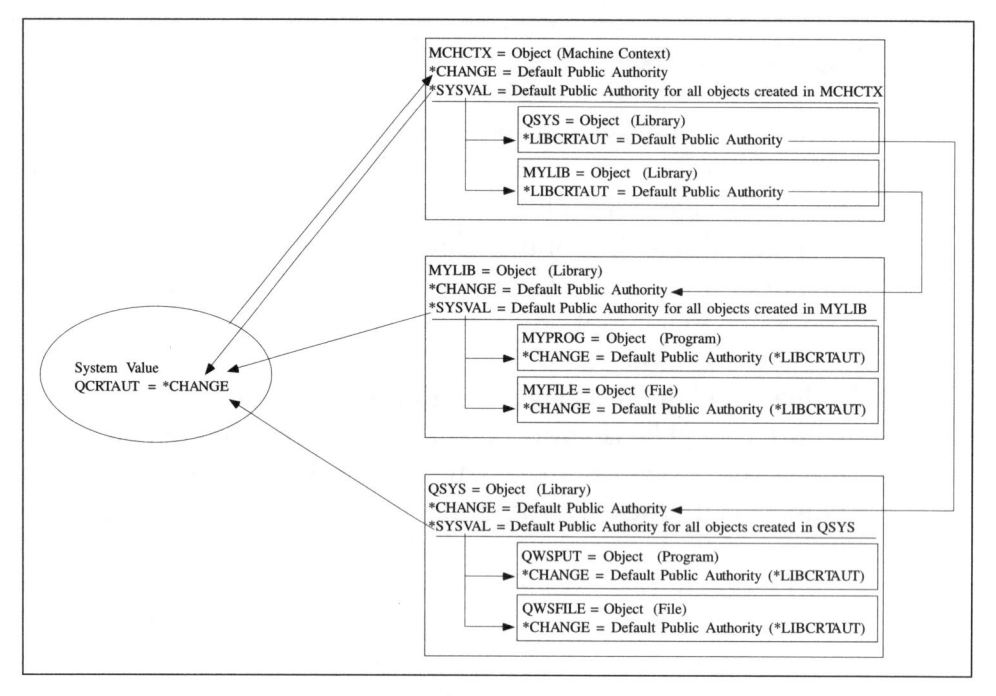

```
MCHCTX = Object (Machine Context)
*CHANGE = Default Public Authority
*SYSVAL = Default Public Authority for all objects created in MCHCTX

    QSYS = Object (Library)
    *LIBCRTAUT = Default Public Authority

    MYLIB = Object (Library)
    *LIBCRTAUT = Default Public Authority

MYLIB = Object (Library)
*CHANGE = Default Public Authority
*SYSVAL = Default Public Authority for all objects created in MYLIB

    MYPROG = Object (Program)
    *CHANGE = Default Public Authority (*LIBCRTAUT)

    MYFILE = Object (File)
    *CHANGE = Default Public Authority (*LIBCRTAUT)

QSYS = Object (Library)
*CHANGE = Default Public Authority
*SYSVAL = Default Public Authority for all objects created in QSYS

    QWSPUT = Object (Program)
    *CHANGE = Default Public Authority (*LIBCRTAUT)

    QWSFILE = Object (File)
    *CHANGE = Default Public Authority (*LIBCRTAUT)

System Value
QCRTAUT = *CHANGE
```

Figure 2.1 Default public authority propagation.

The purpose of these system values is to discourage users from leaving their terminals unattended, because of the obvious security breach that could occur if an unauthorized person takes advantage of the workstation. Unfortunately, even the best laid plans to guard against this type of negligence may be inadequate, since it only takes a minute to overcome an entire security network if an intruder gains access to a privileged user's workstation. On the other hand, it may be unreasonable to ask everyone to sign off their terminals when they need to use the washroom and sign back on to the program that took several minutes to get to in the first place. In view of this situation, if one assumes that intrusion may be imminent within the organization, one would be required to educate, monitor, and enforce adherence to sign-off procedures. If the disciplinary consequences of leaving workstations unattended are not enforced, internal security measures will be compromised sooner or later. In my own personal observations, I find that most of the security-conscious individuals in the AS/400 community realize the benefit of these values and allow AS/400 to take specific action within a reasonable time frame; however, these same individuals are not so strict at enforcing the consequences of leaving workstations unattended, nor do they feel overly concerned about the possibility of an internal security breach. This suggests that most AS/400 professionals are securing their systems against external intruders rather than internal ones, a philosophy that should be kept in mind when exploring system integrity issues.

The most sensible settings for these values seem to include a time interval of 30 minutes for the QINACTITV and use of the example program INACTMSGQ provided in the appendix to determine the course of action for each inactive workstation. Limiting all users, including the security officer and privileged users, to a single workstation is recommended. Programmer-class users with dual address workstations can be supported as needed by overriding the system value at the profile level. However, specific authorization must be granted to devices to allow privileged users to sign on from them. It is acceptable to allow a remote privileged user to sign on using a remote workstation so long as the authority is granted just prior to initiating a call-back unit and is revoked right after termination of the session. It is best to plan ahead and authorize a number of workstations at various strategic locations within the organization that allow privileged profiles and security officers to sign on. Remote location call-back processing is a must for any privileged account, and no more than three sign-on attempts should be allowed. A legitimate user will understand the inconvenience of having to call the operations staff to have the device and the profile reset; an intruder will have to find another way.

The QRMTSIGN parameter is used to control the process of how one signs on to another AS/400. If communication with other AS/400s or PC workstations is not necessary, then this value should be set to reject (*REJECT) any request and the related system value QAUTOVRT should be set to 0. However, in most AS/400 environments, communication to both PC workstations and other AS/400s is the norm; if this is the case, this value should be set to verify (*VERIFY) the incoming profile and the password. If further discretion is required, a user-written program may be associated with this parameter. The user-written program specified will be invoked both before and after the passthrough session.

Audit Controls

One of the security manager's primary weapons to detect and identify an intruder is the use of the system auditing controls. It is absolutely vital that these control values are utilized to ensure the security and the integrity of the system. System auditing features may appear to be a complex and technical maze. In reality, they provide multiple layers of usefulness, ranging from general-purpose detection mechanisms to very specific pinpointing devices, all using a relatively simple yet ingenious approach.

System auditing does not provide all the answers to the questions that arise from the data it collects, nor does the system provide the means to correct some of the problems it reports. It does report, to the best of its ability, any attempts made to circumvent the operating system's security and integrity.

The best way to explain the implementation of the AS/400's security is to compare it to boarding an airplane at an airport. Airline passengers pass through three main security checkpoints. Guards inspect all passengers to ensure that no dangerous weapons are being carried on board. Boarding attendants check all passengers to make sure they have the proper boarding tickets. Armed guards detain anyone loitering around the flight deck who doesn't have the proper ground control identification. When IBM implemented the AS/400's system integrity, the first of the three security checkpoints is represented by the verification of the program validation value during a restore operation. If the program's instruction stream or the program's validation values have been altered since its creation, the change will be noticed by the restore operation. The system will identify, report, and log all exceptions only under security level 40 or above. Security levels below 40 can be easily bypassed, presenting an unacceptable risk. The second checkpoint is represented by authority management. Only the user with the authority to use an object will be allowed to "board the plane." If an unauthorized person attempts to use an object, that action will be logged along with the person's profile in the security audit journal.

The third and final guard is represented by enforcement of the state/domain boundaries. Operating system programs are, for the most part, assigned *system state* attributes and may utilize any other program in the system, providing the caller has the necessary authority. User-created programs are defined as *user state* programs and can only reference other user state programs. An exception to this rule is that a user-created program may call an operating system program that was specifically made to interact with user programs. These special operating system programs are designated as system state programs, but reside in a *user domain*. (This is analogous to a ground control person whose job is to deliver a passenger's message from the terminal to the flight deck.) All objects created on the system are in the system domain with the exception of user programs, SQL packages, user spaces, user indices, and user queues—no other objects may be directly accessed by any user-created program. When an attempt is made to cross this boundary, it is prevented and logged, or simply logged, depending on the security level setting.

Figure 2.2 illustrates the relationship between OS/400 object domains and program states. The User Domain/User State objects (right) can only access objects within their own boundaries (User Domain/User State) or those within the neighboring User Domain/System State boundary (center). They are not allowed to directly access System Domain/System State objects (left). Any attempt to do so will cause a system integrity violation and will either be logged or disallowed based on the system security level value. However, User Domain/User State objects may employ User Domain/System State objects to access System Domain/System State objects. User Domain/System State objects are collectively known as Application Program Interfaces (APIs) and are provided by the operating system.

System Domain/System State
Most OS/400 Programs
Most user-created non-executable objects
(files, commands, data areas, etc.)

User Domain/User State
All user-created programs
User-created spaces, indices, and queues

User Domain/System State
QCMDEXC
Operating System
Application Program Interfaces
(APIs)

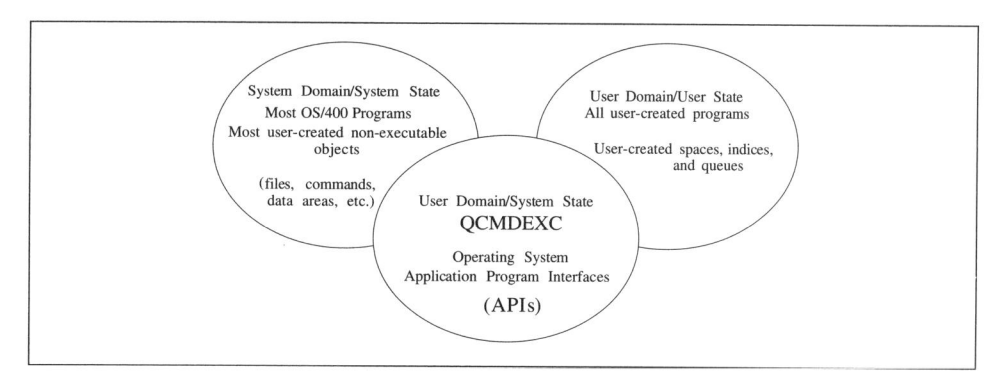

Figure 2.2 OS/400 domain/state processing.

System audit values should be used to identify a particular anomaly. Once an anomaly has been found, system auditing tools may be used to collect more detailed information about the anomaly. The eventual goal is to pinpoint the cause of the anomaly and determine whether it is an intentional intrusion or an unforeseen peculiarity of normal daily processing. The audit control (QAUDCTL) should be set to its home state of *AUDLVL. This value may later be changed to the object audit (*OBJAUD) setting once the general audit records determine that further scrutiny is necessary on a given object.

The audit end action control (QAUDENDACN) specifies what actions are to be taken if the auditing system could not record an audit journal for whatever reason. Under C2 security guidelines this value must be set to power down the machine. However, under normal circumstances, shutting down the system in the middle of a busy workday may be too drastic a measure. It is recommended that this value remain at the default of *NOTIFY. A message will be issued to the system operator every hour until further action is taken to rectify the problem.

The auditing level (QAUDLVL) determines what security-related actions are deemed worthy of recording in the security journal. The security administrator walks a fine line in determining this setting; if not enough security violations are recorded, anomalies may pass through without being detected. If too much data is collected, attention to an obscure but significant abnormality may be clouded by hundreds of extraneous entries.

It is strongly recommended that system audit level parameters not be used to identify specific abnormalities, but more broadly defined events that may lead to a specific user or an object. To that end *AUTFAIL, *OFCSRV, *PGMADP, *PGMFAIL, *SAVRST, and *SERVICE parameters are recommended as default values to be associated with audit level settings. Each of these parameter values will generate a specific type of security record in the audit journal. These records should be analyzed using the software provided and the procedures outlined in the Auditing chapters.

If a questionable item appears in the system audit journal, narrow the scope of the search to an individual or a set of objects. For example, if the program failure analysis report determines the use of an object by a particular profile that resulted in a domain violation, then narrow the scope of audit by specifying the *OBJAUD parameter in the audit controls system value, and start a supplementary audit of the user of the offending program. This procedure will provide a more detailed analysis of the actions relating to that user and in some cases will reveal the intent of the offending program. In most instances, users are not aware that they have violated system integrity. The software creator, however, is very much aware of such a program's violation of AS/400 system integrity. Identifying and working to eliminate or at least minimize such integrity problems can be one of the most time-consuming tasks in security management.

The recommended audit level parameters discussed in this chapter will record various authorization violations, unauthorized access to other people's electronic mail, access of objects through an established gateway or an unknown back door, illegal crossing of the state/domain boundary, restoration of patched programs, and the use of system service tools. Most of the time the security logged entries are explainable, but once in a while a dormant worm may become active. That's the reason for the practice of religiously analyzing the security audit journals.

It is also recommended that a security journal analysis be performed every day. Use of a scheduler to initiate the analytical reports may help to ease the daily burden. It is imperative to keep up with the daily analysis, for it would be unbearable to analyze and follow through with a month's worth of data. Furthermore, the disk storage space will be quickly consumed if the reviewed journals are not removed from the system. Again, a job scheduler is highly recommended to automate such a clean-up operation.

CHAPTER THREE

User Profiles

A user profile represents the closest thing possible to a complete dossier of a user. While a profile does not necessarily identify a person, it provides crucial information about the user associated with it. Let's look, for example, at the fictional profile Kermit. The name of the profile tells us nothing about the identity of the user; it does, however, describe a set of authority limitations for whoever may be using that profile. When a user enters the Kermit profile with a password, the AS/400 verifies the user's authority to use the Kermit profile according to the accuracy of the password. This system leaves a lot to be desired as far as secrecy is concerned; nonetheless, it is the password which serves as the definitive means to identify an individual on the AS/400. The profile, on the other hand, serves as an information repository for the management of resources within a given system, not necessarily an integral part of the identity verification process itself.

Although users are required to enter the profile name in addition to the password on the AS/400, the most significant reason for the entry of a profile is to provide the system with information as to what identity the user wishes to assume while working in the system. Indeed, the same password could be associated with many different profiles.

Profiles and Portraits

There exists a fair argument to the effect that the construction of user profiles should be as random and vague as possible in order to elude a potential security threat. The underlying principal says that if profiles are named with an arbitrary set of characters, an intruder will be less likely to pair profiles and passwords or detect the importance of a particular profile. This seems logical and reasonable. However, the use of completely random profile designations is not without cost in terms of both systems management and user relations. Consider having to remember what amounts to two passwords in order to use your ATM card.

A reasonable user may ask to understand the logic behind arbitrary profile names and the necessity for these measures. Given that most AS/400 security administrators are more concerned about external intrusions rather than internal breaches, the logical explanation would be that arbitrary profile designations inhibit external intruders from being able to guess profile names.

A serious hacker will almost never connect to a system blindly and try to sign on by guessing profiles and passwords. The last thing an intruder wants to do is to leave a trail—or worse yet, set off an alarm. Only an amateur or someone who is familiar with the system would make such a clumsy endeavor. And the chances of an amateur intruder *guessing* a correct password within three tries is nearly nonexistent, provided the security administrator has in place the security guidelines recommended in this book. If the person is familiar with the system, then the profile and the password may already have been compromised; this is usually the case. Experienced hackers can usually count on the average AS/400 shop's conformity to defaults when dealing with an apparently complex communications network, so connecting to a target system is usually not a problem for them.

Gaining access to the system, though, is another matter entirely. It has been said that hackers are well versed in the area of social engineering (in other words, getting others to volunteer information without using force). If the hacker succeeds in learning this much, the most arbitrary profile name and the most secret password will not secure the system. Therefore, the potential risk of using conventional profile naming standards rises directly in proportion to the amount of amateur hacking that is taking place on a given system. It is the security administrator who must weigh these values and decide whether the potential risks outweigh the ongoing inconvenience.

There is one other possibility, however. The fundamental concept of disassociating a person's identity from his or her profile designation is certainly worth considering. As a matter of fact, this principle has been employed for a long time. The U.S. armed forces use such methods every day in order to thwart the enemy's efforts to detect the friendly forces' command size and significance. A coded name such as "Kermit" is just as effective in deterring an outsider as GHJ456KL; both bear no relation to the identity of the actual person, nor do they detail that person's authority. However, "Kermit" is much easier for the user to remember than GHJ456KL.

Although code names need not be readily recognizable, the idea of using an alias that a user can easily remember may be worth a try. Perhaps the profiles should identify a member within a group, such as GONZO of the MUPPETS or CHARMED of the QUARKS. The traditional method of using standardized profile designations based on locations or the user's name will always be available should an alias or random characters present too many administrative problems. Be advised, however, that although the OS/400 operating system allows profile names of 10 charcters, some communications methods and licensed software packages limit the length of profiles to eight characters.

Work Groups

When creating profiles, consider using group profile strategy. Group profiles represent a set of users who require similar working boundaries. This boundary can be as specific as that for a clerk who may only need to access the Accounts Payable files, or as broad as that of a security officer class user who needs to access all objects on the system. Most users may be grouped together according to their primary function, such as AP, GL, AR, and so on. The group profile itself should not have passwords, but should host a variety of special authorities as required. Only the individual profiles should be allowed to sign on to the system. The individual profiles should generally be created under a *USER class and assigned to a particular primary group with limited capabilities. If the user requires authorities to other objects in different applications, supplementary group profiles (up to 15) may be designated to augment the primary group profile.

Objects, on the other hand, should be assigned to their respective primary groups in order to maximize efficiency in resolving the requester's authority to the object. When an individual profile creates an object, it should be defined as belonging to the group rather than to the individual. Individual ownership of objects not only conflicts with the principles of group management, but also becomes a nightmare to manage when the owner needs to sever its relationship from an existing group in favor of a new group.

Most importantly, the use of private user authorities should be limited. The fewer user-specific authorities granted in the system, the faster the system will respond to the authorization validation process. For example, all Accounts Payable clerks should be grouped together under a *USER class, group profile AP. The primary group profiles of all objects in the Accounts Payable library should be designated as AP with *CHANGE authority. If the same person requires access to the General Ledger system, add supplementary group GL to the user profile. The owner of the objects in the Accounts Payable and the General Ledger libraries may be the original vendor profile with *USER class special authorities. Use caution when ordering the supplemental group profile designations. The most often used group name should precede lesser used group names. Figure 3.1 illustrates an overview of object authority validation process.

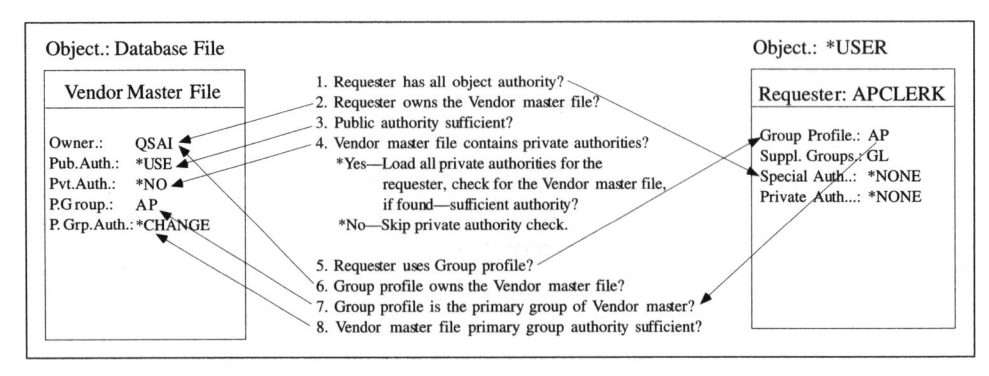

```
Object.: Database File                                                        Object.: *USER
┌─────────────────────┐                                                  ┌──────────────────────┐
│  Vendor Master File │       1. Requester has all object authority?    │  Requester: APCLERK  │
│                     │       2. Requester owns the Vendor master file? │                      │
│                     │       3. Public authority sufficient?           │  Group Profile.: AP  │
│  Owner.:    QSAI    │       4. Vendor master file contains private authorities? │  Suppl. Groups.: GL  │
│  Pub.Auth.: *USE    │          *Yes—Load all private authorities for the        │  Special Auth..: *NONE │
│  Pvt.Auth.: *NO     │                requester, check for the Vendor master file, │  Private Auth...: *NONE │
│  P.Group.:  AP      │                if found—sufficient authority?   │                      │
│  P. Grp.Auth.: *CHANGE │       *No—Skip private authority check.      │                      │
│                     │                                                  │                      │
│                     │       5. Requester uses Group profile?          │                      │
│                     │       6. Group profile owns the Vendor master file? │                  │
│                     │       7. Group profile is the primary group of Vendor master? │         │
│                     │       8. Vendor master file primary group authority sufficient? │       │
└─────────────────────┘                                                  └──────────────────────┘
```

Figure 3.1 Authority verification process.

Other special authorities should be used sparingly. The group profiles for programmers should be created with the *PGMR user class, and the system operator group profile with *SYSOPR class special authorities. A network administrator may be given an *IOSYSCFG special authority as well as the *JOBCTL special authority. In addition, all group profiles' status parameter should read *DISABLED, and only those who require the use of commands should be allowed to use the command lines.

Secret Passwords

When a user profile is first created, it is a good idea to specifically designate an arbitrary password and set it to the expired state. This will force the user to change the password on the next sign on. The password expiration interval should default to the system value; the default system profiles' passwords should be changed from their shipped values immediately. The QPGMR, QRJE, QSRV, QSRVBAS, QSYSOPR, QX400, and QUSER profiles' passwords should be changed to *NONE and the QSECOFR password to something other than the shipped value. Starting from version 3 release 1 of the OS/400 operating system, all system default profiles are shipped with no passwords, but the security officer's password will still need to be changed. Also, a seldom used Dedicated Service Tool system profile's password should be changed using the CHGDSTPWD command as soon as possible.

The AS/400 is said to employ a double encryption mechanism in storage of the passwords in the system. There are those who believe that encrypted passwords cannot possibly be reversed—that the system uses one-way encryption. If that is the case, how then is the password entered by a user compared with the stored value? One of two possibilities exists—either the password entered each time is encrypted to a similar pattern, then compared, or the encrypted password in the file is deciphered to match the password entered during the sign on. The first scenario is more likely to be used than the second.

Although the process of password table deciphering has intrigued some hackers, many resort to other methods with more success. Unbeknownst to most, an experienced hacker can assign a password to an operating system profile such as QSYS in a matter of seconds; it is also

38 MANAGEMENT

possible to create programs to automate the password entry process to operating system profiles. This is rather difficult to believe, since the operating system is supposed to prevent any such attempt. Nevertheless, the ability exists and has been successfully demonstrated, as evidenced in Figures 3.2 and 3.3. Therefore it is the security administrator's responsibility to display a list of all authorized users from time to time and ensure that there are no passwords associated with the following operating system profiles: QDBSHR, QDFTOWN, QDOC, QDSNX, QFNC, QGATE, QLPAUTO, QLPINSTALL, QSNADS, QSPL, QSPLJOB, QSYS, and QTSTRQS. Because the general AS/400 population assumes that it is a fact that the operating system disallows modifications to these profiles, patching these profiles is seldom detected.

Even when the evidence is clearly displayed on the screen, unless the person is specifically looking for such an invasion, this type of patch is usually overlooked. For instance, Figure 3.2 shows one of the most widely used AS/400 panels. A closer look, however, reveals a subtle discrepancy. The job PCS116S1 in QINTER subsystem is signed on to the system using the QSYS profile which should not be possible, since QSYS profile does not possess a password as shipped from IBM.

```
                       Work with Active Jobs                    GONZO
                                                     08/13/94  15:39:17
CPU %:    16.7      Elapsed time:   00:00:07    Active jobs:   36
Opt   Subsystem/Job   User        Type   CPU %   Function       Status
 __   QBATCH          QSYS        SBS     .0                    DEQW
 __   QCMN            QSYS        SBS     .0                    DEQW
 __     PCS116        QSYS        EVK     .0   * -PASSTHRU      EVTW
 __   QCTL            QSYS        SBS     .0                    DEQW
 __   QINTER          QSYS        SBS     .0                    DEQW
 __     PCS116S1      QSYS        INT    14.7   CMD-WRKACTJOB   RUN
 __   QPGMR           QSYS        SBS     .0                    DEQW
 __   QSAI            QSYS        SBS     .0                    DEQW
 __     IPLMONITOR    QSAI        BCH     .0   DLY-02:00:00     DLYW
 __     LCLMONITOR    QSAI        BCH     .0   PGM-JSPSCH04     MSGW
 __     QSCHEDULER    QSAI        ASJ     .0   PGM-JSPSCH00     MSGW
 __     RMTMONITOR    QSAI        BCH     .0   PGM-JSPSCH04     MSGW
 __     WRKMONITOR    QSAI        BCH     .0   PGM-JSPSCH04     MSGW
 __   QSNADS          QSYS        SBS     .0                    DEQW
 __     GONZO         QSNADS      BCH     .0                    EVTW
 __     NEWTON        QSNADS      BCH     .0                    EVTW
                                                                 More...
===>
F21=Display instructions/keys
```

Figure 3.2 Work with Active Jobs. The job PCS116S1 in the QINTER subsystem is signed on to the system using the QSYS profile.

```
                    Display User Profile - Basic
User profile . . . . . . . . . . . . . . . . :   QUSER

Previous sign-on . . . . . . . . . . . . . . :   08/13/94   15:37:44
Sign-on attempts not valid . . . . . . . . . :   0
Status . . . . . . . . . . . . . . . . . . . :   *ENABLED
Date password last changed . . . . . . . . . :   08/13/94
Password expiration interval . . . . . . . . :   *SYSVAL
Set password to expired  . . . . . . . . . . :   *NO
User class . . . . . . . . . . . . . . . . . :   *USER
Special authority  . . . . . . . . . . . . . :   *NONE
Group profile  . . . . . . . . . . . . . . . :   QSYS
Owner  . . . . . . . . . . . . . . . . . . . :   *USRPRF
Group authority  . . . . . . . . . . . . . . :   *NONE
Assistance level . . . . . . . . . . . . . . :   *SYSVAL
Current library  . . . . . . . . . . . . . . :   *CRTDFT
Initial menu . . . . . . . . . . . . . . . . :   *SIGNOFF
  Library  . . . . . . . . . . . . . . . . . :
```

Figure 3.3 Display User Profile. This QUSER profile is patched to be a member of a restricted system profile QSYS.

The best method to determine whether any of the system profiles have been compromised is by reviewing each of the reserved profiles for their previous sign-on dates. Obviously, they should all be blank. Listing all authorized users on the system may show which profiles are being used by an uninvited guest.

An attacker who is capable of this kind of invasion, though, possesses the capability to be far less obvious. The same technique could be used to introduce the QSYS profile as a group profile to a non-privileged, QUSER-type profile as illustrated in Figure 3.3. This type of infiltration may be more difficult to detect, since system profiles are not altered but only referenced for their authority. The only way to detect a profile that borrows a system profile's authority may be to review each user's group profile individually. It is sufficient to say that user profiles and passwords may be compromised in many different ways.

Other Significant Threats

Although the Accounting Code parameter in the user profile definition is usually not given much attention, it can help to determine the time period and the amount of system resources used by each user or group of users. The Information Resource Accounting report generation programs provided with this book may be used not only to substantiate the growth patterns for a given enterprise, but also to track the perpetrator's actions and cycles. Once an assailant has been detected on the system, the primary focus should change from one of vigilance and defense to that of a silent hunter. Initiating a new accountability procedure during the hunt is a bad idea. Any activity or sudden changes in the system configuration outside of the norm will alert the intruder. Therefore, options such as the Accounting Code definition in each user profile should be designated as a matter of course, and the accounting level system value should be set to capture the appropriate data, as suggested in the Implementation chapters.

One of the parameters associated with user profiles is a default message queue for the user with an indicator showing what action should be taken when a message arrives to that queue. Defaults for these values usually specify the profile name and instruct that the user be notified when a message arrives. The message queues of the privileged profiles should be reviewed while the user is signed on to the system. A commonly known program called a message queue break handler may be associated with the privileged user's message queue; this program may be used to execute commands on behalf of another user. Such a program, when attached to a person with sufficient authority, may receive messages and execute a message as a command using the authority of the receiving person. Although one cannot simply assign a message queue break handler to someone else's workstation while in use, when we consider that even the most observant security officer leaves the workstation unattended once in a while, and that it only takes one message to create a permanent back door, we see that it is worthwhile to browse the message queues from time to time.

Let's consider one of the back doors that could be created by using a message queue break handler. A command could be sent to the security officer's message queue to grant a *USE authority to one of the privileged user profiles. Then the clever assailant could submit a batch job using the authority of the privileged profile. The batch job would, of course, create more subtle back doors.

It is necessary for readers to understand that it is not sufficient to protect against internal and external harm; it is also necessary to take proactive steps to capture a perpetrator. There is nothing more degrading to hackers than being outsmarted and having to face the consequences of their actions. If an assault is simply terminated in progress without consequence to its instigator, it only invites the assailant to play a more dangerous game the next time. Once hackers gain access to a system, one of their first priorities is to secure alternative passages in the event the primary route is discovered. The assailants may be back, and this time, revenge may fuel their determination.

CHAPTER FOUR

Object Management

Objects are at the heart of the OS/400 operating system. The construction of an operating system that is based on the object concept is significatnly and fundamentally different from that based on files. In lay terms, *object* essentially defines a single logical entity against which any number of actions may be taken. This entity may be a single unit or a group of units, such as an engine or a tire. As with an automobile, a variety of different objects are needed in order to make an operating system work properly.

All OS/400 objects share certain basic attributes. For instance, all objects have owners; they also have default authorities that describe who may or may not use the object, and they are all created by the operating system using a set of predetermined rules and template values. Therefore, the creator of an object has very little to say about the object's construction, only how the object is to be used.

Anatomy of an Object

All OS/400 objects are said to be *encapsulated*. In short, encapsulation ensures that all objects are utilized through an established interface. This process provides uniformity, stability, and integrity to the operating

44 MANAGEMENT

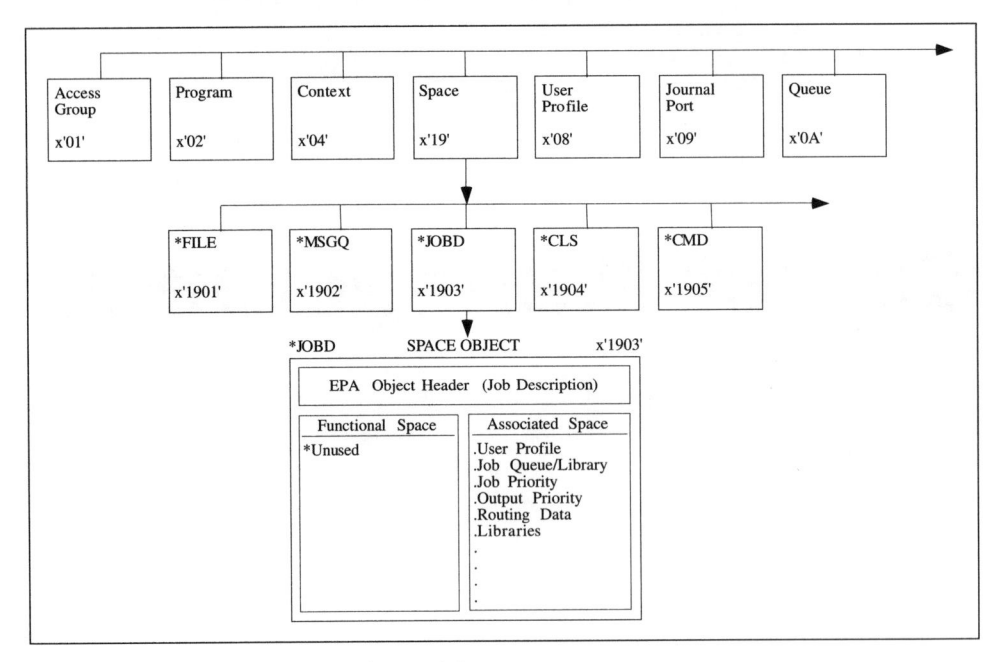

```
┌─────────┬─────────┬─────────┬─────────┬─────────┬─────────┬─────────┐
│ Access  │ Program │ Context │  Space  │  User   │ Journal │  Queue  │
│ Group   │         │         │         │ Profile │  Port   │         │
│  x'01'  │  x'02'  │  x'04'  │  x'19'  │  x'08'  │  x'09'  │  x'0A'  │
└─────────┴─────────┴─────────┴─────────┴─────────┴─────────┴─────────┘
                                    │
        ┌───────┬───────┬───────┬───────┬───────┐
        │ *FILE │ *MSGQ │ *JOBD │ *CLS  │ *CMD  │
        │x'1901'│x'1902'│x'1903'│x'1904'│x'1905'│
        └───────┴───────┴───────┴───────┴───────┘

              *JOBD     SPACE OBJECT         x'1903'
         ┌─────────────────────────────────────────┐
         │   EPA Object Header (Job Description)   │
         ├──────────────────┬──────────────────────┤
         │ Functional Space │  Associated Space    │
         │ *Unused          │ .User Profile        │
         │                  │ .Job Queue/Library   │
         │                  │ .Job Priority        │
         │                  │ .Output Priority     │
         │                  │ .Routing Data        │
         │                  │ .Libraries           │
         │                  │ .                    │
         │                  │ .                    │
         │                  │ .                    │
         └──────────────────┴──────────────────────┘
```

Figure 4.1 Machine interface object types.

system environment. All OS/400 objects are identified by their type, subtype, and name designations, as illustrated in Figure 4.1. The type and subtype designations are currently implicitly assigned by the operating system. The name of an object, however, may be assigned by the operating system or by the creator of the object. Although the OS/400 user interface only allows 10 characters to be used in an object name, the internal length of an object name may be as long as 30 bytes.

Every object is described within the Encapsulate Program Architecture (EPA) header information (Figure 4.2), a block of data at the beginning of each object that tells the OS/400 its type, subtype, name, size, version, release, public authority, creator's authority, and the creator's profile, along with other attributes. This information is vital to the workings of the operating system, since without it, the OS/400 would not know what type of object it was or how to manipulate the object's contents.

All OS/400 objects are constructed in two distinct parts: functional spaces and associated spaces. These are used to host a variety of object-type specific data. In a program object type, the functional space may contain

OBJECT MANAGEMENT

```
    DISPLAY/ALTER/DUMP                          JPARK USER PROFILE                          09/10/94  18:43:31  PAGE
USER PROFILE               SUBTYPE:  01    NAME:  JPARK                         ADDRESS:  0053  01297500 0000
SEGMENT HEADER   (YYSGHDR)
   TYPE  01    FLAGS  91   SIZE  0020   EXT  0053   OBJ  01297500 0000    SPLOC  01297600 0020
EPA HEADER    (YYEPAHDR)                                                                    Public Authority
   ATT1   80           JOPT   00              TYPE   08          STYP   01
   NAME   JPARK
   SPATT  80           SPIN   40              SPSZ   992         OSIZ   00000032      PBAU   3800
   VER    0101         TIME   08/09/92  20:01:27                 UP0    0003 00023800 0000
   AG0    0000 00000000 0000                   CT0    0000 00000000 0000              OHDR   0053 01297500 0000
   RCVV   00020000     PERF   01000000        MDTS   09/10/94  17:48:01               JP0    0000 00000000 0000
   COB0   0000 00000000 0000                   JID    00000000000000000000             OWAU   FF00
   IPL#   0000002C     AL1    00000000000000                                Owner Profile
01297500 0000    01910020 00538000   00530129 75000000   00000000 00000000   00530129 76000000   *...........
01297500 0020    80000801 D1D7C1D9   D2404040 40404040   40404040 40404040   40404040 40404040   *....JPARK
01297500 0040    40408040 000003E0   00000032 38000101   72BD1EF5 A44000C0   00030002 38000000   *.........5..  Owner Authority
01297500 0060    00000000 00000000   00000000 0D000000   00000000 00000000   00020000 01000000   *...........
01297500 0080    767B0E54 8E00004C   00000000 00000000   00000000 00000000   00000000 00000000   *.#.........
01297500 00A0    0000FF00 0000028C   00000000 00000000   00000000 00000000   00000000 00000000   *...........
                                                                                                           More...
```

Figure 4.2 Encapsulated Program Architecture segment header.

Machine Interface instructions. In a message file object type, on the other hand, the functional space may contain index entries that describe where the actual messages may be found in the objects own associated space. Many OS/400 objects share the common object type of Space object. These Space objects are used for different purposes, the most common of which perhaps is to store information that may be used by the operating system at a later time. The operating system recognizes what information is contained in these Space objects by their subtype designations.

Ownership Authority

The object owner's authority and the creator's profile pointer are part of the object header data and therefore are stored with the object itself. If the requester of the object is also the owner of the object, then the authority validation process may be shortened due to the implicit object ownership authority, which includes all data rights as well as object management rights as a default. The owner of an object has the ultimate authority over the control of the object, including deletion. Because creator's names are in effect imprinted with each object, when a creator is to be deleted, all objects belonging to the creator must have their ownership transferred to another user. Otherwise there will exist objects whose owner may no longer be on the system, which would create tremendous problems for the operating system. The object ownership configuration can become a nightmare to manage, especially when users are often transferred from one workgroup to another.

The primary means used to simplify the management of object ownership is through the use of group profile object ownership as opposed to individual profile object ownership. Group profile ownership simplifies object ownership management by assigning the group profile as the owner whenever an object is created by a member of the group. The end result is that individuals may be transferred from one workgroup to another or removed from the system without the system administrator having to go back and reassign objects that they have created.

Public Authority

Public authority signifies default access permission, and may be given to all users on the system for a specific object. Each object hosts a default public authority in addition to the owner's profile and authority. The public authority value may grant all rights, reserve all rights, or designate some authority in between. The public authority value of an object is used only if there are no specific authorities designated for the requesting profile.

The initial public authority value for an object defaults to the object creation authority parameter contained in the library (*LIBCRTAUT) of which the object is going to be a member. Therefore, if a particular library's object creation default authority is designated to be *EXCLUDE, then all objects created into that library would have *EXCLUDE as their default public authority unless specifically overridden. Figure 4.5 illustrates the authority validation procedure.

Private Authority

Private authorities are authorities given to a specific profile for a particular object. All private authorities and ownership authorities are stored with individual profile objects illustrated in Figure 4.3. If a profile owns or is authorized to many objects, the profile's object storage area may become excessively large. This may cause problems if a user profile has a defined maximum storage size allowed as part of its profile definition. Additionally, working with an "overloaded" profile may adversely affect

```
OBJECT TYPE-        USER PROFILE                           *USRPRF
NAME-        QUSER                    TYPE-     08  SUBTYPE-      01
LIBRARY-     MACHINE CONTEXT
CREATION-    02/04/92  14:40:15       SIZE-     0000003400
OWNER-       QSECOFR                  TYPE-     08  SUBTYPE-      01
ATTRIBUTES-        0000               ADDRESS-  00024800   0000
USER PROFILE-
   000000    00FFFF00 00000080 0801D8E4 E2C5D940 40404040 40404040 40404040 40404040   *            QUSER             *
   000020    40404040 40404040 C0000000 00000000 000003E0 40010000 00000000 00000000   *         {          \          *
   000040    00000000 00000000 00000000 00000000 00000000 00000000 00000000 00000000   *                               *
   000060    E0600000 0E000000 7FFFFFFF 00000000 80000000 00000000 00000000 00000000   *\-        "                    *
AUTHORIZED OBJECTS-
   19 02 QUSER                     04 01 QUSRSYS                    FF80 3F00 00385E000000
   12 01 QPACTL01                        MACHINE CONTEXT            FF80 3F00 004FFA000000
   10 01 QPADEV0001                      MACHINE CONTEXT            FF80 3F00 00F9A7000000
   19 02 QPADEV0001                04 01 QSYS                       FF80 3F00 00F9A9000000
   08 01 QUSER                           MACHINE CONTEXT            7F00 0040 000248000000
   19 01 TEMPORARY                                         +:£_C    3F00 3F00 0034C1000000
   08 90 TEMPORARY TEMPORARY       04 C1 QTEMP                      3F00 3F00 0034C7000000
                                                        Private Authorities   Public Authorities
```

Figure 4.3 Object authorization table in user profiles.

system performance during save or restore operations. Although the group profile object ownership notion is strongly recommended, this is one of its disadvantages.

The OS/400 operating system provides the Work with Objects by Owner (WRKOBJOWN) and Edit Object Authority (EDTOBJAUT) commands to help effectively manage object ownership and private authorities. Object ownership may be transferred and private authorities may be revoked by using these commands.

Authorization Lists

An authorization list is an object that associates many user profiles with specific authorities to a list of objects (Figure 4.4). A user profile may only be associated with a single authority. This single authority governs all objects in the authorization list. For example, if profile Debbie is associated with an authorization list having *USE authority, she would be able to use all objects in the current authorization list as well as any other object that may be added in the future. Conversely, if Karen is *EXCLUDED from the same authorization list, she would be restricted from all objects assigned to that authorization list now and in the future.

One other restriction that the use of an authorization list imposes is that an object may only be a member of a single authorization list. This means that an authorization list can not be used to secure Debbie from using objects A and B, but not C. This problem may be solved by creating two authorization lists, the first containing objects A and B, the second

48 MANAGEMENT

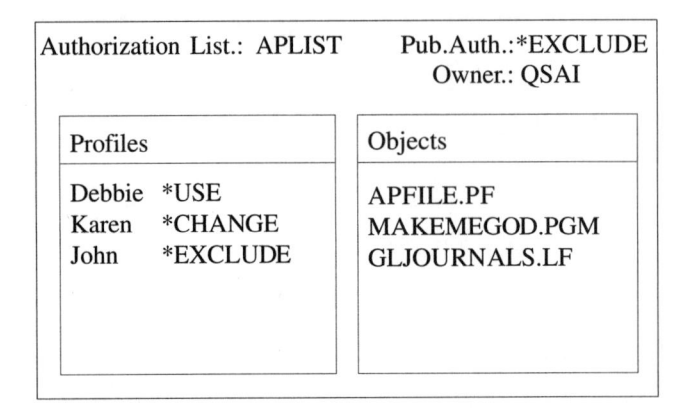

```
Authorization List.: APLIST        Pub.Auth.:*EXCLUDE
                                   Owner.: QSAI

   Profiles                 Objects

   Debbie   *USE            APFILE.PF
   Karen    *CHANGE          MAKEMEGOD.PGM
   John     *EXCLUDE         GLJOURNALS.LF
```

Figure 4.4 Authorization list usage.

containing object C. Then profile Debbie may be authorized to use the objects in the first list, but restricted from the use of the objects in the second list. If, in addition, Karen needed to access objects A and C, but not B, the two authorization lists would need to be reconfigured into three separate authorization lists, each having only one object, with appropriate authorities for Debbie and Karen profiles. This may be more cumbersome to manage and to maintain than using private authorities.

Unlike the group profile concept, where all objects created by the group's members are owned by the group profile and all members are thus given implicit authorities to any new objects created, there is no mechanism on the OS/400 to assign an object to an authorization list as it is created. Objects must be specifically added to authorization lists. Some authorization list usage may be quite helpful, however. For example, authority to an office document may be given to various individuals simply by associating the document with an authorization list; the individuals and group profiles attached to the authorization list would immediately be able to access the document or be restricted from it.

Authority Holders

Authority holders may be used to specify authorities to program-described database file objects that may not exist on the system. If authority holders

OBJECT MANAGEMENT 49

are used, the database file object's private authorities are ignored in favor of the private authorities associated with the authority holder. Although this feature is most often used in the System/36 environment, authority holder management commands are indistinguishable from those of the native AS/400 environment. Commands such as Grant Object Authority (GRTOBJAUT), Revoke Object Authority (RVKOBJAUT), Display Object Authority (DSPOBJAUT), and Edit Object Authority (EDTOBJAUT) will function as if the authority holder is the actual program-described database file.

It is appropriate that the only users who may use the Create Authority Holder (CRTAUTHDR) command are those with privileged *ALLOBJ authority, because if intruders were to acquire knowledge that a company is using program-described database files, they could potentially create authority holders with the same database file names, giving them ownership privileges to those databases. This is possible because in the System/36 environment, most databases are program-described rather than externally described, and programs are often designed to delete old data files and re-create them as necessary. If a system detects the existence of an authority holder during a database file creation, the ownership of the database file is implicitly given to the owner of the authority holder, creating the potential for an intruder to gain full access to the database file as well as existence authority to destroy it.

Authority holders are automatically created during System/36-to-AS/400 migration. However, authority holders are only needed for those databases that are deleted and re-created. Therefore, any authority holders for database objects whose existence is static should be removed using the Delete Authority Holder (DLTAUTHLR) command. It is also recommended that System/36 migrated programs be changed to avoid deleting and re-creating databases in favor of clearing files for the same reasons.

Authority Adoption

Programs, service programs, and SQL packages may be created to execute under the influence of the owner's authority rather than under the requester's authority. This feature is available in the OS/400 operating system for many reasons and is known as the "authority adoption" feature. The main purpose of this function is to allow temporary access to secured objects through an established and controlled path. For example, users may be restricted to all objects except those associated with their main menu. Each option from their main menu would execute the selected function using the adopted authority of the called program. In this way, no user would be able to access the data directly without using his or her menu. The menu program, in turn, would be secured so that only selected users could gain access to those menu functions.

In theory, this approach to securing a system is viable. In practice, however, it becomes quite cumbersome to manage this "intentional release of control"[1] throughout the system. There are numerous pitfalls that could present themselves if this scenario were to be followed literally.

The most reasonable use of this feature is in situations where normal object authority assignments cannot address the users' authority requirements. For instance, suppose that the only information Marc needs the ability to view is the General Ledger journal information, except during month end periods. He may be given the *USE authority to browse that data at any time. At month end, however, *USE authority would not suffice, and Marc would require at least a temporary *CHANGE authority. A program could be created to service Marc's needs by using the authority adoption feature. This program, when called, would execute using the authority of the program's owner, who has the necessary authority to the database objects.

The authority adoption concept is relatively simple as has just been stated. However, there are a few security-related issues that should be considered prior to designing programs that will adopt owners' authorities. The most obvious of these concerns is that as a default, all programs are created to take advantage of and propagate the adopted authority unless it is specifically stated otherwise. For example, if MAKEMEGOD program was created to run under the creator's privileged authority, the authority associated with the creator of MAKEMEGOD program would still be in effect in all subsequent programs that MAKEMEGOD invoked. The subprogram DELETEALL might thus gain sufficient authority to delete more than what it would have been able to without the adopted authority. If, on the other hand, the MAKEMEGOD program were to inadvertently or on purpose invoke the command entry program (QCMD), security would be

---

1. AS/400 Security Reference Guide, IBM SC41-8083-02, Third ed., November 1993.

nonexistent for that user. Such a user could grant any authority to any object within the boundaries limited to the authority of the owner of the MAKE-MEGOD program.

Additionally, a less known but potentially damaging loophole exists when using OS/400 commands that resolve and update pointers in the user's job space. When an adopted authority program adds additional libraries to the interactive job's library list in order to carry out its function, but neglects to remove those libraries before the end of the program, those libraries from which the user was originally restricted become available to the user after they are called. When libraries are added to the user's job space, the pointers and authorities to the libraries are resolved, and the pointers, not the library names, are added to the requester's internal job space. This means the requester's job will not need to revalidate authority to the libraries already in its job space. The end result is that in such situations, a user would gain residual authority to access the libraries and may have enough public authority to view the data kept within those libraries. This scenario is all too likely to occur, since many AS/400 professionals group objects together in a library and revoke the authority to the library from users in an effort to secure objects within the library, rather than revoking an individual object's authorities within each library.

Because of the issues surrounding the use of authority adoption, OS/400 offers extensive fail-safe mechanisms. For instance, the authority gained by the authority adoption process can be manipulated in such a way that it is only effective within the program that actually adopts the owner's authority, and does not propagate such authority to subsequent programs. This may be accomplished by changing programs so that they do not allow the use of adopted authority via the Change Program (CHGPGM) command. Also, the designers of the OS/400 were cautious enough to automatically suspend the use of adopted authorities during system request, group jobs, debugging, job submission, user-defined message handling, and attention key processing.

The restore operation also ensures that if a person other than a security administrator, a privileged user with *ALLOBJ authority, or the owner of the object tries to restore a program that executes under the owner's authority, all private and public authorities will automatically be revoked. In addition, if the owner's profile does not exist on the system where the object is restored, the restored object's owner designation will be automatically changed to the OS/400 default user profile of QDFTOWN.

One peculiarity exists, however; if a program is designed to execute under the owner's authority, and is replaced by one of the OS/400's compilers via a program recompilation process, the compile process purposely ignores the program creation parameters that disable the authority adoption function. Rather, the existing program's authority adoption controls are copied to the new program before the old program is displaced into the QRPLOBJ library. Therefore, all authority adoption controls should be modified by using the Change Program command, and, as a precaution, the program compilation parameters should not be relied upon.

Primary Group Authority

Every object in the system contains a flag that determines whether or not there exists any specific object authorities granted to specific profiles other than the owner's profile. Each profile, in turn, maintains a list of objects that it owns or to which it is authorized in a temporary queue accessible only through the user profile's associated space. When a request is made to access an object, the object's private authority existence flag is checked. If the flag value suggests that there are specific private authorities relating to the object, then the requesting profile's list of specific authorizations is searched for the desired object. This process of looking up the requester's specific authority to the object occurs even if there are no entries in the queue matching the object's identity. The look-up process is simply controlled by the object's private authority existence flag. Figure 4.5 illustrates the AS/400 object authority validation procedure.

Although the process of searching the requester's authorized list of objects is a relatively quick one, as the number of private authority assignments to objects increases, more specific searches into the requester's queue must be performed, which, in turn, degrades system performance. It is for this particular reason that the use of the object primary group feature is more desirable than the use of the private authorization scheme alone. The primary object group feature will allow security administrators to restrict a majority of system resources while streamlining the authorization vali-

OBJECT MANAGEMENT   53

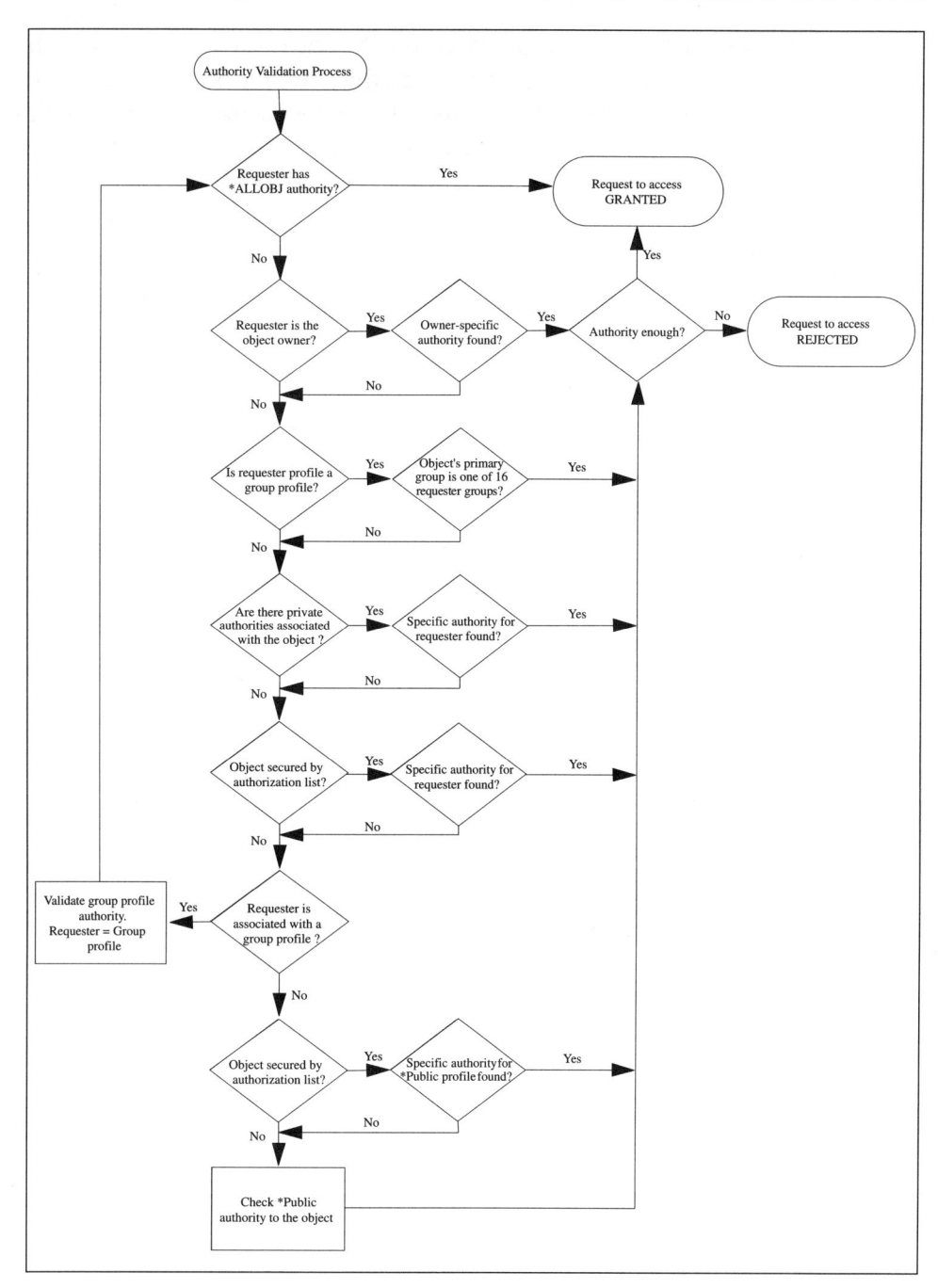

Figure 4.5 Aulthority validation procedure.

dation process to avoid searching the individual profile's authorizations list for each object requested. When the primary object group feature is used properly, the authorization validation procedure should have significantly fewer object specific authority assignments to process, since most authorities to objects for the requester are resolved by either Yes or No answers, or at the most, a look at 16 group profile names that may be associated with each user.

CHAPTER FIVE

Communication Management

Although AS/400s are generally not considered to be vulnerable systems today, the threat of break-ins is always more than just a possibility, increasingly proportionally as AS/400s gain popularity among corporate systems. It is clear that IBM intends to make the AS/400 one of the key components in its corporate information hierarchy. It is gaining market share as a file server and mid-range business system, and is quickly replacing yesterday's high-end multiprocessor mainframes. IBM is also addressing business's need to interconnect AS/400s using nontraditional SNA communication protocols, understanding that there are as many variations in communication protocols and configurations as there are requirements.

A brief chapter is certainly not sufficient to address the intricacies of AS/400 communication, nor is that the focus of this book. There are dozens of acronyms that are supposed to mean something that many of us simply don't have the time to learn and would rather leave to someone else to figure out. In this world of communications connections, already difficult to understand, there exists a dichotomy. Why is communication so often linked with hackers when it requires attention to so many tedious details just to establish the connection? I remember a threat by an employee who stated that if he were to damage the system, he would call his destruction in from a phone booth, implying that he need not be present at the office to create havoc.

It might seem reasonable for the management staff to assume that if proper precautions are taken, corporate assets will be safe from outside intruders attempting to gain access via communication channels. This assumption is based on the belief that without some knowledge of the target system's communication configurations, the chances of a remote intruder guessing several network-related values is very low. This assumption would be reasonable, except for two minor points: underestimation of hackers' social engineering abilities as practiced with unsuspecting end users, and overuse of default communication values due to lack of time or understanding of the subject matter. These minor but critical issues plague the digital communication industry both inside and outside the AS/400 world.

To make matters worse, once a working network model has been established, it is seldom modified, enhanced, or further secured. Many AS/400 operations and network administrators simply leave it alone in fear that it will go down for some mystical reason. Such a feeling of uncertainty is further reenforced by random bad cables, minor variations in parameters, mismatched location passwords, and a variety of other mishaps. Hence, even experienced network administrators often rely on staying with what works rather than understanding and applying the principles behind each communication configuration parameter to determine network problems. Eventually, other AS/400s are added to the network and the same techniques used to configure the first are repeated on subsequent systems.

While an information system staff slowly acquires network education by trial and error, the users' demands grow exponentially with each technical success. The lack of widespread knowledge in implementing solid communication security contributes, in some degree, to the popularity of software like the Kerberos network security system, which allows end users to sign on once and be able to hop across multiple systems and platforms with appropriate authorities. After all, computers should provide an optimum environment for users to address business functions; and if the security administrator is unable to secure the network, it would be far simpler to purchase a package than to reengineer the business around the lack of experience. Thus, pressure to make the network more accessible and user-friendly grows by leaps and bounds, while the major emphasis in the network establishment is simply to make it work and to survive staff turnover.

It is unfair to say that this scenario applies to all businesses and networks. However, it does apply to many, if not the majority. From an intruder's point of view, any networked system is only as strong as its weakest link. Once the weak link has been compromised, the intruder simply uploads the tools necessary to explore the rest of the network at leisure. The weak link may be one of hundreds of small AS/400s from satellite offices connected to the main office (e.g., that of an automotive dealership). The staff of a small local retail outlet might not even be aware of someone other than the corporate office dialing in to their machine, and even if they became suspicious, might not be able to do much about it.

This chapter, like the other chapters in Part One, is geared toward the management staff; hence the discussion will be limited in its use of technical terms and acronyms, instead using, where possible, objective-driven abstract concepts. The Implementation section, however, does describe and recommend specific values and present applicable program codes for technically inclined readers.

Fundamental Concepts

Implementing security on an AS/400 network may be broken into five discrete areas:

- The physical security of communication equipment
- The assignment of resource authorities associated with communication objects
- Establishment and validation of communicating entities
- Confirmation of communication conversation-specific validations
- Establishment of function security based on profiles

Physical security is mostly dictated by common sense: locking computer rooms, avoiding excessive temperatures, using temporary power supplies, and so on. Some concerns may not be so obvious—for instance, securing telephone closets.

Resource authority involves making sure a requester has enough authority to use the line, controller, and device descriptions, as well as job descriptions and other related AS/400 objects. For instance, a user who needs to update a remote database using a distributed data management (DDM) application must first possess the authority to the local system's DDM file associated with the remote database. Furthermore, the requester is also required to have the appropriate authority to access the actual database on the remote system.

The procedure used in identifying and validating the physical entities involved in the communication process, known as BIND, validates the source and target systems by using encrypted location passwords. If the source and target systems are operating at security levels above 10, the BIND process is said to be secured when the location passwords match. Conversely, if one or more systems are operating at security level 10, BIND is not considered to be secure even when the location passwords are in sync. If, on the other hand, the location passwords do not match regardless of security levels, a BIND failure occurs which terminates communication linkage. The AS/400 provides a default location password of *NONE, which translates to eight null characters as the location password. Although using this default value is convenient when managing a large network, consider specifying unique passwords for each AS/400, or at least for all X.25 networks and switched communications. The location passwords become increasingly important as the number of dial-ups and X.25 nodes increases. This is due to the uncertainty of the physical unit attached to the other end of the telephone line. For example, it is quite possible to tap into a network of AS/400s by redirecting the physical telephone line connection to another AS/400 or attaching a different AS/400 into the network for which the assailant has the complete authority to the new AS/400.

Once the BIND is complete, the next hurdle to cross is the communication conversation configuration associated with APPC (advanced program-to-program communications) applications. It largely determines whether or not guest users should be asked to prove their identity before being allowed to access the host system. This procedure is controlled by the Secure Location (SECURELOC) parameter either in a device description or in the configuration list entry. If the host is told (configured) that

Table 5.1 Bind Validation

	Target Qsecurity = 10	Target Qsecurity >10 LocPwd = *BLANK	Target Qsecurity >10 LocPwd = FRED
Source Qsecurity = 10	BIND Unsecured	BIND Unsecured	BIND Unsecured
Source Qsecurity >10 LocPwd = *BLANK	BIND Unsecured	BIND **Secure**	BIND Failed
Source Qsecurity >10 LocPwd = FRED	BIND Failed	BIND Failed	BIND **Secure**

the guest system is a secure system and that the BIND is secure, then the host allows the guest to use either the same profile or another profile, providing the password sent is correct for the substitute profile. If the host is told that the guest system is not a secure system, the communication subsystem's default user profile is used to initiate jobs on the host system. Until recently, the password sent across communication channels for the substitute profile in an APPC conversation request was not encrypted, but enhancements in the version 3 release 1 of the OS/400 include a feature equivalent to encryption to prevent intruders from learning profiles and passwords through line tapping.

User Exits

The final guardians in communication security are user exits that determine what actions are to be taken when the local system detects remotely submitted network jobs, PC Support requests, passthrough sessions, and distributed data management accesses. These user exits may be used to discriminate for or against specific functions based on the profile of the requester. For example, the QRMTSIGNON system value may be used to initiate a user-written program that would ensure that only a selected group of users found in a database would be able to pass through from a remote system or a PC. The PC Support Access (PCSACC) network attribute may be used to reject all PC Support access requests, to allow access in accordance with object authority validation rules, or to further discriminate, in addition to the object authority validation, the access based on a user-specified exit program. The Distributed Data Management Access (DDMACC) network attribute is similar to that of the PC Support access network attribute in that it is used in PC Support shared folders support, and submission of remote commands. Lastly, the Job Action (JOBACN) network attribute specifies whether jobs submitted remotely through the Submit Network Job (SBMNETJOB) command should be rejected, or filed for approval, or whether a table should be searched for the appropriate action to be taken.

The PC Support access network attribute is used to determine whether file transfer capability is allowed for a given user. In many instances, object authority is not sufficient, since all users have the ability to create objects and work with objects that they have created. This ability, coupled with the ability to restore objects or libraries and start REXX procedures, introduces a potentially dangerous security exposure situation if not managed properly. Distributed data management access provides PC Support users with the capacity to use the AS/400 as a server of word processing documents and PC objects. It is capable of transferring the contents of an AS/400 database to PC documents, and vice versa. It is also involved in executing remotely submitted OS/400 commands from a PC. The DDM and PC Support access user exit programs accompanying this book should be modified and used to limit access to the AS/400 based on profiles and functions.

Client/Server Connections

The attractiveness of the AS/400 file server is multifold. Among the most notable features are a comprehensive integrated database, a proven, stable operating system, and a security system far better than those of PC-based operating systems available today. The AS/400 also provides true multitasking capabilities by utilizing multiple processors, supports transparent distributed data management features, and communicates with just about anything. The only ability it lacks is an intuitive graphical user interface found on most PCs. To that extent, a combination of a PC-based user interface with the power of AS/400 seems an ideal choice. Therein lies the logic behind the birth of an AS/400-based client/server system.

A variety of connections may be used to implement client/server applications. Among the earliest of these connections was made possible by the use of 5250 emulation software. If a PC is to be locally attached to an AS/400, then a local 5250 emulation card, rather than a remote 5250 emulation card is required. [The local 5250 emulation card is connected to an AS/400 by a twinaxial cable, whereas a remote 5250 emulation card is really a Synchronous Data Link Control (SDLC) communications adapter that needs to be connected to the AS/400 via a pair of synchronous modems.] The 5250 emulation software essentially mimics an AS/400 workstation and/or a printer. These 5250 cards are primarily used to provide a dumb terminal interface without having to purchase the PC Support software from IBM.

Another popular method used to connect a PC to an AS/400 is by way of an AS/400 ASCII workstation controller, which is capable of communicating with local or remote PCs using common ASCII terminal emulation software. Software packages such as Procomm or Terminal that are capable of emulating the VT100 device are sufficient to connect to an AS/400. The only requirement to communicate, aside from the AS/400 ASCII workstation controller, is an asynchronous modem at both ends. Although the ASCII emulation connection is generally slower than 5250 emulation at equivalent modem speeds, the functions it provides are equivalent.

The IBM PC Support product is probably the most widely used means of connecting independent PCs to AS/400s. Although the hardware requirements for asynchronous PC Support differs from that of synchronous PC Support as in 5250 and ASCII emulation configurations, PC Support software is identical for both types of connections. Unlike the 5250 and the ASCII workstation emulation software, the PC Support software provides file transfer capabilities, submission of remote AS/400 commands, integrated messaging functions, and shared folders, in addition to multiple workstation session conversations. Although PC Support's abilities to send messages and commands and to emulate workstation devices are of significant importance, it's the ability to access the AS/400's database files that is most significant for the client/server environment. The ability to transfer

62 MANAGEMENT

database files to and from a PC provides the AS/400 with the means to export specialized functions to other processors, even though those functions are limited and have their drawbacks as far as security is concerned. The use of the shared folders function is also of significance, since the folders serve as a common storage area for all PCs, and access to this area is governed by OS/400 object authorization rules.

Shared Folders

The objects contained in today's shared folders and tomorrow's integrated file systems may become increasingly more important, due in part to the ability of the OS/400 v3r1's image integration feature. As of v3r1, AS/400 may not only process OfficeVision/400 documents, among other files, but also image objects (TIFF, PCX, and IOCA). These image objects may be displayed using native AS/400 display logic units (3489V) or PC emulation software that supports the new enhanced nonprogrammable terminal user interface (ENPTUI) capabilities (Figure 5.1).

This development may pose a security risk beyond that of the word processing document area. If the stored images are those of payroll

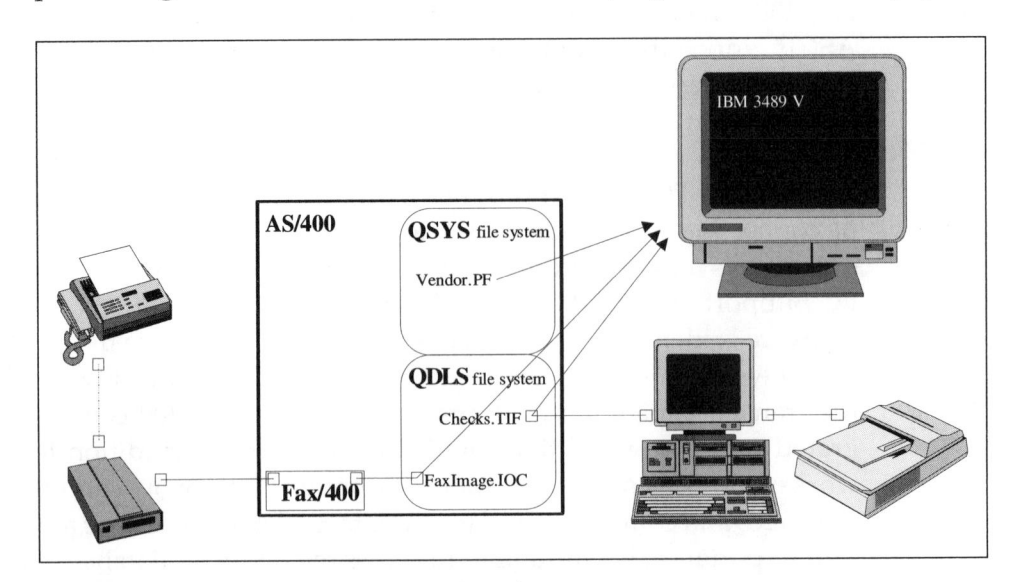

Figure 5.1 Integrated image processing.

checks, personnel records, medical records, and so on, the sensitivity of these images would be of great concern. The ability to access these image files or documents must be carefully controlled for every PC Support user.

Do not assume that securing shared folders is the same as securing directories on a PC network. The documents within AS/400 shared folders may be accessed by any users who have the authority to the object, even if they have no authority to the folders preceding the current folder for which the document is a member. For example, if folder B is a subfolder of A, a user who is restricted from folder A but authorized to folder B will still be able to access documents within folder B although it is a subfolder of A. This is unlike most PC network operating systems, where subfolders are also restricted if the parent folder is restricted.

The object within a shared folder may be accessed directly if one specifies the full folder path and the object name and has the appropriate authority for the object. Furthermore, the objects in shared folders may not be secured by group profile as they can with the other OS/400 object types, since these objects are considered to be in a different file system than that of the QSYS. The QSYS file system, which controls the libraries, programs, database files, and so on, abides by the rules enforced by the QSYS file system structure, whereas shared folders contents are controlled by the QDLS file system structure. Additionally, AS/400 supports POSIX-compliant QOpenSys file system, Windows compatible QPWXCWN file system, and LAN Server/400 QLANSvr file system structures (as illustrated in Figure 5.2). All these file systems are part of the AS/400's native Integrated File System (IFS) design, which is made possible largely due to the object-oriented design of the AS/400. In absence of the group profile authorization mechanism, the best way to secure objects in these hierarchical file systems may be to use the authorization lists and private authorities.

Integrated File System

The Integrated File System (IFS) is not a new architecture created on the AS/400 to host the client/server technology, but an exploitation of the already existing possibilities that AS/400 architecture allows. The QSYS file system with which traditional System/38 and AS/400 bigots identify is implemented through the use of a system object called Machine Con-

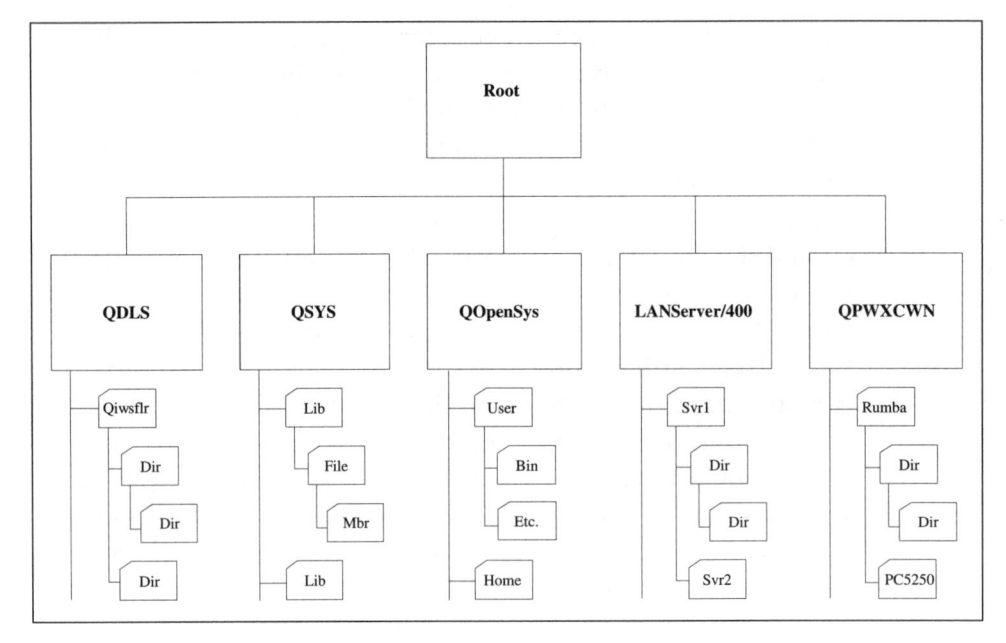

Figure 5.2 Integrated file system.

text. This Machine Context describes and maintains all library objects for which QSYS is a member. The Machine Context also describes and maintains other file systems in addition to the QSYS file system, such as the Document Library Services (QDLS) file system. The QDLS file system is referred to as a nonrelational byte stream–oriented file system, or a Hierarchical File System (HFS). The Machine Context keeps track of QDLS file system's directories and files in a tree-like relationship that differs considerably from the traditional QSYS file system. The rules associated with using each file system may be independently developed as new file systems are introduced, avoiding the re-creation of the OS/400 operating system.

This design serves as the basis on which many other file systems, including the POSIX, Client Access, and LAN Server, will undoubtedly be introduced in the future. It is also the "magic" behind the ability of OS/400 software developers to create and maintain application-specific file systems. Its most stunning feat, however, is the ability to manipulate and use data across multiple file systems through the OS/400 operating system commands.

The security issues surrounding the use of these file systems are not as clear-cut with the release of OS/400 v3r1, since the 64-bit RISC processor, which is supposed to drive the various environments (or "personalities," the term IBM has coined) is not yet generally available. However, if the history of OS/400 security measures is any indication, there will undoubtedly be viruses that go undetected by the operating system.

PC Workstations

Although many AS/400 data processing professionals realize that the traditional AS/400 terminals are not going to be the only way of communicating with AS/400s, and that most likely, those terminals eventually will give way to PCs as the de facto workstations for many users, these same professionals have not yet fully alerted the mainstream data processing industry regarding the potential security exposures involved in using PCs as workstations. Some of the early habits developed while using PCs as workstations have not yet been revisited for an evaluation of their effectiveness in practicing security measures at the workstation level. For example, through all the trials and tribulations of using IBM's PC Support software, many IS professionals have mastered the art of pre-loading the necessary device drivers and assigning the common user identifier with a piped-in password for all PC Support users. This made life easier for many users, since the connectivity to an AS/400 was made relatively transparent for them. The problem is that anyone could turn on the PC and gain access to the AS/400. What's more, the use of a common user identifier may further confuse a security administrator as to the identity of the person that is behind a common group name. The use of a common user identifier even undermines the use of PC Support and DDM user exit programs, since these are most effective when they allow or disallow requests based on various user profiles.

Although one may think the use of the hardware protection schemes accompanying a PC such as a lock and key or low level PC bios based password protection, in addition to individualized user identifiers and passwords, may suffice, the crux of the problem is not solved by such physical or low level PC security measures—although they will help the security practice in general, if they can be enforced. The crux of the problem is that both the AS/400 password and the corresponding profile are kept in a PC that may be compromised independently of the host system. Even under lock and key with password protection, a PC may be easily accessed by prying open the case, which is usually secured only by a strip of plastic, and disconnecting the battery or altering a jumper setting in order to reset the password. Once it has been compromised, the entire network is in jeopardy. Therefore, do not assign common user identifiers, and do not allow passwords to be piped in from a data file. Ask users to enter these values during the start-up process or use a PC Support router that asks for the user ID and password when they are needed rather than at start-up.

Data Encryption

Whether the AS/400 is communicating with a PC workstation via modem or with a locally attached terminal through a twinaxial cable, the data transmitted thereby is vulnerable without the use of an encryption mechanism. Granted, locally attached devices are far less susceptible to tampering than remotely attached workstations; that does not, however, excuse the local devices from being considered a security risk.

This is not to suggest that every cable originating from the back of the AS/400 should have an encryption device attached. It does, however, represent a basis against which any self-imposed compromises may be compared. Many entities (the U.S. government among them) have varying degrees of secure transmission requirements. For instance, as early as 1982, the U.S. government employed laptop computers (GRiD Compass computers) attached to frequency modulated radio sets to transmit the status of front-line infantry units via KY-12 scramblers. These scramblers are used in pairs, with each scrambler containing a sandwich-like cartridge that opens in half, exposing the encryption keys to be used for the next 24 hours. These encryption devices not only are vastly superior to the Data Encryption Standard (DES) used by the CIA and NSA, but are also made from materials that induce self-destruction with the slightest of effort. This is an example of the extent of security that one must practice in order to save lives on the battlefield.

Although corporate assets may not be compared to lives, they are of considerable value to those who wish to protect them. To that extent, encryption security measures may be prudent, especially for remote dial-up lines. When considering the availability of the different communication diagnostics hardware and software that may be used to monitor data transmission for both synchronous and asynchronous communications, the use of encryption hardware may be more of a required reactive response to the uncertainty of data security through a public network than the proactive measure with which one would normally have associated encryption hardware a decade ago, thus the justification and investment for the Clipper chip technology by the U.S. government. The AS/400 is not without indigenous encryption capabilities, however. IBM offers the AS/400 Cryptographic Support licensed program product 5738-CR1, which enables an application to encrypt and decrypt data before and after transmission. When such encryption technology is used in conjunction with call-back modems, one can be reasonably assured that corporate assets are secured from unauthorized eyes.

If, on the other hand, such encryption technology is not considered feasible or warranted, consider the possibility of compression. Although compression is not encryption, many data processing professionals and lay hackers who are not familiar with encryption techniques may find that compressed data appear as if they were encrypted over the wire. Compression has the added advantage of being free and available, and it requires fewer data packets being transmitted over the communication lines. There are two indigenous OS/400 compression algorithms that may be used—Terse and Lemple Ziv 1 (LZ1) algorithms. The Terse algorithm compresses data faster, at the expense of the compression ratio. The LZ1 algorithm can compress reports so that they are reduced in size as much as 95 percent. These reports may then be transmitted to other AS/400s, where they may be expanded or saved onto a PC for archival purposes. The appendix contains the necessary program codes to enable this kind of compression.

Device Configuration

Sometimes the best way to discourage intruders is to ignore them. If the situation allows for a switched line configuration not to answer an incoming call automatically, then specify *NO for the AUTOANS parameter. Additionally, use the remote location name (RMTLOCNAM) and the exchange identifier (EXCHID) where applicable in the communication controller configuration. Also, the use of a location password (LOCPWD) for APPC devices is encouraged, as well as the secure location (SECURE-LOC) value of *NO for all but the most confident systems in the network.

One last note regarding network security concerns the importance of utilizing the value 3 in the maximum sign-on action (QMAXSGNACN) system value. Many AS/400 sites, especially those with several AS/400s, pay little or no attention to the importance of specifying an arbitrarily large number associated with the QAUTOVRT system value. If the value associated with the action to be taken when a user fails to sign on within a specific number of consecutive attempts is specified to "VARY OFF" the workstation device, then a potential intruder will have as many attempts at the sign-on process as there are virtual devices available. When only the workstation device, and not the user profile, is varied off, the intruder may simply initiate a passthrough function again, which will either create a new virtual device automatically or select one of the available virtual devices that has not yet been varied off. This would, in effect, give an intruder ample opportunity to try multiple profiles and passwords in the attempt to break into the system. It is acceptable to specify any number deemed necessary for the QAUTOVRT as long as the QMAXSGNACN value remains at 3 for security reasons.

CHAPTER SIX

Client/Server Issues

There are various ways to look at client/server computing. It can be defined as any two or more computing devices used in conjunction to accomplish a particular task, or a centralized database machine serving the data needs of many applications residing on other computing platforms. For the purposes of this book, we will adopt the latter description. In such a case, a server's function is to provide accurate, up-to-date, centralized data to anyone who has proper authority. The client, on the other hand, is responsible for the processing of data according to application-specific rules and timely presentation of requested information to the user.

The particular security issues in a client/server environment mainly involve an individual client application's ability to determine the requester's need, deliver only the information necessary, and properly secure the data received. Other issues, such as choice of an operational platform, communication establishment, and division of client and server responsibilities, can arguably be looked upon as connectivity or implementation security issues and are not necessarily indigenous to the client/server environment.

There exist many similarities between a server-based application accessed remotely via a communications channel and a client-based application requesting data through the same communications channel. Both are concerned with communications security, both require identity verification, and they are equally dependent on the accuracy of the data they will eventually receive. The client-based application has another concern, however. The client application's ability to store received data from a server and provide an equivalent set of functions for those who cannot always connect to a Server on the road is crucial to the client/server environment. The storing of data in a client machine does not itself necessarily pose a security risk, but the theft of a laptop client—and the data it contains—is a significant security concern. This chapter discusses some of the issues and concerns surrounding the distribution of corporate databases and applications from traditionally centralized host machines to PC networks, mainframes and mid-range computers, and the fast-growing population of mobile dial-up clients.

Client/Server Concept

There exists some confusion as to the conceptual difference between a client/server environment and the distributed data management, distributive processing, and cooperative processing technologies. For the sole purpose of clarifying this book's approach to client/server implementation, a brief—and by no means comprehensive—discussion of each technology follows.

Distributed data management technology provides seamless access to a desired database regardless of its physical location. The main difference between DDM's access and client/server's access of data is that under DDM, there is a single logical requesting entity that controls the access, selection, and manipulation of data. The host simply allows the requester to access the resource. The *distributive processing* concept is, arguably, similar to that of cooperative processing, in that they both provide pieces of application logic that, when used in conjunction, perform a desired function. The underlying theory in using this technology is that the strength of the collective processing power will eventually outweigh that of any single centralized processor machine. An example of this concept in practice is a PC network where each user may perform independent functions using his or her own PC but shares a printer attached to the network. Although the term "cooperative processing" implies a peer-to-peer relationship among the processors, whereas "distributive processing" suggests a hierarchical organization, these implications are often not reflective of actual usage or configuration.

Neither cooperative processing nor distributive processing technology precludes the use of distributed data management capabilities. For example, the MS Windows for Workgroups software provides the ability to share folders among workgroup users while also allowing them to use any of the printers attached to the workgroup members. Although, strictly speaking, DDM technology is IBM's standard for logically accessing any database through an APPC interface, the notion of dynamic data access from a source not physically located in one's own machine applies even to an application such as MS Windows. Using a combination of DDM and distributive processing, one could create an application that accesses remote databases, transparently shares programs, and cooperates with remote PCs so that the application may use any of the attached devices in order to perform its function. However, this process of sharing physical and logical resources is often limited to homogenous operating system environments such as DOS, Novell, OS/2, NT, and OS/400.

Although the need for sharing resources was identified long before the arrival of DDM and cooperative processing, it has always presented technical difficulties in crossing multiple operating system environments transparently. For example, unlike the access to shared files of any single homogenous operating system network, access to the AS/400 database from a foreign platform such as NT, OS/2, or Novell cannot be directly accomplished by a requester as it could within the requester's own operating system environment. It takes some help from an OS/400 operating system's built-in support to complete the database access request. Furthermore, cooperative processing takes on new meaning when one is interacting with foreign operating systems programs, since PC programs cannot directly invoke an OS/400 program via OLE2 (object linking and embedding) support. In addition to technical difficulties, cost issues enter the picture, making it seem a questionable business venture for any single organization to produce one operating system that can support all other operating systems environments.

Today's business community, however, demands that its computing machines have the ability to seamlessly share data and cooperate with one another in order to accomplish tasks more efficiently. The notion of a

72 MANAGEMENT

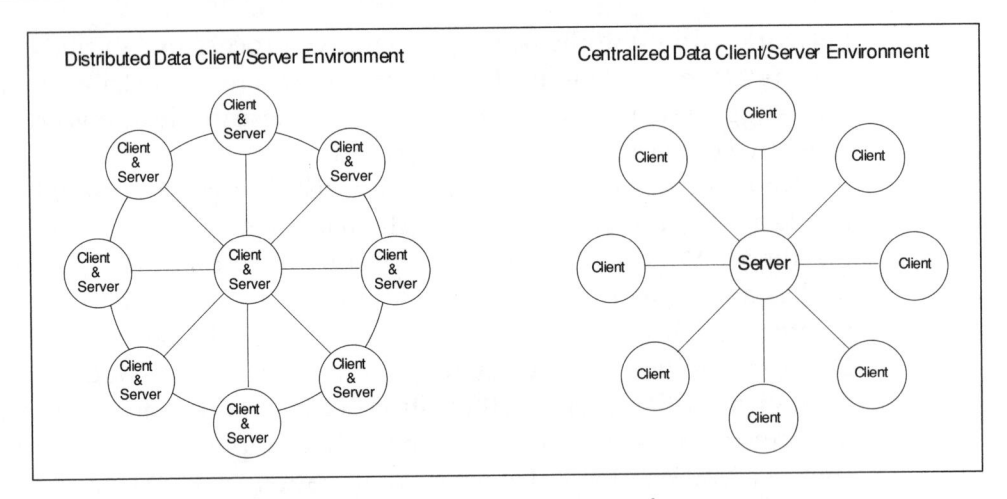

Figure 6.1 Single and multiple data server environment.

client (requester) and a server (provider) has surfaced in response to this demand. Under a client/server environment, any machine may assume the part of a client or that of a server (as illustrated in Figure 6.1). Each client machine must possess the ability to properly form requests for a specific server, no matter what operating system or type of machine the server may be. If the server is able to understand a common database access language such as SQL (Structured Query Language), then the requester's job is simplified. However, if the interface to the server is unique, then the requester must abide by the rules set forth by the server. Each server machine, on the other hand, must be able to fulfill its tasks in a manner consistent with the request. Theoretically, this division of responsibilities and roles will provide cohesiveness and efficiency in a world of varying standards and incompatibilities. In short, I believe, client/server technology is simply the most recent of the efforts to standardize all computing machines, created out of necessity in this time of fierce market competition.

Client Platforms

In the world of client/server application development, there are many client/server platforms to choose among for the purposes of application development. These range from an industry standard interface such as an Open Database Connectivity (ODBC) driver used over an IBM PC Support/400 router, to a set of user-written API calls over a vendor-specific router. An ODBC driver is a set of programming interfaces that enables high-level language application programmers to access a variety of databases from many dissimilar platforms using SQL as a common thread. Lower level user-written programs that interact with PC Support/400 APIs are unique to the AS/400 system.

The database access method chosen by the client application may be independent of the client application's execution environment. In other words, an AS/400 router supplied by a third-party vendor may be used in combination with API calls (created in house) to access database records from a FoxPro environment within an MS Windows platform.

End users generally do not concern themselves with the intricacies of data retrieval, ODBC or otherwise. However, users are interested in knowing that their applications are capable of disseminating information appropriately with respect to individual authority. Therefore, all client applications must address certain inescapable obligations when managing security issues within their applications.

C/S Role Topology

Client/server technology allows the freedom for any client to acquire data from one or more Servers either through a fixed cable attachment, a public telephone system, or frequency-modulated radio waves. This feature is significant to the development of client/server applications, since designers of C/S applications must allow users to be able to use a customer master file in one system against the orders file in another. The greatest impact of this feature is not realized, however, until one tries to secure data while preserving the flexibility of client/server technology. For instance, consider all the operational, administrative, and authority management issues that exist in addition to application-specific issues in a centralized AS/400 data server supporting 100 PC clients, as compared with the same issues in a distributed and mixed platform server environment supporting the same number of clients. The management responsibilities across all data processing areas will be significantly more extensive for a mixed platform C/S environment than they would be in a single centralized server environment. However, since the whole idea of client/server technology is to utilize the best resources to solve the business's needs, regardless of computing platforms, IT professionals can't simply ignore this option solely based on resource intensiveness. Rather, an efficient means should be found to manage resources and limit security exposure as much as possible.

Since the intuitive user interfaces available on various PC platforms are one of the major benefits of using PCs as clients, much of this chapter deals with graphical user interface constructs, such as windows and icons, in vendor-supplied desktop environments. In addition, an object-oriented approach to security planning and implementation is reinforced in developing PC client/server applications. In discussing the above mentioned topics, most of this chapter assumes that the server is connected to its clients in some way, so that the server has the means to process the requests received from clients. The impact of portable clients on system security is addressed in the last section of this chapter.

C/S Environment Security

One of the earliest issues that a developer of a client/server application must tackle is where to store client-specific authority data. Traditional host-based applications control the user's authority to access various applications and functions based on his or her designated authority in the authorization tables. When a user requests to sign on, the user's profile and password are validated by the OS/400 operating system. This action provides the OS/400 with the information about the user needed to effectively manage the object authorization process. For instance, the requesting client may be authorized to view the customer master file, but not to change its contents or add any new customers. If profile/password validation is bypassed somehow, the OS/400 will not be able to differentiate between a supervisor and a clerk. On the other hand, if this process is automated, such as by "piping in" a password to a PC batch program during boot, then the existence of a profile and password as input data on a client machine would represent an unwarranted security exposure.

However the communication conversation is initiated between a client PC and a server AS/400, the requester's identity must be established. There are some choices as to how this verification may be accomplished. The client program may initiate a conversation with the AS/400 under a common user profile, prompt the user for the profile and a password on the client system, and relay that information to the server for verification. If the verification is successful, the server would process all requests originating from that client under the verified profile's authority. Another method is to have the server communicate directly with the user on the client system during the C/S application start-up process. This eliminates the use of a common user profile, but may take away some flexibility and control from the client application itself. A major security benefit under the second scenario is that the security administrator on the AS/400 will always be able to identify the clients that the server is currently servicing. Neither of these methods takes into consideration a detached, portable client.

Folder Object Security

Once a user's identity has been verified, his or her authority to various information stored in a server or servers must be determined. For example, if a particular C/S application utilizes the object-driven concept, then a client should be able to access any folder (menus) containing various icons (functions) for which he or she has authority. A folder, in such a case, would represent an object, and therefore would be associated with authority attributes independent of any icons or subfolders that it may host. If a client is not authorized to access the folder, then he or she is also restricted from accessing any of the functions available within that folder. This is much like the OS/400's library/object access authority, in that one must first obtain the authority to use the library before one can access the objects within that library. However, unlike the OS/400's library/object implementation, the C/S application folder object contains a group of logical, not physical, objects, such as an Accounts Payable application's Voucher Entry icon, an Order Entry application's Customer Maintenance icon, and so on. These icons may be associated with other folders with different folder authorities, thus allowing individual clients to build their own folders with icons that

76 MANAGEMENT

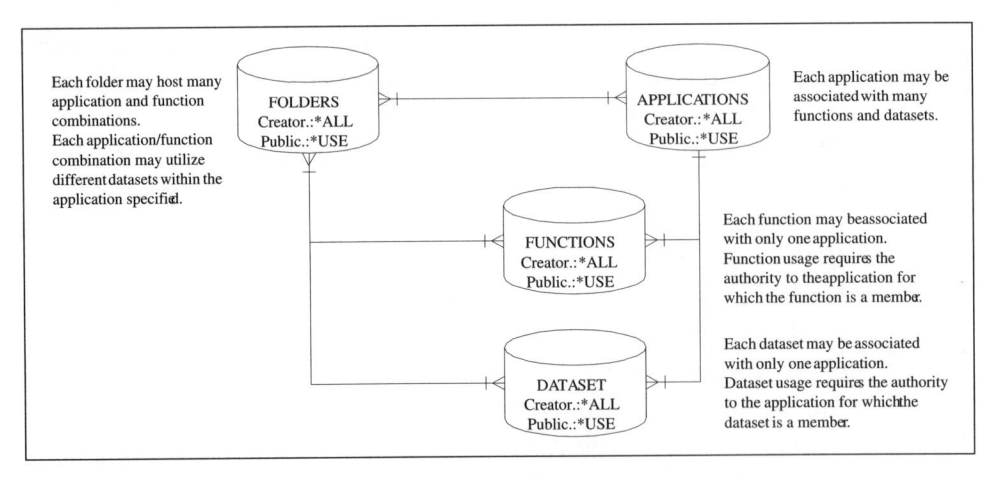

Figure 6.2 Client/server application object concept.

[Figure 6.2: Entity-relationship diagram showing FOLDERS, APPLICATIONS, FUNCTIONS, and DATASET objects, each with Creator.:*ALL and Public.:*USE attributes.

- Each folder may host many application and function combinations. Each application/function combination may utilize different datasets within the application specified.
- Each application may be associated with many functions and datasets.
- Each function may be associated with only one application. Function usage requires the authority to the application for which the function is a member.
- Each dataset may be associated with only one application. Dataset usage requires the authority to the application for which the dataset is a member.]

they utilize the most, provided the client first obtains the necessary authorities to the application functions and to the application itself. Figure 6.2 illustrates the folder, application, function, and dataset object concept.

Because of this variety of folders and the varying authorities required to use those folders, the client/server application must be able to recognize whether or not an individual user is authorized to access one folder versus another prior to displaying the initial C/S application desktop, since any unauthorized folders should be made unavailable (grayed out). This may be accomplished by utilizing a master server that maintains all individual authorities to specific folders. This, however, means that all clients must connect to the master server before the application can be made to function properly.

An alternative solution requires duplication of the master server's security database to other servers or to individual clients. If the security information is duplicated onto other servers (AS/400 only), then the burden of maintaining the accuracy of duplication will grow with each server put into service. If, in addition, the duplication of security information must cross operating system platform boundaries, then each server platform's indigenous security system represents the effectiveness of the entire client/server application security network. For example, if a copy of the client/server application's security database is distributed to a PC server, any PC program able to print the server machine's disk sectors would represent a serious security breach for the entire C/S network. On the other hand, if individual clients maintain a complete copy of the C/S application's security information, the loss of one portable client machine would jeopardize the entire security network, not to mention the enormous task that would be involved in synchronizing such databases among all clients. Conversely, if portable clients maintained only their own profile's security information so that they would not have to connect to a server on the road, then each client machine would only be useful to the individual to whom it was originally assigned, since each client would only recognize the assigned person's profile and password. This may seem appropriate in theory, but in practice client machines often change owners, and sales representatives borrow each other's laptops from time to time in haste to complete sales.

Without considering portable clients for the moment, the most reasonable recommendation would be to keep the security information on an AS/400 server or servers. If the security information must be duplicated among various servers, it may be best for the master server to distribute to other servers only the security information that the secondary servers would need to validate those clients who would gain access to the network via the secondary server. Automated synchronization of security information is highly recommended using any viable means, including APPC (advanced program to program communications), DDM (distributed data management), FTS (file transfer support), SNADS (system network architecture distribution services), and so on.

Application Object Security

Client/server applications are subject to the same rules and regulations that govern traditional host-based applications; in addition to folder security, it should be possible to secure each application from a user or a group of users. For example, an AP clerk should have authority to access the Accounts Payable application functions, but not the General Ledger functions. Opening a folder for which the clerk is authorized that contains General Ledger functions should automatically disallow the selection of unauthorized GL application functions.

In order to accomplish such authorization flexibility, logical applications must be made to behave as if they were physical objects. The

78 *MANAGEMENT*

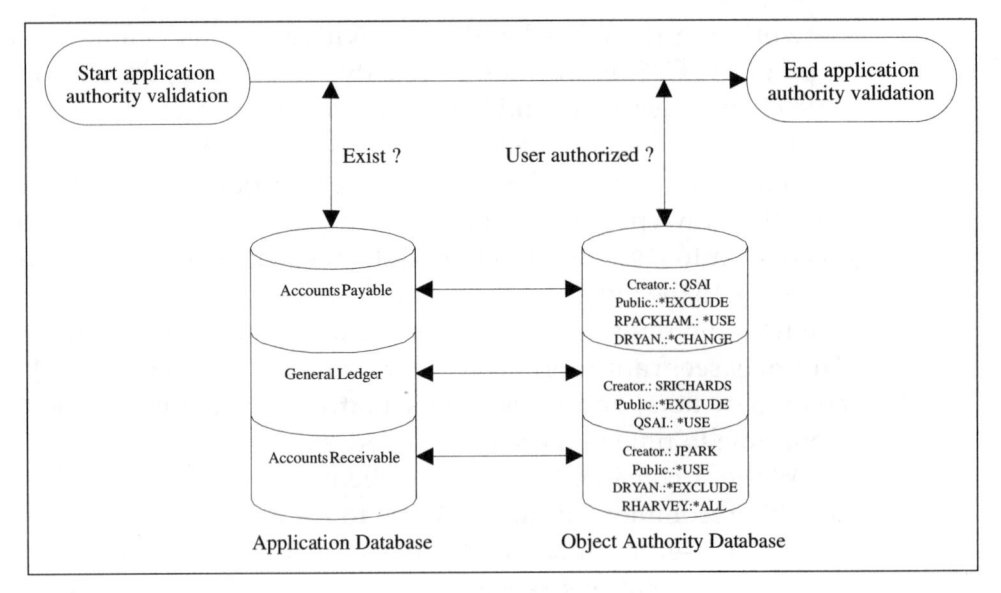

Figure 6.3 Application authority validation.

authority attributes of such logical application objects are stored in another database that contains the owner and public authorities of the application as well as any specific or group profile authorities associated with the application. This concept is illustrated in Figure 6.3. Any references to use functions within an application are verified through an OS/400 operating system authority validation-like routine.

An application definition record, on the other hand, may contain the server's name, data path, and routing designations as well as any prerequisite environment controls prior to executing any functions that belong to that application. For instance, if an Accounts Payable application resides on a secondary AS/400 server or a PC LAN Novell server, then application definition routing procedures may be used to automatically retrieve the necessary data from a remote server without the client's knowledge. If a work space must be created in a temporary directory or a library prior to the initiation of a particular application, the application path configuration may be used to find the temporary directory name.

In addition to such application-specific configurations, encryption keys, color palettes, function key assignments, and other application attributes may be defined by the application administrator rather than being permanently assigned by the application developer.

Dataset Object Security

The implementation of a dataset allows any application function within a folder to utilize a particular set of information rather than just one set of databases. For example, a programmer working to correct a problem in a General Ledger application is allowed to access only the test copy of the GL dataset rather than the production dataset. The application definition and the programs associated with the function being tested may be identical to those of the production environment, but the databases allowed to be accessed by the development staff are limited to the test dataset as illustrated in Figure 6.4.

In order to enforce such restrictions based on user classes, dataset definitions associated with an application must be manipulated as conceptual objects, with authorities stored externally, as in application definitions. Unlike application definition records, which are necessary because they provide a default dataset, among other application-specific information, additional dataset records for applications are not necessary for the proper execution of an application—they simply provide additional secure working environments for various classes of users. Having multiple dataset environments may allow a General Ledger accountant the ability to compare the previous year's reports against the current year's data in a PC LAN platform where the previous year's data may have been purged into separate data directories apart from the current dataset location.

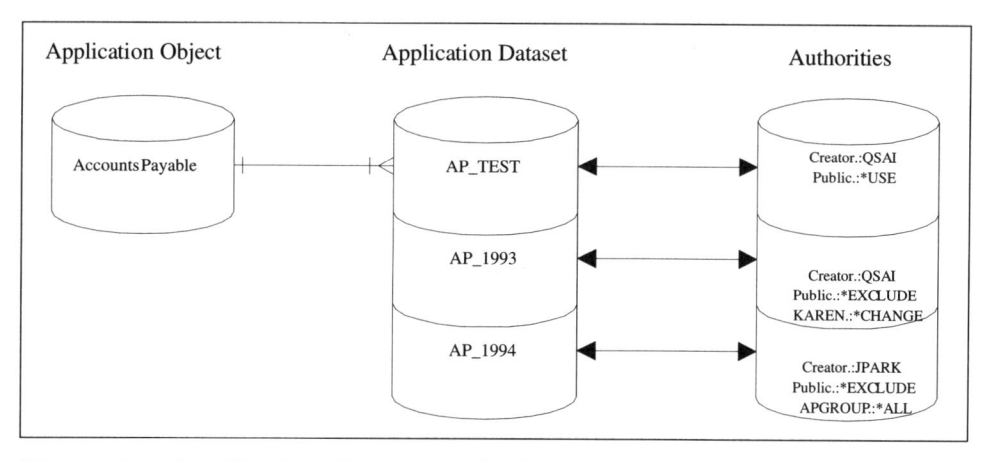

Figure 6.4 Application dataset authority.

Function Object Security

There are some obvious reasons to support function-level security within an application. A user who has authority to use an Accounts Payable application will also have the authority to use the check processing function, which is contained in the Accounts Payable application, if there have been no additional authority requirements at the function level. As a folder is opened by a user who has the necessary authority to the folder object, the client/server application should verify each icon found in the folder for its respective application authority, function authority, and any specified dataset authority. If any of these validation checks results in a failure condition, the icon should not be selectable by the user. As in the folder, application, and dataset security measures, function security should also be implemented through an object-oriented approach as previously illustrated. This particular approach to security will create an artificial view of applications, functions, and folders where each of these items will seem to represent an independent tangible entity and yet will implicitly work in conjunction with the others to present only the authorized folder options for any given profile. Any authority changes made to a single object will immediately have a cascading effect on the rest of the user profiles on the desktop.

Function Option Security

In addition to folder, application, function, and dataset securities, each application function is created with certain action bar options that will cue performance of the desired functions. These action bar options are usually pulled down to reveal a menu of choices. In a multiuser client/server application, a particular user may only be authorized to browse the information and not add, delete, or change the records in the database. In such a case, the choices to add or delete on the action bar pull-down menu must not be available for the user to select. The same function may allow another user to execute the full suite of options available from a pull-down menu. To differentiate one from the other, the client/server application developer must first create a set of programs that is capable of inheriting the user's authority attributes and perform client-specific functions. For example, when Karen activates the Accounts Payable Voucher Entry function from a folder, the system must build the initial voucher entry screen with function options specific to the user Karen or authorized to Karen from a default set of options assigned to the function.

If such a process were to be accomplished by each program of every function, application maintenance would become overwhelmingly difficult. Therefore, a reusable dynamic link library module should be used to build a part of the voucher entry function's initial panel structure. The Dynamic Link Library module (DLL) responsible for the screen build process should reference a database file where the authorities to the default action bar options and pull-down menus may be found. This DLL module would pre-build the action bar options and the associated pull-down menus using the authorities found in the database for the current profile, then initiate the application function originally chosen. By the time the chosen application function is displayed on the screen, only the appropriate action bar options are made selectable, thanks to the DLL module. If function option security is implemented in this way, the action bar options and the pull-down menu items for each action bar option may also be managed as discrete objects with authorities. The DLL module would simply apply the same logic that was used to gain access to the Accounts Payable Voucher Entry function.

Field Object Security

In an application such as Payroll, there are situations in which it may be desirable to only display, allow to edit, or completely hide a field from a screen. However, application developers cannot always predict the fields that a customer would wish to secure in this fashion. Removal of a field from a screen seldom involves just the data, but also the text associated with the field as well as any functions allowed to be executed on behalf of the field itself (e.g., field help text and field lookup values).

In implementing field-level security, one must first determine whether or not the field is to be secured for a given user throughout the application or for a specific screen. The second consideration is whether to limit the fields that could be secured by the customer. The final issue concerns how to minimize the maintenance of each program while preserving maximum flexibility when securing user-specified fields.

In a PC client environment, the best solution seems to be to make a dynamic screen generator that uses a default panel design, and subsequently remove the specified field groups (field name, text, and associated function calls) from the default panel record. On the AS/400, however, there are at least three different approaches to consider when securing fields. The first uses a logical file to subset the data available to the application program. This mechanism creates many unnecessary objects, and customers are often restricted by the degree of foresight of the application developer in securing fields. Consider that a screen with just four fields would require the creation of as many as sixteen logical files in order to completely cover the possible field protection combinations. Although it is highly unlikely that a customer would want, for example, to hide a description field associated with an employee's wage code, still, if that is what the customer wants, it should be made possible dynamically, and not through a logical file creation and application code recompilation.

The second method involves the creation of duplicate display files in the QTEMP library, and alteration of those display files in such a way that the requested fields display only or are hidden altogether. This process does not change the original display file and is only used for those who are subject to such security. It has the added benefit of being completely outside of the application program's control—thus no maintenance is required, and it may secure any field that the customer chooses in the future. The fields to secure for a given user may be stored in a database file or specified as command parameters in the initial program that is used to secure the fields for the specified profile. The negative side to this procedure is that the duplicate display files in the QTEMP can be deleted purposely, thereby exposing the data that should have been secured. (It should be noted, however, that IBM has supplied a user domain, system state API object QDDDUPDF program to at least one software vendor for just such a purpose!)

The third option is to intercept the screen output data being written to the workstation and alter the image to reflect the customer's field security options. This procedure is technically superior to the other two methods, but the software will sustain system integrity violations, since it must interact with restricted system domain OS/400 objects. Therefore, the best way to secure fields for a PC client may be to use a runtime screen painter; on an AS/400, ask IBM for the field-level security API or purchase a third-party solution using IBM's field level security API.

Data Security

Security based on data contained in a record in a file is sometimes referred to on AS/400 applications as *company group security*. Essentially, this type of security allows a user or a group of users to work with a particular set of data within a file that contains or does not contain a specified value. The value and the location of the value within the record is completely dependent upon customer configuration. For example, a customer may configure the data security routines to show only those records whose discount amount field values are greater than 123. Although this technology is often used to secure users from or to a range of companies, it can secure the same users based on any arbitrary field value.

The most effective means to achieve this type of security is to match the data retrieved from the server with the data structure of its field locations, then compare the field values in the retrieved data to that of the specified security values kept elsewhere. As in function option security, the client module interacting with the server may filter out undesirable records and only provide the client application with those records that match the security requirements. This form of data security is essential for any financial application.

Portable Clients

Supporting portable clients may wreak havoc with the design of a client/server application in a most fundamental way. The portability of the client machine means that the users of the portable units must first connect to a server via a public telephone network, or they will only be able to use their laptops for purposes other than accessing client/server applications, since C/S application data is most likely not going to reside on the portable itself. In this case, one may question the use of portable systems at all! This argument is further spirited by the fact that many corporate sites utilize digital phone switches that do not support most dial-up modems. Additionally, many senior managers may expect to have the ability to at least browse important information wherever they happen to be through the use of a portable notepad. After having spent a considerable amount of money to implement a "new world order" featuring client/server technology, the idea of not receiving what they perceive to be any tangible benefits due to technical difficulties may not be acceptable. Therefore, a client/server application designer may be forced to construct a mechanism that must satisfy one of the most challenging tasks of supporting portable clients without requiring portable clients to be always connected to a server.

If a portable client is to be able to function independently as well as within the network, it must have provisions to detect whether it is connected to a server. If it is connected to a server, should the profile/password identification process be different than if it wasn't attached to a server? If the process remains the same, then there must exist a data file on the PC that contains the profiles and passwords for the user or all users who may access the network. This constitutes a large potential security breach, as well as maintenance overhead. If the validation process is disregarded when the portable is not attached to a server, then the C/S application may not know what authority the user has in relation to the locally stored data. A logical choice may be to have an independent validation process for the server and the client in such a way that users are asked to sign on to the server only when the server connection is present. Although this seems redundant and restrictive, it satisfies both the server's requirements and the client application's independence. It should be remembered that the client application may also need to enforce application-, function-, and option- specific securities in addition to the data access authority that the server requires.

If the portable client is to be independently usable by anyone, then C/S environment security information, as well as the authorities for each application, function, and dataset, must reside within each portable unit. The C/S application start-up process must be able to detect whether or not the client is attached to a server. If attached, then the data provided by the server should be utilized, and the local database automatically synchronized. If the client is not attached to a server, then the local security and application information should be used to identify the user and provide the same authority-sensitive access to folders and icons as if the user were attached. To minimize the security exposure represented by the duplication of such sensitive information on a portable client, the C/S application should be designed to encrypt any information when updating or writing onto a client's local storage medium. This process will reduce the risk of compromising the C/S network and any application-specific information contained within lost laptop clients. In addition, consider storing application summary information on portables and allowing only the browse ability when not in communication with the server.

CHAPTER SEVEN

Object States and Domains

The concept of object states and domains was introduced with the announcement of the OS/400 operating system version 1 release 3. Prior to this release, all objects on the system were accessible by anyone with necessary authority to them. The need to differentiate objects did not occur until it was widely known, in AS/400 technical circles, that the OS/400 operating system had serious integrity problems. The AS/400 operating system's integrity was compromised slowly and quietly by a few technical giants at an early stage, dating back to the days of the infant System/38. Although many consider the AS/400 to be a computing platform that is distinct and separate from its predecessor, the System/38, the two machines' operating systems are as closely related to one another as the various PC Disk Operating System versions. The OS/400 operating system on AS/400 was built on the foundation laid by the System/38's CPF operating system, so the experience and knowledge gained in dissecting the late System/38's internal microcode not only is transferable, but provides invaluable insight into the workings of today's AS/400 client/server platform. Although many technological advancements have been implemented on the AS/400 platform, not much effort has been expended in blocking security exposures until OS/400 version 1 release 3. The reason for this may have been because OS/400 security modules were considered the best in the industry—or perhaps because IBM discounted rumors of rampant security breaches within System/38 technical circles. Whatever the reason, once IBM was notified of the breaches through formal channels, they did address some of the problems.

Background

To understand the reasons for the introduction of the OS/400 operating system's object state and domain designations, one has to first understand the problems that they were meant to solve. The operating system security implemented on the AS/400 is very similar to that of the System/38. The AS/400 operating system integrity problems did not suddenly occur one day, but rather they evolved slowly from the weaknesses of the System/38 operating system which were exploited by some users who then applied the same techniques on the AS/400. That the System/38 did not employ the object state and domain concept was IBM's most significant oversight. If IBM had employed the object state and domain concept from the beginning, today's AS/400s might not be so plagued by problems with system integrity. In reality, the technology needed to enforce the object state and domain concept was already in use in many System/370 architecture machines when the System/38 was announced—proving, once again, that hindsight is indeed better than foresight and that the computer industry has a nasty habit of underestimating the ingenuity of end users!

The CPF operating system security on System/38 was fundamentally based on the object authorization validation routines embedded deep within the microcode. For most System/38 users, the object authorization routines were not only sufficient, but simple and effective in controlling large groups of users with varying authority requirements. By the mid-1980s, System/38 techies had discovered the layered architecture design of their machines and started to explore the layers below the System/38's CPF operating system. The first layer they encountered was the Machine Interface (MI) layer. This discovery was made relatively easily, since every program, regardless of the programming language used, compiled the programmer's work into this MI text, which the compiler, if asked, would obligingly print out. Therefore, an average programmer could see clearly what happened to his or her HLL instructions as they were compiled into lower level language. Most who made the discovery were intrigued— enough, at least, to inspire interesting small talk. Others, however, wanted to master the machine interface instructions and write programs using those instructions exclusively—eliminating the "middleman" conversion process. And those who realized that IBM itself had published and sold manuals telling them how to use the MI instructions (IBM System/38 Functional Reference Manuals 1 and 2, GA21-9331) not only were able to decipher the rules of the MI instructions but also were given an important clue as to what was beneath the Machine Interface layer of the System/38 machine. Additionally, IBM made the CPF operating system code and the Vertical Micro-Code (VMC) source instruction text available to anyone who had the money to purchase them in a microfiche format. This microfiche source text further educated curious techies about MI language programming techniques. Thus, there were enough sources of information to learn how to program using the Machine Interface instructions for those who were interested, although those who knew the "secret" seldom divulged their knowledge to others.

The problem for those educated, curious, and now impatient techies was that there was no way for them to apply their knowledge, since there weren't any operating system commands that would create programs from the Machine Interface instructions that they had learned. The operating system only allowed for the creation of expected programs from High Level Language compilers sold by IBM, and none of these publicly available compilers were designed to accept the MI source text. There was, however, an IBM-sanctioned MI compiler with restrictions for those that IBM had approved to use privately; this was not widely known at the time. Some software vendors did purchase the IBM-sanctioned MI compiler—others engineered their own solutions.

The first underground MI compiler, I recall, was written using the PL/1 language. However, not too many System/38 shops had the PL/1 compiler, so another unofficial MI compiler emerged that hoodwinked the System/38's CPF operating system Control Language compiler into accepting and creating programs from an MI text source member. While this was going on, a few techies, including myself, concentrated on a different route to the same solution—the creation of an executable program using MI instructions. This "road less traveled" approach was inspired by the existence of the patch program command, which was on System/38. The patch program command allowed users to overwrite the Machine Interface template with other instructions and values as long as the replacement data were deemed correct by the operating system. Furthermore, once the MI template was patched, a command key could be used to create a replacement program with the altered instructions. However, not many bit twiddlers undertook this journey, since to do so would require them to educate themselves about the complexities involved in the System/38's program compilation process and the role in which the MI template was meant to serve.

Program Compilation Process

When a programmer executes a command to create an RPG program, the pseudo-English text known as the program source code is presented to the RPG compiler. The RPG compiler, which must be purchased separately in addition to the operating system, accepts the source code, and verifies whether the source code satisfies all of the rules pertaining to the RPG programming language. If the compiler's requirements are satisfied, then it converts the RPG programming language text into a common intermediate text unique to the System/38 and the AS/400. This text is widely known as the Machine Interface (MI) source text, although some IBM documentation refers to it as the Intermediate Representation of Program (IRP).

As far as the System/38 and AS/400 RPG compilers are concerned, once the RPG source text has been translated into the MI source text, the compilation task has been completed. The translated MI source text is then presented to a suite of operating system programs, known collectively as the Program Resolution Monitor (PRM), that assembles the MI source text into a binary representation of the English-like MI source text. The result is a stream of binary digits describing the program's intent as well as the attributes and options associated with creating the final executable object. This stream is the Machine Interface template. It is also the binary data that the System/38 patch program command allows programmers to change in order to re-create the program from the altered

MI template. Therefore, if one was proficient in writing programs following the rules and regulations of the MI template guidelines using only binary digits, then one did not have to create an MI compiler. A dummy RPG program could simply be created and patched using the System/38's patch program command which overwrites the original instructions with the "real" intent in a hexadecimal format; one could then request to have the operating system re-create the program using the altered MI template. The program compilation process finally terminates after the Program Resolution Monitor presents the MI template to the VMC translator module. It is the VMC #XLATOR routine that translates the MI template data into processor-executable instructions and assembles the proper housing for the program that is created. The binary representation of the MI source text, the MI template, is kept with the final executable program object. The MI template, therefore, serves as a focal point for all high-level language compilers and is a compiled program's link back to the source code where it had originated. Indeed, if the MI template data is removed from an executable program, although the program would execute as it always had, the operating system would no longer be able to assist the developer of the program in identifying a field as it had been named in the original source code. Without the MI template, the link between the source and the object would be lost. Figure 7.1 illustrates the program compilation process.

The Road Less Traveled

The problem with writing programs using MI template opcodes and operands is that it is extremely time consuming, difficult, and error prone. The headaches one encounters in dealing with hexadecimal arithmetic in order to calculate proper offsets and addresses as part of the program instructions can scare the hell out of an ordinary bottle of aspirin. Nevertheless, many useful programs were coded in streams of hexadecimal values and given directly to the VMC translator, bypassing all the layers above the MI template. One of the first programs that was created by patching over a dummy object was a program that invoked the VMC translator, passing the MI template data that would then be used to create new programs. Once this command interface was developed, the process

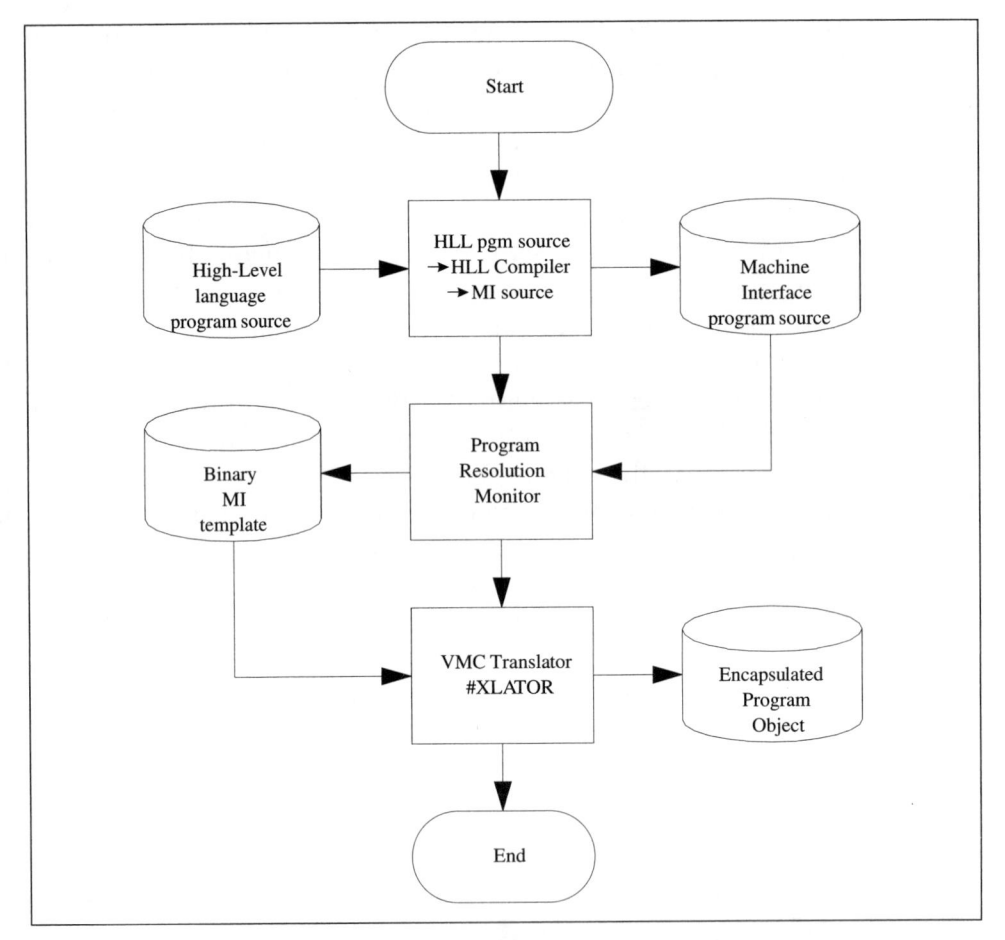

Figure 7.1 Program compilation process.

required to create a dummy program to patch over was no longer needed. One could simply write the entire, albeit short, program in hexadecimal digits, calculate and build the program header information in hex, and present the assembled MI template to the VMC translator via the command interface previously created. In this way, brand new MI-level programs could be created without purchasing or altering an existing language compiler. Furthermore, there were none of the built-in restrictions contained in IBM's MI compiler product.

Looking back, there was one other significant value to having followed such a roundabout solution, rather than simply acquiescing to using the

PL/1 MI compiler or the patched CL compiler from the start. The road less traveled forced its explorers not only to learn MI instructions, but also to manually assemble those instructions and parameters with respect to the other pertinent information that constitutes a program. In doing so, they were forced to dissect, guess, and experiment with various objects and values that were not even visible to high-level language programmers. The more they discovered about the underlying Machine Interface layer, the more predictable, sensible, and uniform the architecture of the operating system was discovered to be. Once having experienced the intricacies of bit twiddling in such a way, it seemed relatively simple to intercept and identify the data being presented to the Program Resolution Monitor (a set of programs that converts the MI source text to the MI template) from high-level language compilers. The pointers and values being passed to the PRM entry program (QPRROOTP) were investigated, identified, and mimicked exactly in order to interface with the operating system's single indigenous compiler that services all high-level language compilers on the machine. The initial interface to the PRM entry program was coded in hexadecimal values following MI template guidelines, and was then assembled into an executable program by the VMC translator.

The first program written using the English-like Machine Interface (MI) language, and not in hexadecimal MI template values, replaced the initial MI template based PRM interface program, thus completing the bridge back from MI template hexadecimal programming to the English-like programming language of Machine Interface text. The low-level homemade interfaces and the techniques used to develop these bridges would later prove to be the base from which the most nefarious viruses and treasured tools have originated on AS/400 systems. Figure 7.2 illustrates the IBM's original program compilation process and the low-level operating system interfaces created by technical users and software vendors.

MI Purpose

Although some have climbed the MI mountain just because it was there, others have climbed it because it offered functions that their RPG compiler simply could not provide. For instance, an RPG program that com-

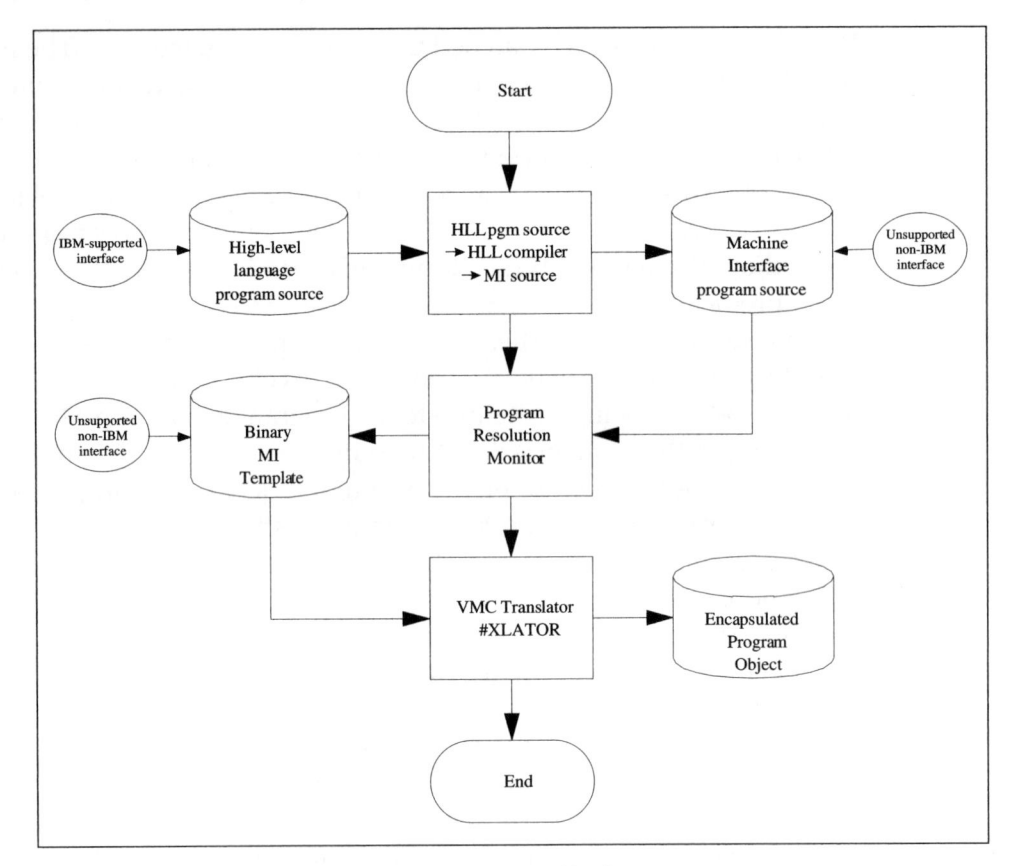

Figure 7.2 Unsupported program compilation process.

pares two strings of text for equality is a simple one, but if it has to compare the same two strings with "wildcard" character considerations, such as "BOB SM?TH" or "B?? S*", the task becomes much more difficult and time consuming to execute. This is especially true if an interactive user enters a request to view an account summary of one of thousands of General Ledger accounts matching a particular pattern. In such an instance, an MI program could be created to provide a yes or no answer using only two instructions, one of which would be used to end the MI program. This simple MI program could cut the processing time for the execution of several often used accounting programs by quite a factor.

Software vendors specializing in technical utilities found many solutions using Machine Interface language, ranging from achieving faster response times to conserving disk storage space; sometimes MI instructions allowed solutions to seemingly impossible situations. Those who mastered and used the MI language enjoyed technical superiority and commanded the respect of their peers and subordinates alike. Those software companies who sought out and employed these techies not only paid premium salaries, but also referred to them as "gurus" and "HMVIPs" (Highly Mysterious Very Important Persons) because these MI jockeys provided an edge over their competitors.

However, these gurus also experimented and created programs that accessed and altered the operating system's internal work areas such as the Work Control Block Table, the System Entry Point Table, and other usually inaccessible areas. Having said that IBM's original intention was not to allow anyone to interact with the System/38's Machine Interface objects directly, let alone to program in that level, the System/38's MI level was rather exposed to security breaches. An average MI programmer was able to create a program that would hunt for a privileged user's or a security officer's authority and assume that authority—and no one would be the wiser, since the programmer was the resident techie. Such "interesting" programs were created to change a user's name to be invisible, or to an arbitrary designation such as "Micky Mouse." They could even be used to hide the active workstation from everyone's view. More mature programs that inserted passwords to system profiles designed not to host any passwords came later, as well as programs that would initialize disk drives if activated properly. What's more, some software vendors knowingly shipped their products with these homemade bombs. In one particular case, correct positioning of the cursor followed by a series of command keystrokes would have displayed all profiles and passwords of users on a particular System/38. Figure 7.3 illustrates the potential security risks associated with using MI-level programming.

A for Effort

As the System/38 became more popular in the mid-to-late 1980s, the existence of MI technology and the capabilities of MI programmers became more widely known in the System/38 industry. Almost every

96 MANAGEMENT

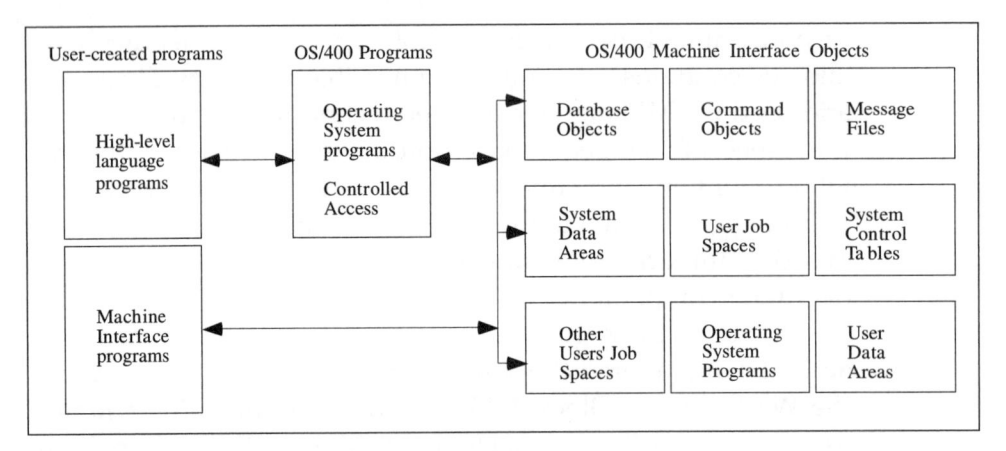

Figure 7.3 Machine interface access.

software vendor had at least one programmer with casual knowledge of MI language who usually had an exaggerated understanding of what MI could do. At about the same time, IBM readied the next generation System/38, code-named the "Silver Lake" project. It was introduced in the spring of 1988 and was named the Application System/400 (AS/400).

The AS/400 project team, acknowledging the rampant use of the MI language on System/38, took this opportunity to protect the AS/400's operating system by automatically re-creating all System/38 programs from their MI templates. Those customers who did not have MI templates with their programs were required to re-compile their programs manually before the programs could be transported to the AS/400. Furthermore IBM, without warning, disabled the use of nearly half or more Machine Interface instructions that were considered by IBM to be "hazardous" for the AS/400. This caused many MI programs to be forever bound to the System/38, since the required and automatic re-creation of MI programs from their respective MI templates failed during System/38-to-AS/400 transition if they used any AS/400-restricted MI instructions. To those MI programmers who could not transport their MI programs to the AS/400, this, of course, meant war.

IBM was so sure that this protection scheme would filter out all undesirable MI programs that they even made the new MI layer, with its reduced instruction set, available to everyone via an API (Application Program Interface). Moreover, IBM published sample programs that a high-level application programmer could follow to create an MI program.

Many System/38 MI programmers did give up their homemade MI compilers and joined the ranks of techies who settled for using the IBM-supplied MI compiler. However, the IBM-controlled MI compiler on the AS/400 could not be used to create some of the programs that software vendors required, since many "sensitive" instructions were restricted from being used on the AS/400. IBM addressed these issues by providing software vendors with specific IBM programs that allowed software vendors to continue their business on the AS/400, providing a vendor's requests were reasonable. All in all, the AS/400 world was a better and safer place, and IBM did regain control of its operating system's integrity—for about two hours.

For those who thrived on challenge, IBM's controlled program entry mechanism into the AS/400 world was a genuine thrill to overcome. Although some Machine Interface language programs were created on the AS/400, other programs that had previously compiled without any problems on System/38 produced errors on the AS/400. Further investigation revealed that the Program Resolution Monitor entry program, QPRROOTP, verified each Machine Interface instruction used in the MI source text. This practice is considered normal for any programming language and is known as syntax check. What was odd was that instructions that were being used in the correct manner were being rejected by the PRM.

When the QPRROOTP program was examined using OS/400's System Service Tools command, it revealed that the MI opcodes and operands referenced in the MI source text were being verified against the QPROCT and QPRODT tables in the system library. It wasn't surprising to find that those tables on the AS/400 did not contain the MI instructions that the corresponding tables on System/38 contained. Having found the crux of the problem, formulating a solution was relatively simple. The answer was to transport the System/38's opcode and operand tables onto the AS/400, create a duplicate QPRROOTP program on the AS/400, and alter it to use the System/38's opcode and operand definition tables. However, there was no guarantee that the MI template with the restricted instructions generated by the PRM would be accepted by the VMC translator. When the theory was put to the test, surprisingly, the rest of the PRM modules, the VMC translator, and all the underlying program compilation processes seemed to work just as they did on the System/38, with the exception of the missing MI instructions. Within a couple of hours, the effort made by the OS/400 designers to keep out MI programs that used dangerous instructions had been circumvented. Some MI programmers dissected the QPROCT and QPRODT entries and added the missing opcodes and operand definitions in the new tables on the AS/400; others may have used a patch rumored to exist that could restore the full MI instruction set. The bottom line was that once again, IBM underestimated the MI community, and "safe enough" simply wasn't.

The Solution

In the fall of 1989 I was talking with Paul Conte, senior technical editor for *News 3X/400* magazine, and made a passing remark about the lack of security on the AS/400. Paul must have thought it would make an interesting article and began to dig for more detailed information with which to confront IBM. When he had enough program examples from myself and others, he approached and presented his case to IBMers who were responsible for AS/400 security. In the end, Paul's article appeared in print in the January 1990 issue of *News 3X/400* magazine and included IBM's official proposed solution to correct the security exposures created by the MI layer compromise. OS/400 version 1 release 3 was shipped later that year, a full two years after the initial release of the AS/400. The proposed solution was to implement the object state and domain concept that OS/400 employs to this day.

The object state/domain concept is a simple one. The state attribute is given only to executable objects such as programs, both operating system and user created. The domain attribute is given to all objects on the system, except the VLIC (Vertical Licensed Internal Code, originally called the VMC on System/38) and HLIC (Horizontal Licensed Internal Code, or HMC on System/38) modules. All system state programs may use any object on the system for which the requester has the necessary authority. User state programs, however, may only reference a user domain object that includes other user-created programs, user spaces, user indices, and user queues. It further followed that all user-created programs would be assigned user state and user domain attributes. The vast majority of the OS/400 operating system programs, on the other hand, were given either system state/system domain or inherit state/system domain attributes. Some operating system programs were given the attribute of system state/user domain so that user programs would be able to activate these system programs. These system state/user domain operating system programs serve as intentional and controlled interfaces that allow user programs to access operating system functions such as database read/write operations. These programs are collectively known as Application Program Interfaces (API); some were meant to be used by high-level language application programmers and others only by high-level language compilers. Nearly all user-created non-executable objects, such as database files, commands, and job description objects, were given the attribute of system domain. This meant that database files created by an application programmer could only be accessed through IBM-supplied operating system APIs. It also meant that none of the user-created programs would be able to activate operating system programs that were not designed to interact with user-created programs. Figure 7.4 illustrates the object state/domain concept.

The establishment of the object state/domain concept essentially made all user-created MI programs that violated the object domain boundary unusable, as built-in OS/400 security enhancements disallowed such violations from processing. Additionally, for all user state programs, the security enhancements also verified at program execution time, that the instructions to be executed were not contained in the defined set of restricted MI instructions. Furthermore, to ensure that no other user-created programs that violated enhanced security rules could be restored onto a system, IBM also coded each program with a program validation

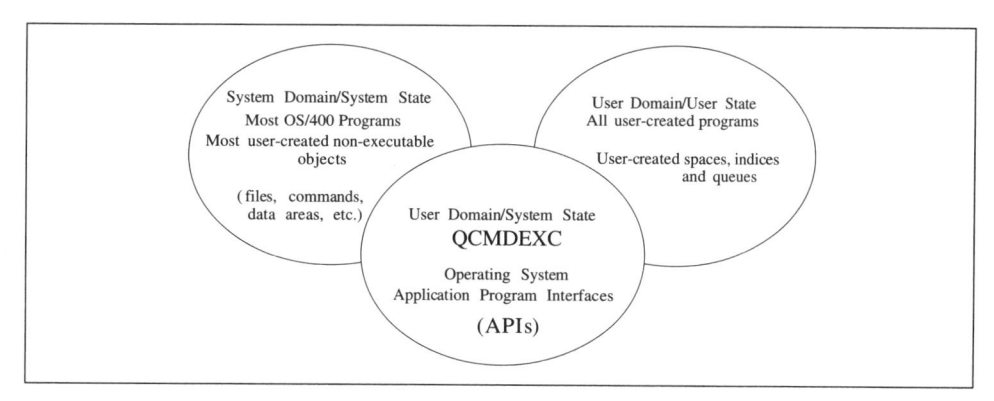

Figure 7.4 OS/400 state/domain processing.

value. The program validation value was calculated and stored with the program so that if the program was altered in any way after it had been created, the operating system restore process would reject it or notify the user of a potential security breach in using such a program. All in all, IBM delivered an outstanding solution to a thorny problem. However, IBM delivered this enhanced security processing as an option that customers could choose to implement rather than as a rule. For those who weren't aware of security exposures, the enhanced security measures were nothing more than superfluous additions to the operating system.

In Practice

The ones who were the most distressed at the announcement of security level 40 and its enhanced security features on the AS/400 were the software vendors. Those who had made a living delivering faster, slicker, and more magical solutions suddenly realized that their products would no longer work if their customers chose to implement the new security enhancements. Some of these software vendors were outraged at IBM and voiced their frustrations to IBM representatives behind closed doors at a special COMMON user group meeting. IBM's answer to these concerns was to open up the OS/400 operating system using Application Program Interfaces (APIs). IBM also provided several specialized APIs for specific software vendors, some of which were designed to execute in the privileged system state. Other smaller software vendors were caught off guard and found no easy way to continue to market their software without breaching the built-in security auditing feature of the OS/400 operating system version 1 release 3.

The most significant effect of enhanced system integrity auditing involved the end users of the software that would no longer execute properly. In fact, many customers who were using popular financial applications that had several MI programs that violated the new security enhancements could not utilize the new security functions, since they would disable the software from functioning properly and therefore disturb the normal flow of daily business. However, the decision not to utilize the enhanced security features because of existing security violations meant, as far as IBM was concerned, a calculated and conscious compromise by the customer. To make matters worse, many customers who had purchased AS/400 software did not possess the source code for their purchased applications; this was true specially for the MI language programs that were considered by many software vendors to be proprietary secrets. This meant that customers were completely dependent upon the software vendor's ability to deliver a version of software that was not dependent upon a particular security level setting of the customer's operating system. If the customer was not an active participant in the software vendor's maintenance program, no such enhancements from the software company were forthcoming. Thus the customer's system was doomed to be forever frozen to an operating system security level that was known to be susceptible to integrity problems and other potential security risks.

The only recourse these unwitting customers had was to purchase a new copy of the same software and make the necessary changes or pay the maintenance fees that would enable them to receive the updated software that would work properly with respect to OS/400's enhanced security features. Neither alternative was especially attractive, which may explain why most AS/400 customers are still utilizing the less stringent security level settings on their AS/400s. Many utility vendors exploit this paralysis by offering products that solve business problems only if the customer uses their software under a less restrictive security level environment, further proliferating security concerns.

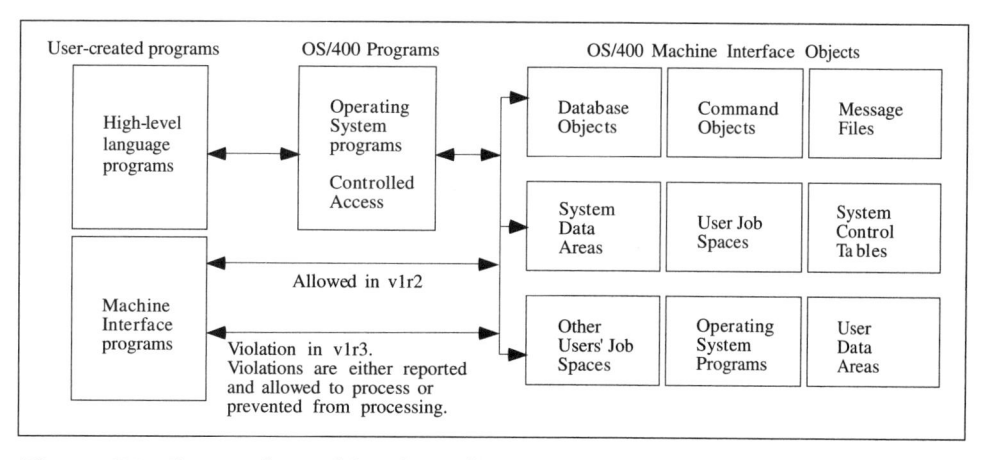

Figure 7.5 Secured machine interface access.

In addition, there are AS/400 professionals who do not clearly understand the benefits of the enhanced security features, let alone the state/domain concept. In their view, security levels of 40 and above are only useful for CIA, NSA, or NASA purposes. Unfortunately, the combined ignorance and indifference on the part of software vendors only serves to establish a de facto security standard within the AS/400 community—the less restrictive security level 30 setting. This is cause for concern when we consider that even the enhanced security levels 40 and 50 have been compromised, as we will discuss in the following chapters. Figure 7.5 compares the traditional Machine Interface access allowed under the v1r2 of the OS/400 operating system to the enhanced security features of the v1r3.

CHAPTER EIGHT

Impact of Altered Objects

Objects have been altered by MI programmers since the early days of System/38. In many cases the initial driving force behind the search for useful object alterations was to satisfy business needs or to enable a particular function that was not allowed by the operating system or the high-level language compilers. However, once the process of circumventing the operating system restrictions was sufficiently explored by altering objects, the new possibilites invited both honorable and not so honorable explorers, who were only limited by conscience in the application of their discoveries.

This chapter concentrates on the security exposures created by object alterations, but in fact there are numerous programs created by these hackers that have actually enhanced the operating system, leading to IBM's approach in providing new API routines as additions to the OS/400 operating system with each successive release. On the other hand, it is also imperative for readers to understand the depth to which such object alterations may make corporate and private assets vulnerable. In that spirit, some of the more commonly known security breaches and operating system patches are explained. One of the more popular alterations known to the System/38 and the early AS/400 machines was the job description object patch. A user could create a job description object and use an MI program to change the user profile parameter of the job description object to QSECOFR or QSYS. The same user could then submit a job using the job description he or she had patched specifying that the profile to use during the submitted job's execution was to be retrieved from the job description object. The submitted job would execute under the authority of the job description object's user profile. This type of object alteration, a simple task for an MI programmer, may now be prevented if the enhanced security level 40 is used instead of the traditional level 30 configuration. Figure 8.1 illustrates a job description object and the user profile parameter that was often patched by MI programmers.

Another popular target of MI programmers was the system work control block table (QWCBT). The system work control block table is a single contiguous space that contains, in 512-byte increments, an entry for each job that the system must manage. It contains many different job types, such as interactive, batch, autostart, and system. MI programmers can easily find their own QWCBT entry by following the offset stored in the individual job's Process Control Space (PCS) as illustrated in Figure 8.2. Once the QWCBT entry is found, the 26-byte job name that identifies a job uniquely throughout the system may be changed to any desired value, including a reverse image attribute or other nondisplayable char-

Figure 8.1 Job description object.

IMPACT OF ALTERED OBJECTS 105

```
DMPSYSOBJ PARAMETERS
OBJ- *PCS
OBJECT TYPE-           PROCESS CONTROL SPACE                      *QTPCS
NAME-        PCS116S1  QSAI        080530    TYPE-     1A  SUBTYPE-      EF
CREATION-    11/15/94  09:05:01              SIZE-     000004BC00
ATTRIBUTES-  0000                            ADDRESS-  A0042D00  0000
PROCESS CONTROL SPACE: NOT MATERIALIZABLE
PRIMARY ASSOCIATED SPACE-
000000   80000000 00000312 025A004E 54000100   00000000 000003AA2 0003002E 9C00191F  *      ! +è              s   æ    *
000020   00000000 00000000 029CC000 E90019FF   00000000 00000000 01F0005C 7C0010FF  *      æ{ Z              0 *0   *
000040   00000000 00000000 029C001D 5C0004FF   80000000 00000000 00030033 35000100  *           æ  *                  *
000340   00000000 00400003 00000000 00000000   00000000 00000000 00000000 00000000  *                                 *
000360   00000000 00000000 00000000 00000000   00000000 00000000 00000000 00000000  *                                 *
000380   80000000 00000000 029CC001 7E001140   00000000 00000000 00000000 00000000  *      æ{ =                       *
0003A0   00000000 00000000 00000000 00000000   00000008 00013D00 00020000 E2000400  *                           S     *
0003C0   00000000 00000000 00000000 00000000   0000C100 40404040 00000000 00000000  *                    A            *
0003E0   00000000 00000000 00000000 00000000   00000000 00000000 C3C4D07 E2E8E2D6   *                                 *
000400   C2D14000 D500000D5 000001F4 00000000   00000000 00000000 00000000 00000000  *BJ  N    N    4        CDMPSYSO*
000420   00000000 00000000 00000000 00000000   00000000 00000000 00000000 00000000  *                                 *
```

```
DMPSYSOBJ PARAMETERS
OBJ- QWCBT
TYPE- *ALL SUBTYPE-*ALL                      CONTEXT-  QSYS
OBJECT TYPE-            SPACE                                    *WCBT
NAME-        QWCBT                           TYPE-     19  SUBTYPE-      D0
LIBRARY-     QSYS                            TYPE-     04  SUBTYPE-      01
CREATION-    02/04/92  15:20:37              SIZE-     00000184000
OWNER-       QSYS                            TYPE-     08  SUBTYPE-      01
ATTRIBUTES-  0800                            ADDRESS-  002E9C00  0000
SPACE ATTRIBUTES-
000000   00FFFF00 00000060 19D0D8E6 C3C2E340   40404040 40404040 40404040 40404040  *      - }QWCBT                   *
000020   40404040 40404040 E0000000 00000000   00018300 00000000 00000000 00000000  *  \           c                  *
000040   00000000 00000000 00030002 31000400   00000000 00000000 00000000 00000000  *                                 *
SPACE-
000000   00000000 00000011 029CA001 AF000AFF   00000000 0000FF99 029CA002 93001A1F  *          æµ        r æµ l       *
000020   002D0000 00000000 0003001D D5000238   00220000 00000000 025A011B B9000238  *                _  N    !    _  *
013D00   D7C3E2F1 F1F6E2F1 4040D8E2 C1C94040   40404040 F0F8F0F5 F3F00000 000000E8  *PCS116S1  QSAI    080530     Y*
013D20   00000000 00000000 029CA004 2D001A1F   00000000 00000400 029C0029 9C0018FF  *          æµ             æ    æ  *
013D40   00000000 00001900 029C0029 9B00195F   00000000 00030033 33001938  *       æ  Ω  ¬                          *
013D60   C9200000 00000000 00000002 61000000   00000000 00000000 029C0029 A100193F  *I           /            æ  ^   *
013D80   00000000 00000000 00000000 00000000   00000000 00000000 FFFF7AC5 D5E4E4E2  *                            :ENUUS*
013DA0   5CC8C5E7 40404040 40404040 40404040   40404040 00000000 00000000 00000000  **HEX                             *
013DC0   00000000 00000000 00000000 00000000   00000000 00000000 00000000 00000000  *                                 *
013DE0   00000000 00000000 0000D8C3 D4C44040   40404040 5CD3C9C2 D3404040 40405CE2  *         QCMD    *LIBL    *S*
013E00   C9C7D5D6 C6C64040 40404040 40404040   40404040 00000076 CDEA34B9 *IGNOFF             +ò²  _*
013E20   00008400 00000000 00000000 00000000   00000000 00000000 00000000 00000000  *  d                              *
013E40   00000000 00000000 00000000 00000000   00000000 00000000 76CDEA34 88C00081  *                          +ò² »{ a*
013E60   5CC4C5E5 C5D3D6D7 D4C5D5E3 40404003   00000000 00000000 00000000 00000000  **DEVELOPMENT                     *
013E80   0000D140 00000000 00000000 00000000   00000000 00000000 00000000 00000000  * J                               *
013EA0   40004040 40404040 40404040 40404040   40404040 40404040 40404040 40404040  *                                 *
013EC0   00D4C3D1 D6C2C440 404040E2 C1C96DD4   C3404040 40000000 00000000 00000000  * MCJOBD    SAI_MC                *
013EE0   00000000 000000E2 C7D6D5E5 D6404040   D8E2C1C9 40404040 AA2F0273 3A920001  *       SGONZO    QSAI    ¦  + k  *
```

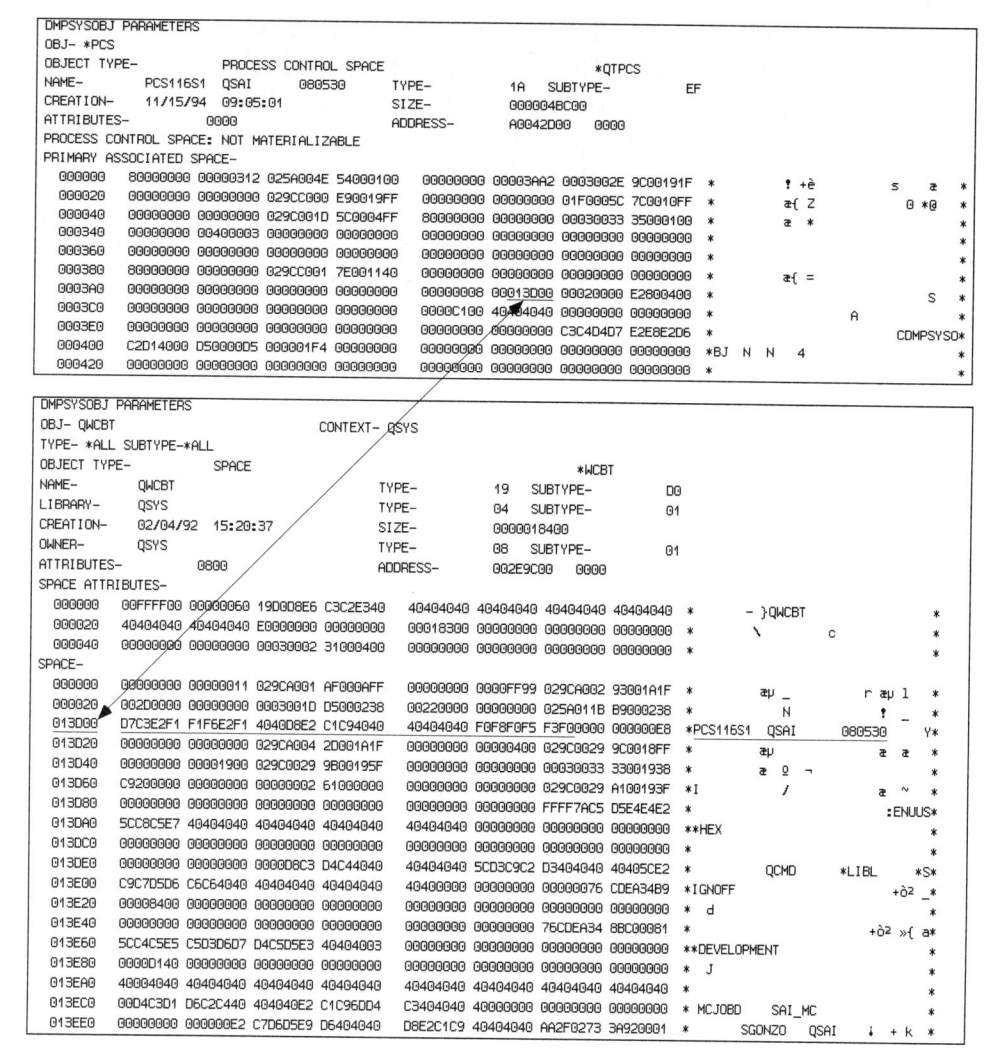

Figure 8.2 System Work Control Block Table.

acters. This technique was used to dynamically change user profile names of any job. It was useful in debugging application programs that were designed to be sensitive to user profiles. For example, instead of signing off and signing on again as a different user, a programmer would simply call a utility to change the system work control block table entry to assume another profile name and activate the desired program. As far as the program was concerned, the user profile was considered to be whatever the work control block table entry contained in its job name location. However, such is no longer the case on the AS/400.

The QWCBT object was also used for other more insidious purposes as well as for practical jokes. It was one of the first places in which an MI programmer was able to locate the pointer to the QSYS profile. (The QSYS profile is a privileged system profile that is used by the operating system at various stages of initial program load as well as during normal system operations. The QSYS profile does not host a password and, therefore, cannot be used by anyone to sign on.) Through trial and error, it was noticed that the first QWCBT entry was always the SCPF job initiated by the QSYS profile with a job number of 000000. It was also noticed that each QWCBT entry housed a pointer back to the job's Process Control Space, where the initiating user profile's pointer could be retrieved. In the case of the SCPF job, following the PCS pointer led to the QSYS user profile, since the initiating profile was always QSYS. Once the QSYS profile pointer was retrieved, an MI programmer would use an altered program to modify his or her own authority with the stolen QSYS profile, thereby assuming the QSYS profile's authority. Altering an interactive user's QWCBT subsystem pointer and the job type had the interesting incidental characteristic of being invisible to the rest of the system. The Work with Active Jobs command seemed to omit work control block table entries that did not belong to any particular subsystem.

MI programmers learned early on that there exists a table that the operating system uses to activate other system programs. This was widely believed to have been done to shorten the amount of time needed to invoke the necessary programs in order to complete the requested tasks. However, the use of such a table also provided an effective means to secure operating system programs from being replaced or intercepted by application programmers. It was considered a challenge among many systems programmers to discover how some operating system commands always seemed to find and execute the correct command processing program (CPP), even though the command was modified to invoke a different CPP.

The key to the mystery was finally found to be directly related to the operating system's use of the System Entry Point Table (QINSEPT) object, which is created during the operating system installation. The System Entry Point Table is an object that contains a list of program addresses. These addresses identify the exact location of each program, wherever it happens to be on the system. (The use of this table is similar in concept to the speed dial feature on a telephone; without this table, the operating system would have to look up each address using a "telephone book.") The QINSEPT object contains more than 3,000 frequently used addresses of operating system programs, and the number grows with each successive release. Since the System Entry Point Table contains addresses and not the names of programs, a program's address stays the same even if the program is renamed. This is also the case when a program is moved from one library to another. Although we may associate a move operation with a physical change of location, OS/400 simply associates the same address with another user-defined physical location name instead. The address for the program remains constant. In the example of an operating system command there is a two-byte binary number hidden from everyone's view which tells the OS/400 to ignore the CPP and activate the program found in the System Entry Point Table at the ordinal position described by the binary number. This is the reason many systems programmers are befuddled when trying to modify an operating system command. Figure 8.3 illustrates an operating system command highlighting the hidden binary offset value into the System Entry Point Table. Discovery of this table was crucial, as it is the primary means to intercept parameters being passed between the operating system programs. By replacing an address in the QINSEPT with a user-created "dummy" program that accepts incoming parameters and passes them along to the original operating system program, normal processing is achieved. However, the MI programmer is now able to debug the sandwiched "dummy" program for the values being passed back and forth between the two

```
DMPOBJ PARAMETERS
OBJ- WRKACTJOB                         CONTEXT- *LIBL
OBJTYPE- *CMD
OBJECT TYPE-          SPACE                                        *CMD
NAME-         WRKACTJOB                     TYPE-         19   SUBTYPE-        05
LIBRARY-      QSYS                          TYPE-         04   SUBTYPE-        01
CREATION-     05/24/93  04:10:30            SIZE-         0000000800
OWNER-        QSYS                          TYPE-         08   SUBTYPE-        01
ATTRIBUTES-           0800                  ADDRESS-      00231300   0000
SPACE ATTRIBUTES-
  000000    00FFFF00 00000060 1905E6D9 D2C1C3E3   D1D6C240 40404040 40404040 40404040  *        -  WRKACTJOB            *
  000020    40404040 40404040 A0000000 00000000   00000700 00030000 00000000 00000000  *          µ                      *
  000040    00000000 00000000 00030002 31000400   00000000 00000000 00000000 00000000  *                                 *
SPACE-
  000000    03DDD8E6 C3C3C4E2 C1C34040 D8E2E8E2   40404040 40400000 5C404040 40404040  * ùQWCCDSAC  QSYS          *      *
  000020    40404040 40404040 40404040 00E0807F   03F70590 D8C3D7C6 D4E2C740 40405CD3  *               \ " 7 °QCPFMSG  *L*
  000040    C9C2D340 40404040 00020000 00000000   00000000 00000000 00000000 00005800  *IBL                            ì *
  000060    00000000 000355A0 00000000 02010000   42039200 6D1488A6 913AC304 01008100  *       íµ        â k _ hwj C   a *
```

Figure 8.3 OS/400 work with active jobs command dump.

108 *MANAGEMENT*

operating system programs. This method may be used to intercept, decipher, and disarm software copyright protection schemes as well as to automatically proliferate undesirable programs or delete random objects throughout the system. It may even be used to intercept save/restore requests and report erroneous completion messages, giving a false sense of confidence prior to deleting all data on the system. Figure 8.4 illustrates the MI programmers' ability to intercept calls to the operating system programs through the System Entry Point Table.

On the lighter side, an April Fool's Day joke that was a big hit involved patching a display file on a System/38 that switched the two Display Active Jobs screens made specifically for the console and a workstation. When a self-proclaimed expert of the System/38, who monitored everyone's work, encountered the patched Display Active Jobs screen that

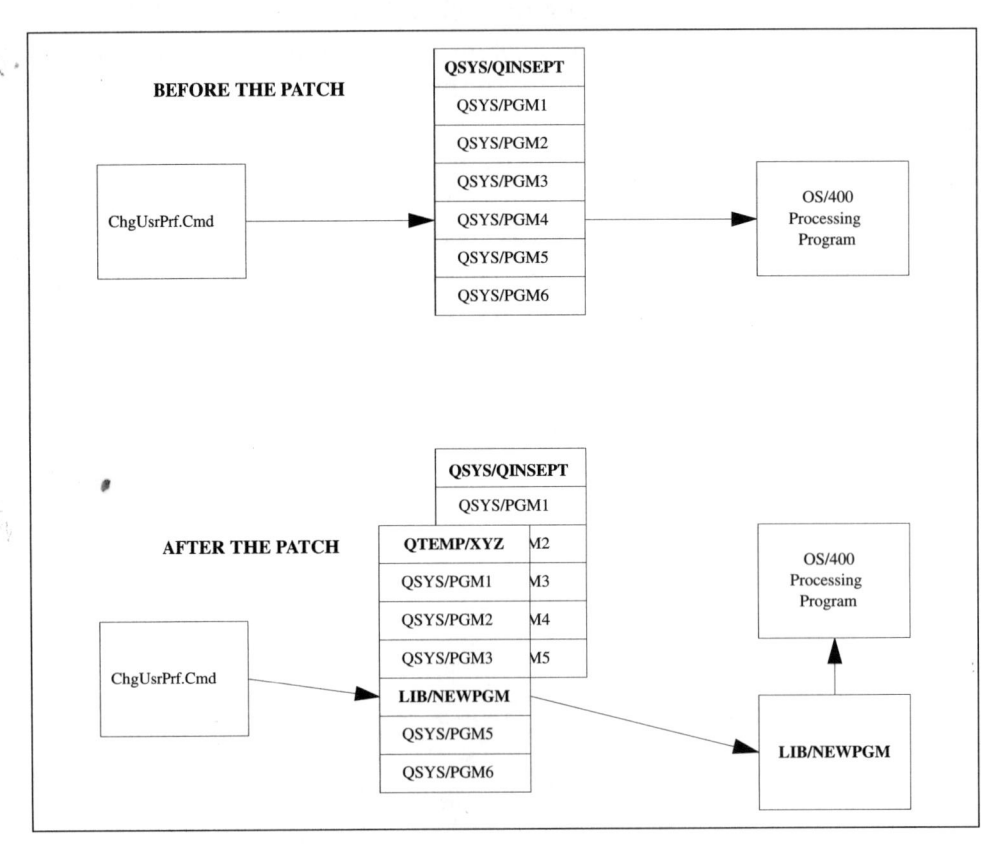

Figure 8.4 System Entry Point Table patch.

painted only a quarter of his workstation, as the System/38 console has a smaller screen size, the expression on his face was truly one of amazement. The same scoundrel responsible for the screen swapping also created and enjoyed a command that enabled or disabled the recognition of the lowercase character on the password field of a sign on screen.

IBM could do a better job of securing some loose ends. Although IBM OS/400 systems programmers may have spent a great deal of time designing and implementing state-of-the-art authority management, process management, and object validation routines, it seems they may have missed the forest for the trees in some instances. A simple and direct assault against the Change User Profiles (CHGUSRPRF) command has revealed that a single-bit patch will allow anyone to insert a password into the QSYS profile. This is an outrageous oversight and should be corrected immediately, as it requires only casual knowledge of the System Service Tools to implement such a patch. To add insult to injury, once a password has been inserted into the QSYS profile, the patched command may be reversed to disallow anyone else from removing the password. The only recourse for an observant security administrator against this kind of infiltration may be to reinstall the operating system. Undoubtedly some readers may feel that the command is not at risk, since the assailant must first have authority to the QSYS profile and the CHGUSRPRF command. However, consider the capabilities of our omnipresent MI programmer. Also consider that it takes less than a minute, using a PC attached to the system with no special authority, to install and execute, using REXX, an MI program that steals a privileged authority, dynamically modifies the Change User Profiles command, and inserts a password that only the assailant can change. The end result is that the assailant will forever be able to gain access to the affected system from any sign on screen. All this may be accomplished today without anyone's knowledge if the enhanced security measures are not utilized. IBM's oversight in not protecting the restricted system profiles, beyond command definition, only provides another route for hackers to gain access to their targets.

When we consider that MI programmers are able to make themselves invisible and assume a privileged user's authority at any time by altering objects, it is certainly fortunate that System/38s and AS/400s are not overrun with viruses and Trojan horses. Readers should also keep in mind that without the v1r3 security enhancements, MI programmers can regain such control over AS/400 authority management within seconds. What's more, if the state/domain processing and the program validation checks are negated in some way, MI programmers will again be able to undermine the OS/400 operating system's security in the most fundamental way. Perhaps after considering these kinds of security risks, AS/400 professionals who are oblivious or indifferent to the enhanced security measures will consider the importance of the security enhancements and implement level 40 security as a rule throughout their organization.

Although the enhanced security measures were designed to counteract and safeguard against those techniques just discussed, they also block the execution of productive application programs. This situation represented an opportunity to a particular software vendor, and as a result, a commercial product is available that creates programs with the benefit of the full MI instruction set executing under the privileged system state. Such a product renders the v1r3 security enhancements obsolete, since anyone can use the product to create system state programs that will go undetected and unchallenged by the enhanced security measures as well as the built-in hardware storage protection mechanisms. The only means to combat the use of this kind of utility is not to restore any non-IBM system state programs, as IBM suggests in the updated version 3 release 1 of the OS/400 operating system. In the OS/400 v3r1, customers may choose to reject the restoration of all system state program onto their machines. This is highly recommended, since legitimate operating system interfaces may be requested through IBM support channels by software vendors, who will receive official APIs from IBM for the desired function.

The Worst Enemy

The worst threat to AS/400 security has yet to be explained, however. There is a silent growing movement within the AS/400 hacker community toward the development of more subtle but far more dangerous user state programs that will execute under the privileged system state at runtime. Prior to the v1r3 security enhancements, there weren't very many reasons to patch programs manually—by that I mean using the SST (System Service Tools) command or equivalent functions, since the Machine Interface instructions could be used to perform most desired tasks. However, with the announcement of the enhanced security level 40, some

MI programs had to be patched at lower levels in order to execute properly. The security enhancements on v1r3, in addition to other security features, also prevented the VMC translator from accepting MI templates with restricted MI instructions if the program being created was a user state program. Therefore, the only recourse left to those persistent MI programmers was to dig deeper into the Internal Micro-Program Instructions (IMPI), which are equivalent to the traditional assembly language instructions. Although many MI programmers could not make the transition to IMPI-level programming, others managed to meet the challenge and began to patch the IMPI instructions in hexadecimal values with growing success. The first and foremost objective for these IMPI programmers was to overcome the object state/domain boundary in such a way that would allow them to cross that boundary at any time with immunity.

Before any IMPI programs could be devised, that factor that identified an object as being in a user domain or system domain, or in a system state as opposed to a user state, first had to be isolated. A logical step toward differentiating system and user domain objects was to review the object description outfile provided by the OS/400 operating system version 1 release 3. In that particular release of the OS/400 operating system, a binary value corresponding to the domain of the object, such as binary 8000 or 0001, was provided. This was a significant discovery, since it not only associated specific internal values to the object domain concept but also provided the length of data to search for within the object. The search for the domain attribute values of binary 8000 or 0001 was further narrowed by comparing a simple object created before and after the v1r3 operating system. This is because the OS/400 operating system not only had to support those objects created prior to the version 1 release 3, but also had to enforce the new security rules over existing and newly created objects. Therefore, if one compared an object that was created with the same set of parameters both before and after the OS/400 v1r3 operating system, one would expect to find some changes that might be attributable to the new operating system features. Surprisingly, there were no significant differences that could not be accounted for using the Dump System Object (DMPSYSOBJ) command. However, those who used the System Service Tools (SST) instead of the Dump System Object command were immediately able to notice the whereabouts of the object domain attribute. Ironically, if it had not been for the helping hand of the operating system's object description outfile, many more IMPI programmers might still be searching for the object domain attribute today. Figure 8.5 illustrates the location of the QHOSTPRT job description object's system domain attribute.

Eminent Domain

The isolation of the object domain attribute led to some interesting possibilities. For example, all database files could be altered to be in the user domain rather than in the system domain. This would render the v1r3 security enhancements ineffective, since the MI programs would access only user domain objects, and not system domain objects as IBM had envisioned. It also meant that most MI programs that were entrenched in many software applications could still be used without any changes, as long as these MI programs only accessed user domain objects. Undoubtedly there still exist software companies that are practicing these techniques in order to avoid the security level 40 restrictions. However, by and large, this type of patch is not a very attractive alternative, because it requires software distributors to ensure, by patching, that all objects are in the user domain in order for their applications to work properly. Additionally, if, for some reason, a customer had to recreate an object, the software vendor would have to explain why the new object could not be accessed by its software under the v1r3 enhanced security levels.

Having discovered these constraints, the next logical step for a vendor was to create a program that could be used to modify the object domain attributes. If such a program could be devised, then it could be incorporated into the software in such a way that before any object was accessed, it could be used to automatically alter the object domain to the desired state. The problem, however, is that Machine Interface instructions cannot be used to access the object header data where the domain value is kept. Thus, v1r3 security measures prevailed.

On the other side of the fence, those techies who were solely interested in taking on the identity of the security officer or QSYS used the knowledge of the object domain location differently. Since under the enhanced security level processing, hardware storage protection restricted user-created programs from accessing the System Work Control Block Table and other system data areas, the QSYS profile pointer could not be retrieved without being detected. Therefore, instead of changing the domain attributes of database files or other non-executable objects, hackers created a duplicate of an operating system program that is known to execute under the QSYS authority in resolving pointers and changed the duplicate program's object domain to the user domain. This modification allowed any user-created programs to activate the copied operating system program that was previously disallowed, since the original program resided in the system domain. The purpose of the patch was to make it possible to use an MI program to retrieve the QSECOFR or QSYS user profile pointer without authority; then the copied operating system program could be used to set the proper authority to the pointer under a privileged state.

This worked just fine. The MI program then used the returned, authorized pointer and overlaid its own profile pointer, assuming QSYS authority once again. There was, however, one major problem that was not noticed until these programs were saved and restored: The copied operating system program and the modified MI program both generated the CPF3848 security violation error during object restoration. Further investigation revealed that if certain values were changed or patched after initial program creation, the altered program always generated the same security violation error. One of these sensitive values was the object domain attribute value. However, only programs were checked in such a way by the operating system. Altered database files restored without incident. Therefore, although the location and the values associated with the object domain represented a significant discovery, they did not help the hacker's ability to subvert the v1r3 security enhancements.

Altered State

Although some hackers may have been disappointed, others continued to be inspired by the challenge. The search continued, concentrating on the object state attribute. It did not take long to find the location where the program state attribute was kept. Having discovered earlier that only programs were associated with object state attributes, the scope of search was limited to the program header section of the service dump. Figure 8.6 highlights the location of the program state attribute. By comparing a

```
MI PROGRAM           SUBTYPE:  01       NAME:  MYPGM                      ADDRESS:    029E  00293C00 0000
SEGMENT HEADER  (YYSGHDR)
  TYPE  01    FLAGS  91   SIZE  0002    EXT  029E     OBJ  00293C00 0000     SPLOC  00293D00 0020
EPA HEADER      (YYEPAHDR)
  ATT1  80                   JOPT  00                   TYPE  02            STYP  01
  NAME  MYPGM
  SPATT  80                  SPIN  00                   SPSZ  480           OSIZ  00000003   PBAU  3F00
  VER  2301                  TIME  11/19/94 19:30:27                        UPQ   0024 00362C00 0000
  AGQ   0000 00000000 0000                              CTQ  0049 00F4F900 0000              OHDR  029E 00293C00 0100
  RCVY  00000000             PERF  01000000             MDTS  11/19/94 19:30:29               JPQ   0000 00000000 0000
  COBQ  0000 00000000 0000                              JID  00000000000000000                OWAU  FF00
  IPL#  0000029E             AL1   00000000000000000
00293C00 0000  01910002 029E0001  029E0029 3C000000  00010000 00000000  029E0029 3D000020  *................
00293C00 0020  80000201 D4E8D7C7  D4404040 40404040  40404040 40404040  40404040 40404040  *....MYPGM
00293C00 0040  40408800 000001E0  00000003 3F002301  76D327C7 FE4000FE  00240036 2C000000  * ............L.G.
00293C00 0060  00000000 00000000  004900F4 F9000000  029E0029 3C000100  00000000 01000000  *.........49.....
00293C00 0080  76D327C9 30800016  00000000 00000000  00000000 00000000  00000000 00000000  *.L.I............
00293C00 00A0  0000FF00 0000029E  00000000 00000000  00000000 00000000  00000000 00000000  *................
                                          User Domain       User State
OBJECT SPECIFIC HEADER    (XPGMHDR)
  ATTR  008120000400000000                             CODE  000210        ISSZ  000238     ISNO  00000006
  LSTB  0002D2              IEXT  029E                 QIS   00293C00 0000  PGEC  000000    QSIC  00293C00 0240
  SICS  00004C              SCEP  000038               QEOL  00293C00 0290  EOLN  0002      EOLS  000038
  QEXD  00293C00 02D0       EXDN  0000                 EXDS  0000          BOMO  0002D0     BOMS  000003
  BSIZ  00                  QTIP  00000000 0000        MECQ  0000 00000000 0000             MDTG  00000000000000000
  MDTS  000000
00293C00 0100  00812000 04000000  00000000 00000000  00000000 029E0029  3C000000 00021000  *................
00293C00 0120  00000000 00060002  38000202 000A5100  00000029 3C000240  00004C00 00380029  *...........K.....
00293C00 0140  3C000290 00020000  38200029 3C0002D0  0002D200 00030000  00030000 00001B572  *................
00293C00 0160  80000000 01100120  00000000 00000000  0000F3F9 417F0000  00000000 00000000  *.........39.....
00293C00 0180  00000000 00000000  02300000 00000000  00000000 00000000  00000000 00000000  *................
00293C00 01A0  00000000 00000000  00000000 00000000  00000000 00000000  00000000 00000000  *................
```

Figure 8.6 Program domain and state attributes.

system state, an inherit state, and a user state program, the allowed attribute values were quickly determined to be either 0080, 0001, or 0000. This knowledge allowed hackers to turn user-created programs into system state programs by manually altering the program state attribute. However, this was no better a solution than patching the object domain attribute, since the enhanced security level 40 always responded with the CPF3848 message if the program's domain or state attributes were altered. It was small consolation to find that under the traditional security level 30 configuration, a patched program could go undetected during the object restore process if the program was in a user state with a null program validation value. However, this vulnerability is widely used today to introduce many undesirable programs onto AS/400 systems that do not employ the security level 40 option. A common delivery method utilizes the Load Run (LODRUN) operating system command that restores objects from the media and executes a patched program that has just been restored. The patched program accesses other restored programs, which are in the user state, and modifies them into a system state by altering the program state attributes. Although this may sound complicated, the actual Internal Micro-Program Instruction patches are minor. I suspect most IMPI programmers are able to perform such a patch within an hour.

Once a program has been altered, it is not validated again at runtime, which is a source of concern even for the OS/400 v3r1. The altered program will execute without further hindrance from the operating system, with the added ability to access the System Entry Point Table, System Work Control Block Table, and other reserved operating system data areas. This essentially negates all efforts made by the IBM OS/400 development staff to contain security exposures. In order to ensure that the altered user-created system state program will work properly, a software vendor may initiate a start-up program that creates a duplicate of a patched program into temporary storage. Then activate the altered program in the temorary storage to transform itself into the system state. Once the altered program has transformed itself to the system state, then it proceeds to change other programs and objects into the desired states and domains as deemed necessary. This way, even if the objects and programs are re-created or set back to their proper states and domains, the next time the application initiates, the start-up program will again modify the required objects. Furthermore, by introducing a duplicate "seed" program into temporary storage, which will automatically be deleted by the operating system, the original Trojan horse program will never be caught in a system state, thereby evading impromptu searches for all user-created system state programs by in-house virus detectors. Fortunately, there is a sure way to stop these unwanted intrusions: Use the enhanced operating system security level 40 or above, and never allow the operating system to restore non-IBM system state programs.

At this point, some readers may be offended that I have exposed information that could be used destructively, but I believe those who are able to patch programs at the IMPI level are already familiar with the locations of the object domain and state attributes. This book does not assist those who are unfamiliar with the Internal Micro-Program Instructions in patching programs. In any case, by avoiding exposure of these intrusions, we are only helping to hide those who wish to remain anonymous. Those readers who are serious about their corporate assets should be aware beyond the shadow of a doubt that two of the three sentinels that enforce the ultimate security on the AS/400 have been compromised by more than just a select few. The first of these sentinels is authority management, bested by MI programs stealing unauthorized pointers from reserved system data areas; the second is represented by object state/domain processing, where the secrecy of object attribute locations have been overcome by casual comparisons. Although one can argue that the second sentinel has not yet been bested, since many are still unaware of what the program's state attribute is being compared against, this too has been defeated by some. The only remaining guardian of AS/400 security is the program validation value calculation. Although knowledge of weaknesses of the first two security measures is worthless without the third and the final piece, if the program validation value calculation process is conquered, there will again be chaos as we have seen in the past. Unfortunately, this too may just be a matter of time, as the next chapter suggests.

CHAPTER NINE

Program Validation Values

If there is one single powerful centurion that refuses to allow those talented IMPI programmers from transforming AS/400 systems into completely chaotic environments, it is program validation value processing. During an AS/400 program encapsulation operation, a built-in operating system routine calculates a value that takes into consideration the object domain, the program state, and the instruction stream, and imprints each program with a set of binary values that may be verified at any time to ensure that the program has not been altered since its creation. It is this value that the OS/400 restore operation verifies, subsequently issuing a security violation message if the validation fails. It is thus not enough for would-be hackers to simply exploit the object domain and program state attributes. They would first have to decipher the program validation value calculation method in order to completely defeat the enhanced security measures.

To IBM's credit, cracking the program validation value calculation algorithm is not an undertaking for the lighthearted. I suspect the validation process has stopped a good portion of the IMPI programming population from achieving success. However, the validation value seems to be derived using a multipart, yet simple, numerical hashing algorithm rather than traditional encryption techniques. This method of securing programs may not be clever enough to deceive the incoming flux of software engineers, some of whom are sure to be familiar with assembling binary codes manually—one bit at a time.

If we assume, for a moment, that the program validation technique has been conquered, then we can expect to find user state programs with proper validation values that alter themselves at runtime to execute in the system state. In this way, even if the operating system disallowed the restoration of system state programs, they would still restore without generating security violation messages. Furthermore, they would also be able to utilize the restricted IMPI level supervisor linkage (SVL) routines to access any object on the system. To prevent this from occurring, IBM could inspect the program validation values prior to activating all programs, which would ensure the program's integrity at runtime. Currently, runtime validation is not enforced. On the surface, it could be argued that such runtime validation may seem excessive, especially at the expense of performance but consider the possibilities. The only restraint standing in the way of a hacker who wants to create a program that will access another program and overwrite the executable instruction stream is the program validation value, which is not checked at runtime. This presents an opportunity for a virus to transform itself to a system state program with full QSYS authority and attach a copy of itself to an unsuspecting program. A runtime program validation inspection would eliminate the possibility, however small, of user-created programs executing in the system state even if the program validation routine is broken in the future.

I had originally planned on exposing the location of the program validation values; several colleagues persuaded me to do otherwise. However, because the primary reason for this book is to use evidence and not hearsay, to convert those who remain indifferent to the issues surrounding AS/400 security, I have included a sample program that could not have been made by any other means, outside of IBM, than patching at IMPI level. Those who are familiar with IMPI instructions will be able to verify its effectiveness. Most significantly, the program dump illustrated in Figure 9.1 is not a result of normal application development—it had to be patched. The most frightening aspect of this program is that it represents a user state program that has been patched at IMPI level and still possesses the correct program validation values. It may be restored onto any AS/400 in the world. The example provides a useful, and otherwise unattainable, function to put or get data from memory loctions of other programs.

The example also exhibits indisputable proof for those doubting Thomases, as well as for the IBM powers that be, that even in this small AS/400 community, there are groups of individuals who will rise to any challenge. For a time, the AS/400 world enjoyed relative obscurity, but that time has passed. More and more computer professionals are joining the ranks of the AS/400 community each day. With this kind of a growing population, the probability of more than a handful of people knowing and exploiting the AS/400's weaknesses will also increase proportionately. Denial is dangerous. Do not rely on a sales pitch. Implement the highest security measures allowed without suffocating your business environment. Remember the old joke that asks the difference between a used car salesman and a software salesman? The answer: The used car salesman knows when he's lying.... Don't let ignorance compromise your system.

Figure 9.1 Patched user state program with correct program validation value.

```
MI PROGRAM              SUBTYPE: 01    NAME: X1                              ADDRESS:  0006 009CCE00 0000
SEGMENT HEADER  (YYSGHDR)
 TYPE 01  FLAGS 91   SIZE 0004   EXT 0006   OBJ 009CCE00 0000   SPLOC 009CD400 0020

EPA HEADER  (YYEPAHDR)
 ATT1   80                    JOPT  00                   TYPE 02                   STYP  01
 NAME   X1
 SPATT  88                    SPIN  00                   SPSZ 480                  OSIZ  00000005               PBAU 3F00
 VER    2301                  TIME  11/22/94 11:37:12                              UP@   0001 00408B00 0000    OHDR 0006 009CCE00 0100
 AG@    0000 00000000 0000                               CT@  0001 003ED900 0000                                JP@  0000 00000000 0000
 RCVY   00000000              PERF  01000000             MDTS 11/22/94 11:37:13                                 OWAU FF00
 COB@   0000 00000000 0000                               JID  00000000000000000000
 IPL#   00000006              AL1   0000000000000000
 009CCE00 0000   01910004 00060001   0006009C CE000000   00010000 00000000   0006009C D4000020   *............................M...*
 009CCE00 0020   80000201 E7F14040   40404040 40404040   40404040 40404040   40404040 40404040   *....X1                          *
 009CCE00 0040   40408800 000001E0   00000005 3F002301   76D68398 95C000A9   00010040 8B000000   *  .....................0........*
 009CCE00 0060   00000000 00000000   00001003E D9000000   0006009C CE000100   00000000 01000000   *............R...................*
 009CCE00 0080   76D68399 D1000045   00000000 00000000   00000000 00000000   00000000 00000000   *.O.J............................*
 009CCE00 00A0   0000FF00 00000006   00000000 00000000   00000000 00000000   00000000 00000000   *................................*
 009CCE00 00C0   00000000 00000000   C0010000 00000000   00000000 00000000   00000000 00000000   *................................*
 009CCE00 00E0   00000000 00000000   00000000 00000000   00000000 00000000   00000000 00000000   *................................*

ASSOCIATED SPACE
 009CD400 0020   00000000 00000000   00000000 00000000   00000000 00000000   00000000 00000000   *................................*
                 14 LINES   009CD400 0040   TO    009CD400 01E0   SAME AS ABOVE

OBJECT SPECIFIC HEADER  (XPGMHDR)
 ATTR   00812000040000 00                     CODE @IS                  ISSZ 0004CC          ISNO 0000001A
 LSTB   00061D                     IEXT 0006  @IS                       PGEC 000000          @SIC 009CCE00 04D0
 SICS   000070                     SCEP 000040 @EOL                     EOLN 0002            EOLS 000038
 @EXD   009CCE00 0580              EXDN 0006   EXDS 0078                BOM0 0005F8          BOMS 000026
 BSIZ   00                         @TIP 00000000 0000    MEG@ 0000 00000000 0000                   MDTG 0000000000000000
 MDTS   000000
 009CCE00 0100   00812000 04000000   00000000 00000000   0000000 0006009C   CE000000 00027000   *................................*
 009CCE00 0120   00000000 001A0004   CC00061D 0013E300   0000009C CE0004D0   00007000 0040009C   *...................T............*
 009CCE00 0140   CE000540 00020000   3820009C CE000580   00060078 0005F800   00260000 00018C2E   *..........................8.....*
 009CCE00 0160   80000000 01100120   00000000 00000000   00006911 A33F0000   00000000 00000000   *................................*
 009CCE00 0180   00000000 01100000   02300000 00000000   00000000 00000000   00000000 00000000   *................................*
 009CCE00 01A0   00000000 00000000   00000000 00000000   00000000 00000000   00000000 00000000   *................................*
                 2 LINES   009CCE00 01C0   TO    009CCE00 01E0   SAME AS ABOVE
```

```
MI PROGRAM                SUBTYPE:  01     NAME: X1                                ADDRESS:  0006  009CCE00 0000
                                                 START CONSTANTS
  009CCE00  0200      D7C1E2C1 40404040  40402000 00000000   00000000 00140000  *PASA           ................*
  009CCE00  0220      000020A0 00000000  00280000 000020A0   00000000 00000000  *.............................*
  009CCE00  0240      00500000 000020A0  00000000 00640000   000020A0 003C0000  *.............................*
  009CCE00  0260      40000000 00000000  00000000 00000000   00000000 00000000  *  ...........................*
            DISPLAY/ALTER/DUMP                                                             11/22/94  11:37:45  PAGE  3


MI PROGRAM                SUBTYPE:  01     NAME: X1                                ADDRESS:  0006  009CCE00 0000
                                                 AUTOMATIC INITIALIZATION CODE
  ADDRESS          LOCATION       OBJECT TEXT              SOURCE STATEMENT
  AUTO INIT CODE IS INCLUDED WITH THE CODE GENERATED FOR THE MI INSTRUCTON AT THE ENTRY POINT AT OFFSET   000274
            DISPLAY/ALTER/DUMP                                                             11/22/94  11:37:45  PAGE  4


MI PROGRAM                SUBTYPE:  01     NAME: X1                                ADDRESS:  0006  009CCE00 0000
                                                 IMPI INSTRUCTIONS
  ADDRESS          LOCATION       OBJECT TEXT              SOURCE STATEMENT                                         MI# (HEX)
  009CCE00 0270     0270           6F00 0298                BU     X'0298'                                            0001
  009CCE00 0274     0274           15D0                     LR     B13, PGM                                           0001
  009CCE00 0276     0276           0DDD                     LSS    B13                                                0001
  009CCE00 0278     0278           CB47 3168 D20A           MVC    X'168'(72,ICB), X'20A'(B13)                        0001
  009CCE00 027E     027E           94C0 3092                L      B12, X'092'(ICB)                                   0001
  009CCE00 0282     0282           53C0 C040                LA     B12, X'040'(B12)                                   0001
  009CCE00 0286     0286           AC1F C000 0000           MVBIP  X'000'(32,B12), X'00'                              0001
  009CCE00 028C     028C           9440 3080                L      B4, X'080'(ICB)                                    0001
  009CCE00 0290     0290           9450 3092                L      B5, X'092'(ICB)                                    0001
  009CCE00 0294     0294           5350 5040                LA     B5, X'040'(B5)                                     0001
  009CCE00 0298     0298           94B0 401A                LA     B11, X'01A'(B4)                                    0001
  009CCE00 029C     029C           64B2 B000                LVT    B11, X'000'(B11), SPP                              0001
  009CCE00 02A0     02A0           CB03 2000 B000           MVC    X'000'(4,B2), X'000'(B11)                          0001
  009CCE00 02A6     02A6           94C0 4008                L      B12, X'008'(B4)                                    0002
  009CCE00 02AA     02AA           64C2 C000                LVT    B12, X'000'(B12), SPP                              0002
  009CCE00 02AE     02AE           CB03 2130 C000           MVC    X'130'(4,B2), X'000'(B12)                          0002
  009CCE00 02B4     02B4           94A0 4002                L      B10, X'002'(B4)                                    0003
  009CCE00 02B8     02B8           64A2 A000                LVT    B10, X'000'(B10), SPP                              0003
  009CCE00 02BC     02BC           D0D7 A000 0310           CBIBE  X'000'(B10), X'D7', X'0310'                        0003
  009CCE00 02C2     02C2           9460 4020                L      B6, X'020'(B4)                                     0004
  009CCE00 02C6     02C6           6462 6000                LVT    B6, X'000'(B6), SPP                                0004
  009CCE00 02CA     02CA           5116 0001                LWRI   W1, X'0001'                                        0004
  009CCE00 02CE     02CE           9178 2000                LW     W7, X'000'(B2)                                     0004
```

(continues)

Figure 9.1 Patched user state program with correct program validation value. (*Continued*)

ADDRESS				SOURCE STATEMENT		MI# (HEX)
009CCE00 02D2	02D2	5175 7FFF		CLWRI	W7, X'7FFF'	0004
009CCE00 02D6	02D6	6B02 1101		SVLOC	X'11', H	0004
009CCE00 02DA	02DA	5175 0000		CLWRI	W7, X'0000'	0004
MI PROGRAM		SUBTYPE:	01	NAME:	X1	
				ADDRESS:	0006 009CCE00 0000	
				IMPI INSTRUCTIONS		
ADDRESS	LOCATION	OBJECT TEXT		SOURCE STATEMENT		MI# (HEX)
009CCE00 02DE	02DE	6B08 1101		SVLOC	X'11', E	0004
009CCE00 02E2	02E2	3371		ALWR	W7, W1	0004
009CCE00 02E4	02E4	5175 1001		CLWRI	W7, X'1001'	0004
009CCE00 02E8	02E8	6B02 1101		SVLOC	X'11', H	0004
009CCE00 02EC	02EC	9660 31C2		ST	B6, X'1C2'(ICB)	0004
009CCE00 02F0	02F0	CB01 31C0 2002		MVC	X'1C0'(2,ICB), X'002'(B2)	0004
009CCE00 02F6	02F6	B000 31C0 FFFF		ALHI	X'1C0'(ICB), X'FFFF'	0004
009CCE00 02FC	02FC	53F0 0260		LA	B15, X'260'(PGM)	0004
009CCE00 0300	0300	96F0 31CA		ST	B15, X'1CA'(ICB)	0004
009CCE00 0304	0304	AB00 31C8 0000		MVHI	X'1C8'(ICB), X'0000'	0004
009CCE00 030A	030A	EB40 31C0 31C8		MVCL	X'1C0'(ICB), X'1C8'(ICB), X'40'	0004
009CCE00 0310	0310	A102 C000 0000		CWI	X'000'(B12), X'0000'	0005
009CCE00 0316	0316	6E0D 04B2		BC	NH, X'04B2'	0005
009CCE00 031A	031A	A102 B000 0000		CWI	X'000'(B11), X'0000'	0006
009CCE00 0320	0320	6E0D 04B2		BC	NH, X'04B2'	0006
009CCE00 0324	0324	6538 5010		STST	ICB, X'010'(B5), SPP	0007
009CCE00 0328	0328	6472 5010		LVT	B7, X'010'(B5), SPP	0008
009CCE00 032C	032C	A200 7004 0000		CHI	X'004'(B7), X'0000'	0008
009CCE00 0332	0332	6E0D 04B2		BC	NH, X'04B2'	0008
009CCE00 0336	0336	A200 70D2 0001		CHI	X'0D2'(B7), X'0001'	0009
009CCE00 033C	033C	6E0D 04B2		BC	NH, X'04B2'	0009
009CCE00 0340	0340	C631 31C0 7004		ZAC	X'1C0'(4,ICB), X'004'(2,B7)	000A
009CCE00 0346	0346	9377 31C0		LSOP	B7, X'1C0'(ICB), B7	000A
009CCE00 034A	034A	6578 5010		STST	B7, X'010'(B5), SPP	000A
009CCE00 034E	034E	9410 707A		L	B1, X'07A'(B7)	000B
009CCE00 0352	0352	6510 5000		STST	B1, X'000'(B5), SYP	000B
009CCE00 0356	0356	64F2 2110		LVT	B15, X'110'(B2), SPP	000C
009CCE00 035A	035A	96F0 31C0		ST	B15, X'1C0'(ICB)	000C
009CCE00 035E	035E	9650 31C6		ST	B5, X'1C6'(ICB)	000C
009CCE00 0362	0362	54F0 0061		LHRI	H15, X'0061'	000C
009CCE00 0366	0366	5D5D 31C0		SVL1	X'1C0'(ICB), X'5D'	000C
009CCE00 036A	036A	9480 400E		L	B8, X'00E'(B4)	000D
009CCE00 036E	036E	6482 8000		LVT	B8, X'000'(B8), SPP	000D
009CCE00 0372	0372	C509 203C 8000		CLC	X'03C'(10,B2), X'000'(B8)	000D

122

ADDRESS				
009CCE00	0378	6E08 0382	BC	E,X'0382'	000D
009CCE00	037C	1F1F	SVLM	X'1F'	000E
009CCE00	037E	6F00 0328	BU	X'0328'	000E
009CCE00	0382	9490 4014	L	B9,X'014'(B4)	000F
009CCE00	0386	6492 9000	LVT	B9,X'000'(B9),SPP	000F
009CCE00	038A	C509 9000 0200	CLC	X'000'(10,B9),X'200'(PGM)	000F
009CCE00	0390	6E08 03A0	BC	E,X'03A0'	000F
009CCE00	0394	9410 708C	L	B1,X'08C'(B7)	0010

MI PROGRAM NAME: X1 SUBTYPE: 01 ADDRESS: 0006 009CCE00 0000

IMPI INSTRUCTIONS

ADDRESS	LOCATION	OBJECT TEXT	SOURCE STATEMENT		MI# (HEX)
009CCE00 0398	0398	6518 2120	STST	B1,X'120'(B2),SPP	0010
009CCE00 039C	039C	6F00 03A8	BU	X'03A8'	0011
009CCE00 03A0	03A0	9410 7092	L	B1,X'092'(B7)	0012
009CCE00 03A4	03A4	6518 2120	STST	B1,X'120'(B2),SPP	0012
009CCE00 03A8	03A8	6412 2120	LVT	B1,X'120'(B2),SPP	0013
009CCE00 03AC	03AC	4C11 2130	CAL	B1,B1,X'130'(B2)	0013
009CCE00 03B0	03B0	6518 2120	STST	B1,X'120'(B2),SPP	0013
009CCE00 03B4	03B4	94A0 4002	L	B10,X'002'(B4)	0014
009CCE00 03B8	03B8	64A2 A000	LVT	B10,X'000'(B10),SPP	0014
009CCE00 03BC	03BC	D0D7 A000 043C	CBIBE	X'000'(B10),X'D7',X'043C'	0014
009CCE00 03C2	03C2	9460 4020	L	B6,X'020'(B4)	0015
009CCE00 03C6	03C6	6462 6000	LVT	B6,X'000'(B6),SPP	0015
009CCE00 03CA	03CA	6412 2120	LVT	B1,X'120'(B2),SPP	0015
009CCE00 03CE	03CE	51F6 0001	LWRI	W15,X'0001'	0015
009CCE00 03D2	03D2	91E8 2000	LW	W14,X'000'(B2)	0015
009CCE00 03D6	03D6	51E5 7FFF	CLWRI	W14,X'7FFF'	0015
009CCE00 03DA	03DA	6B02 1101	SVLOC	X'11',H	0015
009CCE00 03DE	03DE	51E5 0000	CLWRI	W14,X'0000'	0015
009CCE00 03E2	03E2	6B08 1101	SVLOC	X'11',E	0015
009CCE00 03E6	03E6	33EF	ALWR	W14,W15	0015
009CCE00 03E8	03E8	51E5 1001	CLWRI	W14,X'1001'	0015
009CCE00 03EC	03EC	6B02 1101	SVLOC	X'11',H	0015
009CCE00 03F0	03F0	51E6 0001	LWRI	W14,X'0001'	0015
009CCE00 03F4	03F4	91D8 2000	LW	W13,X'000'(B2)	0015
009CCE00 03F8	03F8	51D5 7FFF	CLWRI	W13,X'7FFF'	0015
009CCE00 03FC	03FC	6B02 1101	SVLOC	X'11',H	0015
009CCE00 0400	0400	51D5 0000	CLWRI	W13,X'0000'	0015
009CCE00 0404	0404	6B08 1101	SVLOC	X'11',E	0015
009CCE00 0408	0408	33DE	ALWR	W13,W14	0015
009CCE00 040A	040A	51D5 1001	CLWRI	W13,X'1001'	0015
009CCE00 040E	040E	6B02 1101	SVLOC	X'11',H	0015

(continues)

Figure 9.1 Patched user state program with correct program validation value. *(Continued)*

ADDRESS		OBJECT TEXT		SOURCE STATEMENT			MI# (HEX)
009CCE00	0412	9660	31C2	ST	B6, X'1C2'(ICB)		0015
009CCE00	0416	CB01 31C0	2002	MVC	X'1C0'(2,ICB), X'002'(B2)		0015
009CCE00	041C	B000 31C0	FFFF	ALHI	X'1C0'(ICB), X'FFFF'		0015
009CCE00	0422	9610	31CA	ST	B1, X'1CA'(ICB)		0015
009CCE00	0426	CB01 31C8	2002	MVC	X'1C8'(2,ICB), X'002'(B2)		0015
009CCE00	042C	B000 31C8	FFFF	ALHI	X'1C8'(ICB), X'FFFF'		0015
009CCE00	0432	EB00 31C0	31C8	MVCL	X'1C0'(ICB), X'1C8'(ICB), X'00'		0016
009CCE00	0438	6F00	04B2	BU	X'04B2'		0017
009CCE00	043C	6412	2120	LVT	B1, X'120'(B2), SPP		0017
009CCE00	0440	9460	4020	L	B6, X'020'(B4)		0017
009CCE00	0444	6462	6000	LVT	B6, X'000'(B6), SPP		0017

MI PROGRAM NAME: X1 SUBTYPE: 01 ADDRESS: 0006 009CCE00 0000

IMPI INSTRUCTIONS

ADDRESS		LOCATION	OBJECT TEXT		SOURCE STATEMENT		MI# (HEX)
009CCE00	0448	0448	51F6	0001	LWRI	W15, X'0001'	0017
009CCE00	044C	044C	91E8	2000	LW	W14, X'000'(B2)	0017
009CCE00	0450	0450	51E5	7FFF	CLWRI	W14, X'7FFF'	0017
009CCE00	0454	0454	6B02	1101	SVLOC	X'11', H	0017
009CCE00	0458	0458	51E5	0000	CLWRI	W14, X'0000'	0017
009CCE00	045C	045C	6B08	1101	SVLOC	X'11', E	0017
009CCE00	0460	0460	33EF		ALWR	W14, W15	0017
009CCE00	0462	0462	51E5	1001	CLWRI	W14, X'1001'	0017
009CCE00	0466	0466	6B02	1101	SVLOC	X'11', H	0017
009CCE00	046A	046A	51E6	0001	LWRI	W14, X'0001'	0017
009CCE00	046E	046E	91D8	2000	LW	W13, X'000'(B2)	0017
009CCE00	0472	0472	51D5	7FFF	CLWRI	W13, X'7FFF'	0017
009CCE00	0476	0476	6B02	1101	SVLOC	X'11', H	0017
009CCE00	047A	047A	51D5	0000	CLWRI	W13, X'0000'	0017
009CCE00	047E	047E	6B08	1101	SVLOC	X'11', E	0017
009CCE00	0482	0482	33DE		ALWR	W13, W14	0017
009CCE00	0484	0484	51D5	1001	CLWRI	W13, X'1001'	0017
009CCE00	0488	0488	6B02	1101	SVLOC	X'11', H	0017
009CCE00	048C	048C	9610	31C2	ST	B1, X'1C2'(ICB)	0017
009CCE00	0490	0490	CB01 31C0	2002	MVC	X'1C0'(2,ICB), X'002'(B2)	0017
009CCE00	0496	0496	B000 31C0	FFFF	ALHI	X'1C0'(ICB), X'FFFF'	0017
009CCE00	049C	049C	9660	31CA	ST	B6, X'1CA'(ICB)	0017
009CCE00	04A0	04A0	CB01 31C8	2002	MVC	X'1C8'(2,ICB), X'002'(B2)	0017
009CCE00	04A6	04A6	B000 31C8	FFFF	ALHI	X'1C8'(ICB), X'FFFF'	0017
009CCE00	04AC	04AC	EB00 31C0	31C8	MVCL	X'1C0'(ICB), X'1C8'(ICB), X'00'	0017
009CCE00	04B2	04B2	AC05 31C0	0000	MVBIP	X'1C0'(6,ICB), X'00'	0018

124

```
009CCE00 04B8    04B8  54F0 0038           LHRI   H15, X'0038'                              0018
009CCE00 04BC    04BC  5D5D 31C0           SVL1   X'1C0'(ICB), X'5D'                        0018
009CCE00 04C0    04C0  A8B0 0000 0000      FNC2   X'000'(PGM), X'000'(PGM), X'B0'           0019
009CCE00 04C6    04C6  A8B0 0000 0000      FNC2   X'000'(PGM), X'000'(PGM), X'B0'           001A

MI PROGRAM                SUBTYPE:  01    NAME: X1                          ADDRESS: 0006 009CCE00 0000
                                                 END CONSTANTS

MI PROGRAM                SUBTYPE:  01    NAME: X1                          ADDRESS: 0006 009CCE00 0000
                                           ACB AND STATIC INIT CONSTANTS

          MAXA   6            MINA   6           ICBSZ  01E0          PASAS  00000020    PSSAS  00000140
PGMHD  009CCE00 0100          PGMIS  009CCE00 0000   PGMEP  009CCE00 0000   PGMOF  0274   PGMEC  009CCE00 0000
IDLOF  0032                   UTOI   009CCE00 0274   PGMAI  028C           UTOIL  0018
009CCE00 04D0  06601E0 00000020  00000140 009CCE00  0100009C CE000000  00000274   *................*
009CCE00 04F0  009CCE00 00000032  009CCE00 0274028C  0018000 01000000   00000000   *................*

MI PROGRAM                SUBTYPE:  01    NAME: X1                          ADDRESS: 0006 009CCE00 0000
                                           STATIC INITIALIZATION CODE
ADDRESS        LOCATION  OBJECT TEXT               SOURCE STATEMENT
009CCE00 0510  0510     971E 3018                  STM    B1, 15, X'018'(ICB)
009CCE00 0514  0514     5390 2040                  LA     B9, X'040'(B2)
009CCE00 0518  0518     ACFF 9000 0000             MVBIP  X'000'(256,B9), X'00'
009CCE00 051E  051E     AC3F 9100 0000             MVBIP  X'100'(64,B9), X'00'
009CCE00 0524  0524     94D0 400C                  L      B13, X'00C'(B4)
009CCE00 0528  0528     94D0 D032                  L      B13, X'032'(B13)
009CCE00 052C  052C     CB07 9010 D032             MVC    X'010'(8,B9), X'032'(B13)
009CCE00 0532  0532     53B0 9010                  LA     B11, X'010'(B9)
009CCE00 0536  0536     65B8 9110                  STST   B11, X'110'(B9), SPP
009CCE00 053A  053A     951E 3018                  LM     B1, 15, X'018'(ICB)
009CCE00 053E  053E     2FEF                       BRL    H14, B15

MI PROGRAM                SUBTYPE:  01    NAME: X1                          ADDRESS: 0006 009CCE00 0000
                                           EXCEPTION DIRECTORY
009CCE00 0580   80000001 00000168  000004B2 0003C3D7  C6000000                              *............CPF...*
009CCE00 0590   80000001           00001174 00000328  00000328 00002201  00040000 00002202  *..................*
009CCE00 05A0                      80000000 00000180  00000001  00000328 00040000 00040000  *..................*
009CCE00 05B0                                         80000001            0000018C 00000328 00002203  *..................*
009CCE00 05D0   80000001 00000198  00000328 00002207                                        *..................*
```
(continues)

Figure 9.1 Patched user state program with correct program validation value. (Continued)

```
009CCE00 05E0    80000001 000001A4 00000328    00040000 00002208    *..............*
MI PROGRAM              SUBTYPE: 01    NAME: X1          ADDRESS:  0006 009CCE00 0000
                                       OBJECT MAPPING TABLE
ODT# (HEX) BASE ADDRESSABILITY         HEX OFFSET FROM BASE         OMTE IN HEX

MI PROGRAM              SUBTYPE: 01    NAME: X1          ADDRESS:  0006 009CCE00 0000
                                       BREAK OFFSET MAPPING TABLE
009CCE00 05F0    80000010 20400000     00008428 10811004 02402288 20400000    *.. ..........*
009CCE00 0610    00000000 0A000000     00000000 4090
MI PROGRAM              SUBTYPE: 01    NAME: X1          ADDRESS:  0006 009CCE00 0000
                                       MI INSTRUCTIONS

MI PROGRAM              SUBTYPE: 01    NAME: X1          ADDRESS:  0006 009CCE00 0000
                                       ODT DIRECTORY VECTOR

MI PROGRAM              SUBTYPE: 01    NAME: X1          ADDRESS:  0006 009CCE00 0000
                                       ODT ENTRY STRING

MI PROGRAM              SUBTYPE: 01    NAME: X1          ADDRESS:  0006 009CCE00 0000
                                       HIGH LEVEL LANGUAGE BOM TABLE

MI PROGRAM              SUBTYPE: 01    NAME: X1          ADDRESS:  0006 009CCE00 0000
                                       HIGH LEVEL LANGUAGE SYMBOL TABLE

****** END OF DUMP ******
```

CHAPTER TEN

The Core War

> The virus had penetrated main storage with little difficulty. No cause for alarm had been detected, no one knew it was there. Posing as a user state program, but designed with special alterations, it had made its way into places where even the most privileged system state programs couldn't venture. It had been scanned for creation validation values when it first entered the system, but at that point, its innocent disguise allowed it to be granted access with no questions asked. That was the beauty of the way it was made; it remained cleverly cloaked until it actually accessed the system, and only then did it take on its current, more ominous form. With the system security level set at 30, there would be little else to impede its slow, destructive journey. Interception of user requests at the operating system's command line interface bought it the time it needed to kill programs from the core memory, and then replace a pointer in the system command entry program. It was quite easy, really. The bustling traffic in the core memory hid the foreign entity well . . . right up until the moment it approached the main storage entry checkpoint and was identified as a system state, user domain program. Here there was nowhere for it to hide. The

> unexpected, second checksum validation process exposed its lack of proper credentials, and the virus now finds itself unceremoniously dumped into the QRECOVER library, where it will eventually be completely unmasked.
>
> Don, in the meantime, has just activated Miss Piggy and is about to settle into his badly needed Monday morning first cup of coffee when the "shake and bake" printer in the corner of the computer room begins to whine. The report it spits out is an unfamiliar one. "User DEBBIE attempted to execute an altered program X0001M in system state. Program has been automatically disabled and relocated to QRECOVER library. Program attributes and statistics have been set to print on default printer." Don's eyebrows rise as he reads. Could the antivirus software package he installed just six months ago actually have snared something in its net? More than likely it's just a harmless program that tripped on authority violation, or maybe even one of Steve's annoying little Monday morning pranks. He returns to his coffee. He'll return to the report later; whatever it is, it can't hurt anything now. It'll wait. He leans back in his chair with his mug, ready for another uneventful week in the MIS department.

As we conclude the management section of this book, I hope I have illustrated the difference that proactive security measures can make when implemented. By taking seriously the possibility of an external threat, as unlikely as it may have seemed, Don averted a potentially crippling disaster for his company—with a minimum of effort. Can you afford to be any less careful?

PART TWO

Implementation

This section of the book outlines in detail what security measures should be taken and the reasons why they are recommended. It also explains, where appropriate, how an intruder may undermine a security system if the measures are not implemented properly. The chapters in this section are designed for those who are directly responsible for security implementation. They provide specific recommendations, warn against potential pitfalls, and tell how to use the tools provided in the appendix. They are meant to be a technical reference guide for the AS/400 security administrator.

CHAPTER ELEVEN

Physical Security

Physical security means more than simply guarding against intruders. It also means safeguarding against the surrounding environment, the effects of mother nature, and even the occasional mishap visited by well-meaning but ignorant operators! For example, in a computer room located high up on the 35th floor of a downtown Boston skyscraper, there were tape drives that appeared to be demonically possessed. Every morning as the sun rose, all the magnetic tape units would suddenly stop reading the tapes and perform a high-speed rewind to the beginning of the reel. Extensive research revealed that the sun's reflection triggered the end-of-tape sensor, causing the tape units to rewind. At another site, an IBM mainframe mysteriously crashed from time to time with no visible cause—but it was observed that whenever a crash occurred, there was always a small pile of sawdust on the floor. The mystery finally unfolded when a maintenance man was seen carrying two-by-fours into the computer room, using the system units as his sawhorse, and cutting the pieces of wood into many smaller pieces. By the time he was done, so was the machine.

The best of these stories I've heard thus far was about a scatterbrained operator whose job was to clean several read-write heads of a system at one of the Los Vegas casinos. The operator diligently cleaned the heads carefully and completely, only to hear the noises of the same read-write heads pinging off the platters as they fell off the actuator arms. The operator had unknowingly used a bottle of acetone instead of alcohol, causing the ceramic heads to become unglued from the metal actuator arms and fall to the disk platters spinning at 360 revolutions per minute.

These kinds of annoyances could have been prevented by implementing a few commonsense precautions, such as controlling entry to the computer room by use of cipher keys or identification badges, designating a computer room away from windows, and perhaps removing unnecessary chemicals from the head cleaning kits.

There are some obvious consequences associated with the lack of physical security. They run the gamut from lost data to system crash. Data loss can occur in an obvious manner; the intruder may simply walk out of the computer room with a cartridge or a reel. A system crash, however, may not be immediately evident. If, for example, a console is left signed on by a system operator, an intruder could disable the system without deleting any objects at all. All that the intruder would have to do is to save the QT3REQIO operating system program to a savefile, then restore it back to the library over the original object. This procedure would essentially render the OS/400 inoperable, as it would no longer be able to communicate with anyone. The reasons why are complicated, but it is sufficient to say that there are many programs that could accomplish this kind of devastation. The existence of such programs does not constitute the actual threat to security, however. The lack of physical security combined with human error in failure to sign off the workstation, in this case, is the culprit.

Phone Phreaks

There are dozens of these stories told throughout the computer industry across all computer platforms. There is also an equal number of stories of computer hackers and phone phreaks breaking into corporate accounts such as AT&T and TRW systems—and these stories, unfortunately, are not nearly as amusing. Among the most widely publicized attacks of this nature came from the original phone phreak, John Draper, also known as Captain Crunch. The nickname was rumored to have come from his ingenious use of a whistle that accompanied a box of Cap'n Crunch cereal.

Apparently the whistle made a sound at the precise frequency used to command the AT&T telephone switching systems to connect the caller to an outbound trunk, thereby allowing the whistler to make free long-distance calls. Draper also created a device known as a "blue box," which simulates tones used by the AT&T switches—again to gain access to the telephone computer systems. He was eventually hired by Apple Corporation—but not before serving time in jail.

There are others who have carried Draper's work much further. In the years following Draper's escapade, the number of would-be phone phreaks soared. Underground newspapers circulated and hacker conventions are still being held. As recently as 1993, unsuspecting corporate operators would regularly transfer an incoming call to an outgoing trunk if asked properly. The most common use of an outgoing trunk is the placing of calls using the home office's WATTS line service, which is cheaper than regular long-distance rates from satellite offices. However, the operator who is used to transferring incoming lines to outgoing trunks seldom stops and asks managers and executives to identify themselves. In occurrences such as this, no amount of physical security may be enough. The operator must be told not to permit such a transfer, or the company should take steps to properly identify the caller prior to granting access to their outbound lines.

Local Switches

Unfortunately most AS/400 data communication is still in the clear because the consensus among the AS/400 information systems professionals is that their duties end where the telephone system begins. In many corporations this means at the internal telephone switching system. Yet, telephone systems are still a mystery to many AS/400 computer professionals. Beyond the fact that normal telephones only require two of the four wires, and that the other two can be used to connect the AS/400 terminals via patch panels and balens, the majority of AS/400 technicians are oblivious to the local PBX's or CBX's operating systems used to route their data from and to the outside world.

As in the AS/400, most telephone switches require passwords that identify authorized profiles. These machines understand commands sent via modem attached to a PC. The PBX or CBX allows configuration of extensions, voice mail passwords, trunk assignments, and much more. A curious listener may eavesdrop on anyone's conversation using a special telephone set known as a lineman's set, purchased through a mail order catalog, by connecting two alligator clips on a 66 block telephone closet. Such a setup will appear to the telephone system to be no more than an extension receiver. This is the domain of phone phreaks. They are well versed in the workings of various telephone system switches.

It is not too difficult to gain access to many private telephone switching systems, since many do not employ a telephone systems expert on-site. In the majority of these cases the telephone switch's access codes either correspond to the assigned customer numbers, which are shown on invoices, or match unchanged default shipped values. This creates a situation similar to that of the AS/400: anyone may easily sign on by knowing that the password for the security officer is QSECOFR, if no one bothered or no one knew enough to change it. Once the switch has been compromised, the assailant may initiate calls originating from that switch, all for free.

Protocol Analyzers

Using the lineman's set, a novice hacker may target an unsecured telephone closet to gain AS/400 user profiles and passwords. A device known as a protocol analyzer may be used to browse digital information being transmitted on telephone lines. Protocol analyzers are sometimes used by phone companies to track down communication problems when customers report digital line failures. A hacker armed with this device only has to identify which lines to analyze in the phone closet. An experienced phone phreak may be able to gain access to your local telephone switch as a systems administrator, if the password hasn't been changed, then monitor trunks from afar. Once the phreak identifies what information is needed to sign on to the AS/400, baring any encrypted location passwords, the rest is academic. To provide an example of what hackers might see if they were to analyze one line, an equivalent function that resides on every AS/400 is explored in the following paragraph as an exercise. (Different protocol analyzers format and display the data differently.)

First, initiate the service tools using the STRSST command followed by option 3 to activate the work with communications trace function

PHYSICAL SECURITY   135

```
                    System Service Tools (SST)
Select one of the following:

        1. Start a service tool
        2. Work with active service tools
        3. Work with disk units
        4. Work with diskette data recovery




Selection
     1
F3=Exit         F10=Command entry        F12=Cancel
```

Figure 11.1 Start service tools.

(Figures 11.1 and 11.2). Start the trace with recommended parameters specified in Figure 11.3.

```
                     Start a Service Tool
Warning: Incorrect use of this service tool can cause damage
to data in this system.  Contact your service representative
for assistance.

Select one of the following:

        1. Error log utility
        2. Trace Vertical Licensed Internal Code
        3. Work with communications trace
        4. Display/Alter/Dump
        5. Vertical Licensed Internal Code log
        6. Input/Output debug utility
        7. Print stand-alone dump
        8. Display hardware configuration



Selection
     3
F3=Exit         F12=Cancel         F16=SST menu
```

Figure 11.2 Start a service tool.

136 IMPLEMENTATION

```
                        Start Trace
Type choices, press Enter.

  Configuration object . . . . . . .   qsai
  Type         . . . . . . . . . . .   1         1=Line, 2=Network interface
  Trace description  . . . . . . .     qsai lind
  Buffer size  . . . . . . . . . . .   1         1=128K, 2=256K, 3=2048K
                                                 4=4096K, 5=6144K, 6=8192K
  Stop on buffer full  . . . . . . .   N         Y=Yes, N=No
  Data direction   . . . . . . . . .   3         1=Sent, 2=Received, 3=Both
  Number of bytes to trace:
    Beginning bytes  . . . . . . . .   *CALC     Value, *CALC
    Ending bytes     . . . . . . . .   *CALC     Value, *CALC

F3=Exit   F5=Refresh   F12=Cancel
```

Figure 111.3 Start trace.

Next, sign on to the system using a device attached to the line description that was specified in the first step (Figure 11.3). Return to the service tools and stop the trace with option 2, then request to format and print the trace with option 6 (Figure 11.4).

```
                      Format Trace Data
Configuration object   . . . . :   QSAI
Type             . . . . . . . :   LINE
Type choices, press Enter.

  Controller . . . . . . . . . . .   *ALL        *ALL, name
  Data representation  . . . . .     2           1=ASCII, 2=EBCDIC
  Format SNA data only . . . . .     Y           Y=Yes, N=No
  Format RR, RNR commands  . . .     N           Y=Yes, N=No




F3=Exit    F5=Refresh    F12=Cancel
```

Figure 11.4 Format Trace Data.

```
                                    Display Spooled File
File . . . . . :   QPCSMPRT                                              Page/Line   4/1
Control . . . .    _____                                                Columns     2 - 131
Find . . . . . .
....+....1....+....2....+....3....+....4....+....5....+....6....+....7....+....8....+....9....+....0....+....1....+....2....+....3.
COMMUNICATIONS TRACE       Title: QSAI LIND              08/22/94  00:31:08               Page:    4
Record      Controller  Data
Number S/R  Name        Type     SNA Data: TH, RH, RU
  397   R               EBCDIC   TH :  FID=2,  MPF=Only         ODAI=1, DAF'=01, OAF'=01, SNF'=0001
                                 RH1 : ('0A9100'X)   REQ FMD, FI, BCI, DR1, ERI, PI
            RU Command . . . . : FMH- 5=200502FF0003D0000000407F0F0F10F0502D8E2C1C90001C2     *......}....001...QSAI..B    *
                                 C1D1C1D9C1E30000                                             *AJARAT..                    *
  398   R               EBCDIC   TH :  FID=2,  MPF=Only         ODAI=1, DAF'=01, OAF'=01, SNF'=0002
                                 RH :  ('019020'X)   REQ FMD, ECI, DR1, ERI, CDI
            RU Data . . . . . : 000AD00100010004041                                          *...}........                *
  399   S               EBCDIC   TH :  FID=2,  MPF=Only         ODAI=1, DAF'=01, OAF'=01, SNF'=0000
                                 RH :  ('030100'X)   RSP FMD, PI
                                 No RU data
  457   S               EBCDIC   TH :  FID=2,  MPF=Only         ODAI=1, DAF'=01, OAF'=01, SNF'=0001
                                 RH :  ('039120'X)   REQ FMD, BCI, ECI, DR1, ERI, PI, CDI
            RU Data . . . . . : 000AD00300010004 1443                                        *...}........                *
  460   R               EBCDIC   TH :  FID=2,  MPF=Only         ODAI=1, DAF'=01, OAF'=01, SNF'=0001
                                 RH :  ('030100'X)   RSP FMD, PI
                                                                                                                More...
F3=Exit    F12=Cancel    F19=Left    F20=Right   F24=More keys
```

Figure 11.5 Display spooled file.

Finally, delete the trace request with option 4, exit the service tools, and display the trace report generated using the work with spooled file (WRKSPLF) command.

As illustrated in Figure 11.5, even to an amateur AS/400 hacker, QSAI and BAJARAT stand out as a possible profile and password. The trace report contains other sensitive information, such as a network identifier, device name, device address, and system name, all of which may be used to connect to the system. As the service tools have demonstrated, if data is not encrypted, it is just as important to secure the telephone system and communication lines as it is to secure the computer systems. The process just described is common knowledge to all but the most inexperienced hackers and ranks among the least sophisticated techniques available.

Encryption Devices

An encryption device may be external, configured to intercept data between the system and the modem, or may be a built-in function of the modem. These units essentially block any protocol analyzers from eavesdropping on the line by enciphering data before it leaves the modem. Incoming data is deciphered once it reaches the modem or before it enters the system, thereby shortening the range in which protocol analyzers would be useful. There are a variety of data encryption devices, from simple stand-alone units to rack-mounted multiline systems with thousands of encryption keys. In addition, switched lines may employ call-back units. When a call-back unit detects an incoming call, it identifies the caller and returns the call to a predefined number. This feature physically requires the caller to be at a specified, authorized location and may even require the connection to be made available only at proper times.

Conclusion

Here is a list of recommendations regarding the physical security of AS/400s:

- A separate computer room should be established and secured with cipher lock or identification badges.
- The system unit's key should be removed and secured.
- A separate secured room within the computer room is recommended for all communication equipment, including the local telephone switching systems. At the very least, secure all telephone closets.
- Secure "telephone lineman's sets" and protocol analyzers when not in use.
- All devices that will allow users to save or restore objects onto the system should be placed in a restricted access area.
- A console and secured printers should be made available only to those who are authorized with proper means of identification.
- Consider using a fireproof cabinet to store system backup media, in addition to establishing a secure off-site storage location.
- If a local telephone switch is used, change the system administrator's password from the default.
- Visitors to the organization should be clearly identified with a badge and should always be accompanied by an internal representative.
- Educate users to route the print of sensitive data to a secured printer.
- Emphasize to all users the importance of signing off their workstations when not being used.

CHAPTER TWELVE

System Values

System values are used by OS/400 operating system commands and programs as default values. Changes to these values may have profound effects throughout the system. Although most of the system values discussed in this chapter relate to the security of the system, some of the parameters are borrowed from other sections governing work management and system controls. The system values discussed in this chapter should be reviewed periodically, particularly when the system environment changes, such as during the installation of new applications or a communications network.

Adjustments

Readers may opt to use the operating system command, Work with System Values (WRKSYSVAL), to review and change parameters as necessary, or to use the command CHGSECVAL, Change Security Values, provided with this book. The advantage of the Change Security Values command is that it provides a single command that will change all security-related values to the recommended settings. Users may then override the changed values individually using the WRKSYSVAL operating system command as necessary. The disadvantage of the CHGSECVAL command is that it is release-dependent and will need to be updated as new security system values and parameters are made available. The source codes necessary to maintain this command are provided with this book.

To use the operating system command to update system values, enter the command WRKSYSVAL at a command line and press command function key F4. Specify the listing of either all values or only security-related values by entering *ALL or *SEC in the system values prompt field. When a list of system values appears, choose the appropriate value to update by selecting it with option 2, as illustrated in Figure 12.1. Some of the system value parameters have prerequisites. For instance, changing the accounting level (QACGLVL) system value parameter from the default of *NONE to *JOB requires that a journal QACGJRN already exist in the QSYS library. The WRKSYSVAL operating system command will not allow this parameter to be changed without first having the prerequisites satisfied. The CHGSECVAL command, on the other hand, will automatically create the necessary objects as they are needed.

In order to use the Change Security Values command, illustrated in Figure 12.2, a user must be authorized to several special authorities. Some

```
                      Work with System Value (WRKSYSVAL)

Type choices, press Enter.

System value . . . . . . . . . .    *SEC         Name, generic*, *ALL, *ALC...
Output . . . . . . . . . . . . .    *            *, *PRINT
```

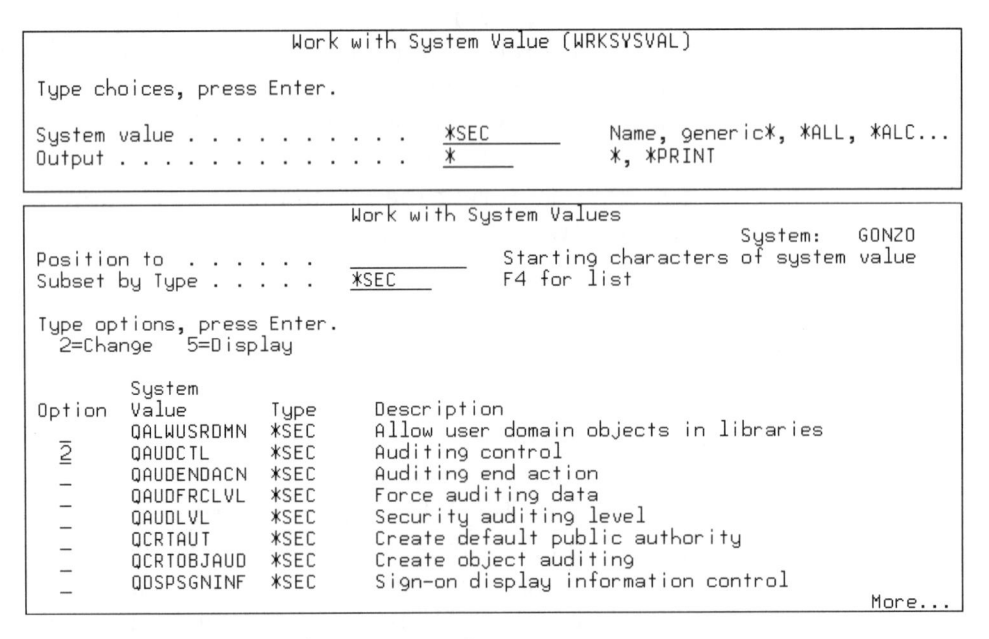

```
                              Work with System Values
                                                              System:   GONZO
Position to  . . . . . .   _____     Starting characters of system value
Subset by Type . . . . .     *SEC        F4 for list

Type options, press Enter.
  2=Change   5=Display

           System
Option     Value        Type     Description
           QALWUSRDMN   *SEC     Allow user domain objects in libraries
   2       QAUDCTL      *SEC     Auditing control
   _       QAUDENDACN   *SEC     Auditing end action
   _       QAUDFRCLVL   *SEC     Force auditing data
   _       QAUDLVL      *SEC     Security auditing level
   _       QCRTAUT      *SEC     Create default public authority
   _       QCRTOBJAUD   *SEC     Create object auditing
   _       QDSPSGNINF   *SEC     Sign-on display information control
                                                                      More...
```

Figure 12.1 Work with System Values.

SYSTEM VALUES 141

```
CHANGE SECURITY VALUES (CHGSECVAL)
```

Figure 12.2 Change Security Values.

system value changes will take effect immediately and others will take effect only after the next IPL (initial program load). If the sample software that accompanies this book has been installed following the setup procedures outlined in the appendix, the CHGSECVAL may be used by simply entering the command and pressing the Enter key. This command will automatically create the necessary journals and journal receivers for the resource accounting and audit control system values. The software has been compiled to execute properly at OS/400 operating system version 2 release 3. It recognizes all system values and their respective parameters from OS/400 v2r3.

Regardless of the methods used to change the system values, if the QLMTSECOFR parameter is to be changed as recommended, be certain to grant explicit object authorities to selected workstation devices for privileged profiles or group profiles. This will allow privileged profiles to use the authorized workstations to sign on. Figure 12.3 illustrates the use of the Edit Object Authorities (EDTOBJAUT) command. This command may be used to grant the necessary authorities to privileged users. The minimum authority required is *CHANGE before the operating system will allow the use of the workstation by privileged profiles.

Also accompanying the Change Security Values command is a Delete Old Journal Receivers command, DLTOLDRCV (Figure 12.4). The use of

```
                          Edit Object Authority
Object . . . . . . . :   DSP010003      Object type  . . . . :   *DEVD
  Library  . . . . . :      QSVS        Owner  . . . . . . . :   QPGMR

Type changes to current authorities, press Enter.

   Object secured by authorization list  . . . . . . . . . .   *NONE

                 Object
User             Authority
QSAI             *CHANGE
*PUBLIC          *CHANGE
```

Figure 12.3 Edit Object Authority.

142   IMPLEMENTATION

```
                    DELETE OLD JOURNAL RECEIVERS (DLTOLDRCV)

Type choices, press Enter.
Journal Receivers  . . . . . . .    q*              Name, generic*, *ALL
Receiver Library . . . . . . . .    qusrsys         Name, *LIBL, *CURLIB, *ALL...
```

Figure 12.4 Delete Old Journal Receivers.

this command is highly recommended, as the resource accounting and security audit journal receivers will need to be changed periodically. The DLTOLDRCV command will automatically remove old journal receivers that have already been analyzed or are otherwise no longer needed. The Delete Old Journal Receivers command is designed to work properly with OS/400 version 2 release 2 and above.

Password Validation

The password validation program provided in the appendix (VLDUSR-PWD) will prevent users from changing their passwords more than once a day. To activate this feature, the system value QPWDVLDPGM must be changed to the program name specified in the appendix as illustrated in Figure 12.5. Once the system value has been changed, the Change Password (CHGPWD) command will incorporate the rules of this program in addition to all the other rules that have been set by the system values. The error message "Password may be changed only once a day" will be issued if the user tries to change passwords more than once per day. Figure 12.6 illustrates an example of how the Password Validation program executes.

```
                              Change System Value

System value  . . . . . :   QPWDVLDPGM
Description   . . . . . :   Password validation program


Type choices, press Enter.

  Password validation program        VLDUSRPWD       Name, *NONE
    Library . . . . . . . .          SECURITY        Name
```

Figure 12.5 Change System Values.

```
                        Change Password
Password last changed . . . . . . . . . . :   08/26/94

Type choices, press Enter.

   Current password  . . . . . . . . . . . .
   New password  . . . . . . . . . . . . . .
   New password (to verify)  . . . . . . . .




F3=Exit            F12=Cancel
Password may be changed only once a day.
```

Figure 12.6 Change Password.

Password validation program will not inhibit authorized users from changing their passwords through the CHGUSRPRF command, however. Also, the CHGUSRPRF command does not enforce any of the password validation rules specified in the system values table.

Recommendations

The following system values are recommended. The values are summarized in Table 12.1. If the Change Security Values command, CHGSECVAL, is used, all these values are automatically updated to the recommended settings.

QACGLVL   This system value should be used to collect system resource accounting information. This information may be used to track suspicious activities during off-peak hours, holidays, and weekends. If an uninvited guest regularly breaks into the system, the resource accounting data can be used to establish a call pattern and length of stay, and to identify resources used during the visit. This feature can also be used to charge back part of the information system's resources to

	individuals or departments within the company for budgeting purposes.
QALWOBJRST	This system value may be used to control whether a system state program is to be restored. This option also controls the restoration of programs that adopt authorities at runtime. The use of this system value to restrict the restoration of system state programs is highly recommended.
QALWUSRDMN	This system value may be used to control placement of user spaces, user indices, and user queues. Under security level 50, only the QTEMP temporary library may host user spaces, indices, and queues. If your system is required by the U.S. government to be secured in accordance with the C2 rating, the system security level should be set to 50 and this value should be set to QTEMP only. Otherwise this value should normally be set to *ALL under the operating system security level of 40.
QAUDCTL	This system value activates or deactivates an audit of a particular object or options that have been specified in the audit-level system value. This value should normally be set to *AUDLVL until a specific object or user needs to be audited.
QAUDENDACN	This system value dictates what the system will do if a security violation has been detected and it is not able to notify the security journal. The default value setting is to notify the system operator. The alternative is to have the system power itself down with an error code. If the system is configured to power itself down automatically, it will restart in a restricted state; a user with *AUDIT and *ALLOBJ special authority will be required to sign on to the system and initiate the rest of the system. Under normal circumstances, the operating system will be able to deliver security journal entries to the journal receiver. However, if the journal receiver is accidentally damaged or if a virus is used to detach job pointers from the security journal, this may not be the case. The detection of such a virus may

require ongoing tests during business hours, since the nature of such a virus may only be visible during runtime. The recommended default is to use the system default of *NOTIFY unless C2 guidelines require otherwise.

QAUDFRCLVL   This system value determines how often the system writes the security journal data to permanent disk storage. Normally, security journals are kept in main storage until the system determines that the journals should be written to the auxiliary storage device. This value forces the system to write more frequently. However, more frequent writing of security journal entries may adversely affect system performance. This value should remain at default for best system performance. If there are a large number of system integrity violations, consider replacing the offending programs, rather than degrading overall system performance to keep track of substandard objects.

QAUDLVL   This system value determines the detail with which the security journal entries are collected. This value should include *AUTFAIL, *OFCSRV, *PGMADP, *PGMFAIL, *SAVRST, and *SERVICE. The *AUTFAIL value generates an audit record anytime a user sign-on fails or access to an object is denied due to authorization failure, as well as when a job submission fails due to lack of authority. The *OFCSRV value will log changes to the distribution directories and will also detect intrusion into other users' e-mail. The *PGMADP value logs all programs that access objects using an adopted authority. The *PGMFAIL value records any program that uses blocked MI instructions, program state validation failures, and object domain access failures. The *SAVRST value records attempts to save or restore objects from the system. It also records restoration of altered programs. The *SERVICE value notifies the security journal if someone has accessed the System Service Tools, or uses the Dump Object or Start Copy Screen command. The QAUDLVL system value, with its various options, is the primary mechanism by which the operating system determines whether or not there is a system integrity violation. Because it is highly unlikely that any software company would acknowledge that its software violates operating system integrity, it is the buyer's responsibility to ensure that operating system rules are adhered to in any software that is used on the system. If there are any problems determined to be caused by a program that violates the operating system's integrity, it is unlikely that any maintenance or warranty agreement will force IBM to assume responsibility. IBM has invested considerable resources in securing the AS/400's operating system from viruses. However, some of the responsibility to ensure that the software being utilized is free and clear of any system abnormalities lies with the purchasing company as well. To that extent, OS/400 provides utilities and mechanisms to isolate potentially dangerous programs through this system value.

QAUTOVRT   This system value determines whether the system should automatically create virtual devices that describe how to establish a communication connection to the physical hardware that an end user is using to access the system. This system value should be changed to 0 if there are no PC workstations and AS/400s connected to the system.

QCRTAUT   This system value specifies the default public authority used when objects are created. This value is best left at the default of *CHANGE. Any exceptions to the default *Change Public Object Authority should be reviewed and changed at individual libraries according to their needs. Figure 12.2 illustrates the default public authority propagation principle, in which this system value plays an important part.

QCRTOBJAUD This system value specifies the method by which newly created objects will be audited. Each object created in the system may optionally be audited as to who, when, and how it is used. In most instances it is not necessary or desirable to create objects with the audit flag on, since that would overwhelm the audit journal with data and it would be nearly impossible to sift through thousands of audit records generated by normal daily operation. The determining factor in deciding whether to create objects with an audit flag resides with the CRTOBJAUD system value. If this system value is set to *USRPRF, the auditing of newly created objects is based on the profile using the object. If the value is set to *CHANGE, any changes to the object are logged to the audit journal. The *ALL option logs all actions taken against the object. It is best to leave this system value at the default value of *NONE. If an audit is required for a particular object, it may be initiated as needed at a later time.

QDSCJOBITV   This system value controls the amount of time that a disconnected job is suspended before being terminated by the system. This value is useful only if the QINACTMSGQ value is set to Disconnect Job (*DSCJOB). Since our recommendation for the QINACTMSGQ is either to End Job (*ENDJOB) or to use a user exit program similar to the one provided in the appendix, this value may be set to *NONE.

QDSPSGNINF   This system value controls whether the user sees an informational display at sign-on that contains the date and time last signed on and the number of invalid sign-on attempts since the last sign-on. This system may remain at the default of 0, since it serves very little purpose to the average user.

QINACTITV   This system value specifies, in minutes, at what point the system should take action on inactive interactive jobs. This system value should be changed to between 30 to 60 minutes from the default value of *NONE. The system will monitor inactivity and automatically take the action specified in the QINACTMSGQ system value after the specified amount of time has elapsed.

QINACTMSGQ   This system value specifies what action is to be taken when the inactive time value (QINACTITV) has elapsed. The recommended value is either to terminate the workstation job or to use the program provided in the appendix. The program in the appendix is capable of taking specific action based on a user, a job, or the name attached to the workstation. This program may be altered further to suit an individual organization's needs.

QLMTDEVSSN   This system value controls a user's ability to sign on at two or more workstations simultaneously. While the use of this setting may be inconvenient for many users, it prompts everyone, especially privileged users, to be more security conscious; users must sign off from workstations they have used before they can sign on to another workstation. It is recommended that this system value be changed to 1 (on) from the default value of 0 (off).

QLMTSECOFR   This system value dictates whether or not users with *ALLOBJ or *SERVICE special authority need explicit authority to specific workstations. Use of this value provides an ideal way to physically limit the authority of these users. Only those devices selected at a particular physical location are capable of hosting a privileged user. This system value will automatically prevent any remote users from accessing the system with a stolen privileged user sign-on. Even if the password used is valid, the device itself will not allow the privileged user to sign on. This system value should be changed to 1 from the default value of 0.

QMAXSGNACN   This system value specifies how the system will react when the maximum number of consecutive incorrect sign-on attempts has been reached. This system value should be set at 3, in order to disable both the offending user profile and the device description.

QMAXSIGN — This system value specifies the maximum number of sign-on attempts allowed. This system value should be changed to 3 from the default value of *NOMAX.

QPWDEXPITV — This system value specifies the number of days for which passwords are valid, thus providing password security by requiring users to change their passwords after a specified number of days. If a password is not changed within the specified number of days, the user cannot sign on until the password is changed. This system value should be changed to 30 from the default value of *NOMAX.

QPWDLMTAJC — This system value limits the use of adjacent digits within a password, thereby preventing the use of such easily guessed passwords as dates and social security numbers. This system value should be changed to 1 from the default value of 0.

QPWDLMTCHR — This system value provides password security by preventing certain characters (vowels, for example) from being used in a password. It can be used to prevent the use of common words or names as passwords. This value should remain at default of 0.

QPWDLMTREP — This system value prevents a user from using the same character more than once within a password. This system value is useful on systems with version 3 release 1 of OS/400, because v3r1 offers the option to disallow only *consecutive* repeating characters. This system value should remain at the default of 0 for all systems whose OS/400 operating system level is prior of v3r1.

QPWDMAXLEN — This system value determines the maximum number of characters that can be used in a password. This value may remain at 10.

QPWDMINLEN	This system value determines the minimum number of characters that can be used in a password. This system value should be changed to not less than 6 from the default value of 1.
QPWDPOSDIF	This system value controls the position of characters in a new password. It prevents the user from specifying a password in which the same character is in the same position as in the previous password. For example, new password MIKE2 could not be used if the previous password was MIKE1. The suggested system value for this parameter is 1.
QPWDRQDDGT	This system value specifies whether a digit is required in a new password, to prevent the user from using only alphabetic characters. The use of this system value is recommended. This value should be changed to 1 from the default value of 0.
QPWDRQDDIF	This system value specifies whether the password must be different than the previous 32 passwords used. The use of this system value is recommended only on systems with version 3 release 1 or later; the maximum selected value for these systems should be no more than 4.
QPWDVLDPGM	This system value allows a user-written program to perform additional validation on passwords. Unless there exists a clear reason to use this procedure, such as validation to ensure that passwords may only be changed once a day, it is not recommended, because it provides one of the easiest ways to capture passwords. If this value is used, make certain that the program being called is secured, and that the source matches the object. Also, never store the password; or, if passwords must be stored, make sure they are encrypted. Be advised that if this system value is used, a hostile user may attempt to replace this program with his or her own and look for a file containing user passwords.

QRMTSIGN   This system value specifies how the system handles remote sign-on requests. If the system has no PC workstations and no communication to other AS/400s, this value should be changed to *REJECT. If automatic sign-on to other AS/400s is not a requirement, this system value should remain at *FRCSIGNON. If automatic signons are necessary, *VERIFY may be used in order to verify the remote user's profile and password before he or she gains access to the system.

QSECURITY   This value represents the global operating system's security level. This value should be set to 40 which provides, in addition to the restrictions specified under the previous levels, the assurance that all user-written programs execute in the user state and that they do not directly access system objects. Patched programs cannot be restored, and only operating system–provided interfaces to system objects are allowed to execute. At security level 40, the system prevents attempts to directly call system programs not documented as call-level interfaces. The system uses the domain attribute of an object and the state attribute of a program to enforce this protection. Figure 12.7 illustrates the domain/state security boundary concept.

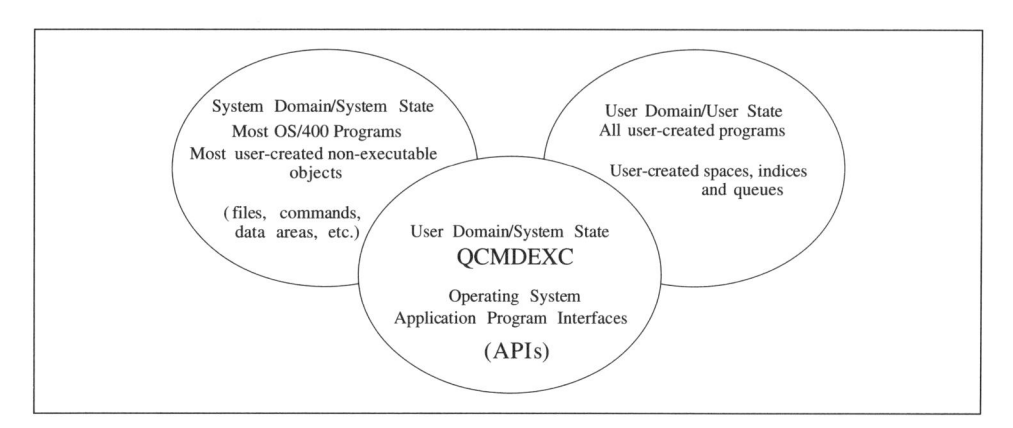

Figure 12.7 OS/400 domain state processing.

Table 12.1 Recommended System Values

System Values	Recommendation	Description
QACGLVL	*JOB *PRINT	Collect resource accounting data to establish a pattern of attack
QALWOBJRST	*NONE	Do not allow altered objects to be restored
QALWUSRDMN	*ALL	Allow user spaces, indices, and queues to reside in all libraries
QAUDCTL	*AUDLVL	System auditing controls should default to the QAUDLVL controls
QAUDENDACN	*NOTIFY	Send a message if audit journal cannot be written
QAUDFRCLVL	*SYS	Allow system to determine when to write audit logs to disk storage
QAUDLVL	*AUTFAIL	Authority failures are logged
	*OFCSRV	Changes to distribution directory and mail handling are logged
	*PGMADP	Programs that access objects with adopted authority are logged
	*PGMFAIL	System integrity violations are logged
	*SAVRST	Save and restore actions are logged
	*SERVICE	Use of system service tools is logged
QAUTOVRT	0	If no PCs and AS/400s are attached
	1–9999	If automatic virtual device creation is desired
QCRTAUT	*CHANGE	Default public authority of new objects created
QCRTOBJAUD	*NONE	Default object auditing value for new object created
QDSCJOBITV	*NONE	If the QINACTMSGQ value is set to *ENDJOB
	30	If the QINACTMSGQ value is set to *DSCJOB
QDSPSGNINF	0 (NO)	Display of sign-on statistics
QINACTITV	30	Length of time, in minutes, a workstation may be idle
QINACTMSGQ	*ENDJOB	What action to take when inactive time has elapsed

System Values	Recommendation	Description
QLMTDEVSSN	1 (YES)	Limit users to one workstation
QLMTSECOFR	1 (YES)	Limit privileged users to authorized workstations
QMAXSGNACN	3	Disable both user profile and device if sign-on attempts fail
QMAXSIGN	3	Limit maximum consecutive sign-on attempts to 3
QPWDEXPITV	30	All passwords should expire within 30 days
QPWDLMTAJC	1 (YES)	Adjacent numeric are not allowed
QPWDLMTCHR	*NONE	All characters are available for password designation
QPWDLMTREP	1 (YES)	v3r1—Restrict only the adjacent repeating characters
	0(NO)	All releases prior to v3r1
QPWDMAXLEN	10	Maximum length of passwords should be set to 10
QPWDMINLEN6	6	Minimum length of passwords should be not less than 6
QPWDPOSDIF	1 (YES)	Passwords characters cannot share the same position
QPWDRQDDGT	1 (YES)	Password requires at least one numeric digit
QPWDRQDDIF	8	v3r1—Password must be different from the last 4 passwords
	0(NO)	All releases prior to v3r1
QPWDVLDPGM	Example Program	Example program ensures passwords are changed only once a day
	*NONE	The use of password validation program is discouraged
QRMTSIGN	*REJECT	Reject all attempts if no PCs or AS/400s are attached
	*FRCSIGNON	Force the users to sign on if automatic sign-on is not required
	*VERIFY	Verify the profile and password if automatic sign on is required
QSECURITY	40	Security level 40

CHAPTER THIRTEEN

Designing Profiles

Defining user profiles on the system requires a fair amount of forethought in order to achieve a balance between management of security and ease of work. The method discussed in this chapter focuses on the roles and duties of individuals within an average corporate environment. Before creating user profiles on the AS/400, first define the logical division of work among the various departments within the company, then identify those individuals whose primary responsibilities lie within those groups. This may be as simple as following the organizational chart, or as involved as defining a complex matrix of individual responsibilities across multiple departments. In most instances, the organizational chart serves as a good starting point.

    The work groups thus defined are used to create OS/400 group profiles. The individuals within each work group will become members within each group profile. Initially, no special authorities are granted to either the group profiles or the individual profiles. Exceptions may be managed after the majority of user needs have been satisfied. Users' authorities to the necessary objects are granted via the use of the object Primary Group and Primary Group Authority designations. This method not only provides reasonable manageability of objects, but also enhances system performance over the use of authorization lists and private authorities. If you associate a group of objects with an organizational group profile, the members of the work group will be able to carry out their primary responsibilities without owning any objects, having special authorities, or requiring private authorities. Also, users who require access to other application groups may be serviced by using the supplementary group designations. There are numerous exceptions to this rule, but the most important principle to keep in mind when creating user profiles is to create a domain in which the individuals may carry out their duties efficiently without granting them *carte blanche* authority to the system.

Work Groups

The identification of work groups may often be most easily achieved by first defining the person or persons heading each section within the larger department. This person is generally responsible for the work produced by that group. For example, within an accounting department, some organizations employ an Accounts Payable supervisor in addition to an Accounts Receivable manager, while others have a controller who oversees all financial transactions. However the organizational structure is laid out, a group of individuals who perform a similar unit of work may constitute a work group.

In a fictional company, ABC, the following work groups are identified: Accounts Payable, Accounts Receivable, General Ledger, Construction Management, Tenant Management, and Lease Management groups (Figure 13.1). In addition, there are management information professionals,

ABC Inc.

Accounts Payable	Accounts Receivable	General Ledger	Construction Mgmt.	Tenant Management	Lease Management
Mgr.: Karen	Mgr.: Karen	Mgr.: Maryann	Mgr.: Susan	Mgr.: MaryKate	Mgr.: MaryKate
Jackie	Darlene	Greg	Peter	Leigh	Sandy
Debbie	Beth	Doug	Rosemary	Margaret	John
Donna	Corinne	Amy		Susan	Janet
Stephanie	Rosemarie	Marc		Gino	Stephen

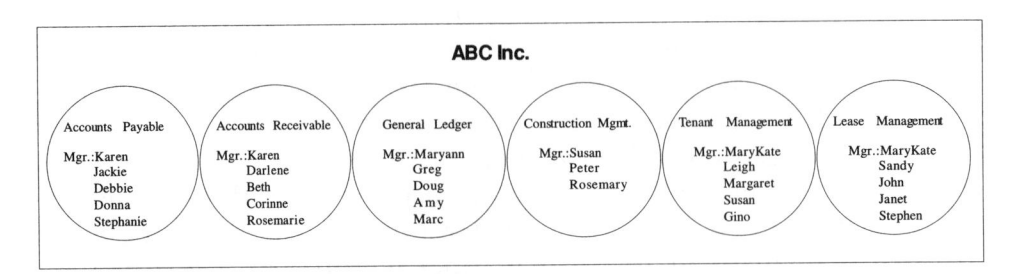

Figure 13.1 Work group definition.

but for now, we'll concentrate on defining the profiles of the nontechnical user community.

Application Groups

Once the user work groups are defined, their counterparts, the application groups, should be identified. Although applications are viewed as logical groupings of functions regardless of their physical locations, the process of identifying application groups requires the names of the libraries on the system: the APOBJ and APDATA libraries. The APOBJ and APDATA libraries contain files and programs that provide end users with the ability to conduct daily Accounts Payable transactions, logically separating the APOBJ and APDATA use from the rest of the system. Sometimes, however, software vendors group all their applications into a single library, as in the FINANCIALS library. This practice makes authority management a bit more difficult for the administrator. For the purpose of this example, an ideal situation is assumed—application groups coinciding with user work groups. These application groups are: AP, consisting of APOBJ and APDATA libraries; AR, containing AROBJ and ARDATA libraries; and GL, containing GLOBJ and GLDATA libraries (Figure 13.2).

Group Profiles

The first profiles to create are the work group profiles. The process of creating these group profiles is identical to that of creating individual

```
                                ABC Inc.
    ┌─────────────────────────────────────────────────────────────────────┐
    │   Accounts Payable   Accounts Receivable   General Ledger   Construction Mgmt.   Tenant Management   Lease Management   │
    │      Group:AP            Group:AR             Group:GL          Group:CM            Group:TM            Group:LM       │
    │      APOBJ               AROBJ                GLOBJ             CMOBJ               TMOBJ               LMOBJ          │
    │      APDATA              ARDATA               GLDATA            CMDATA              TMDATA              LMDATA         │
    └─────────────────────────────────────────────────────────────────────┘
```

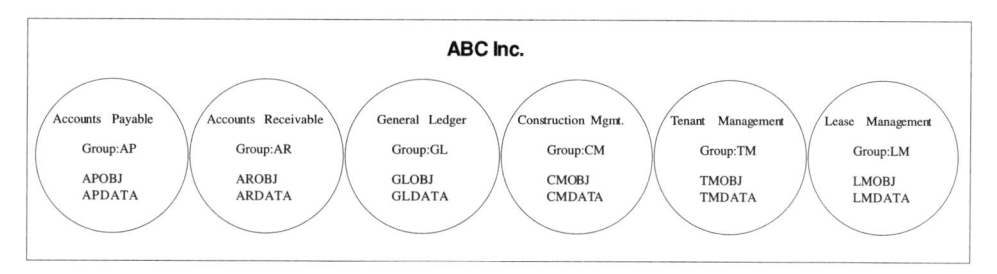

Figure 13.2 Application group definition.

```
             Create User Profile (CRTUSRPRF)

Type choices, press Enter.

User profile . . . . . . . . . . > AP           Name
User password  . . . . . . . . . > *NONE        Name, *USRPRF, *NONE
Set password to expired  . . . .   *NO          *NO, *YES
Status . . . . . . . . . . . . . > *DISABLED    *ENABLED, *DISABLED
User class . . . . . . . . . . .   *USER        *USER, *SYSOPR, *PGMR...
Assistance level . . . . . . . .   *SYSVAL      *SYSVAL, *BASIC, *INTERMED...
Current library  . . . . . . . .   *CRTDFT      Name, *CRTDFT
Initial program to call  . . . .   *NONE        Name, *NONE
   Library . . . . . . . . . . .                Name, *LIBL, *CURLIB
Initial menu . . . . . . . . . . > *SIGNOFF     Name, *SIGNOFF
   Library . . . . . . . . . . .                Name, *LIBL, *CURLIB
Limit capabilities . . . . . . .   *NO          *NO, *PARTIAL, *YES
Text 'description' . . . . . . .   *BLANK
```

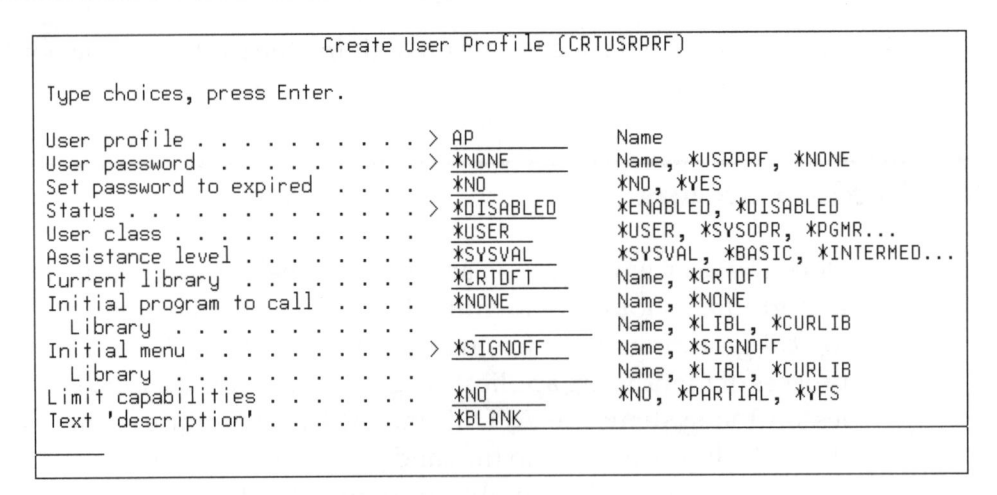

Figure 13.3 Group profile definition.

profiles—only the parameters are different. Group profiles are created using the Create User Profiles (CRTUSRPRF) command (Figure 13.3). Only the security officer, security administrator, or users with *SECADM special authority may create user profiles. Designate all group profiles as user class (*USER) profiles with no special authorities. Additionally, specify that there are no passwords associated with group profiles. This will ensure that only individual profiles, not group profiles, may be used to gain access to the system, thus providing accountability for all users. The group profiles' status should be disabled (*DISABLED), no initial program should be specified (*NONE), and the initial menu should be set to signoff (*SIGNOFF). Ideally, one group profile for each work group and application group pair should be created. For example, group profile AP would represent all users whose primary duties revolve around the Accounts Payable (AP) application group consisting of APOBJ and AP-DATA libraries.

User Profiles

Profiles for the users previously identified within their respective work groups should be created as members within the work group profiles just created (Figure 13.4). The profile-naming convention should have been

```
                    Create User Profile (CRTUSRPRF)

Type choices, press Enter.

User profile . . . . . . . . . . . > JACKIE        Name
User password  . . . . . . . . .     *USRPRF       Name, *USRPRF, *NONE
Set password to expired  . . . . > *YES            *NO, *YES
Status . . . . . . . . . . . . .     *ENABLED      *ENABLED, *DISABLED
User class . . . . . . . . . . . > *USER           *USER, *SYSOPR, *PGMR...
Assistance level . . . . . . . .     *SYSVAL       *SYSVAL, *BASIC, *INTERMED...
Current library  . . . . . . . .     *CRTDFT       Name, *CRTDFT
Initial program to call  . . . .     *NONE         Name, *NONE
  Library  . . . . . . . . . . .                   Name, *LIBL, *CURLIB
Initial menu . . . . . . . . . . > APMAIN          Name, *SIGNOFF
  Library  . . . . . . . . . . . >   FINANCIALS    Name, *LIBL, *CURLIB
Limit capabilities . . . . . . .     *NO           *NO, *PARTIAL, *YES
Text 'description' . . . . . . .     *BLANK


Special authority  . . . . . . . > *USRCLS         *USRCLS, *NONE, *ALLOBJ...
            + for more values
Group profile  . . . . . . . . . > AP              Name, *NONE
Owner  . . . . . . . . . . . . . > *GRPPRF         *USRPRF, *GRPPRF
```

Figure 13.4 User profile definition.

decided by this time. (For simplicity, the figures for the example will use the users' first names as their profile names.) When each user profile is created, it should be given a default password other than the profile name. Passwords should be set to expired, so that they must be changed upon the next successful sign-on. The initial program or the menu should reflect the user's primary function, no special authorities should be granted, and the group profile designation should be specified with the group profile as the default object owner. Additionally, if the users do not require the command line interface, restrict that ability by specifying *YES in the Limit Capabilities parameter.

Primary Groups

The last major step in macro profile management is the primary group assignment of the objects in each application group. As of OS/400 version 3 release 1, objects may host primary group designations in addition to public and private authority flags and owner profiles. The primary group concept is somewhat similar to the *group owner* concept in the UNIX environment. The OS/400's implementation of the object primary group concept essentially allows an alternative to using private authorities when public authority to the object is insufficient. When private authorities are specified on behalf of a user for a particular object, the OS/400 flags the object as having private authorities. Any attempt to use an object that has one or more private authorities will initiate a search of the object's private authority table for the requesting user's profile. This process occurs even if the requester is not one of the users who has specific authority to the object. The loading and the searching of the private authority table for a given object is determined solely by the existence of a private authority flag stored in the object itself. This concept is illustrated in Figure 13.5. This impedes system performance for everyone regardless of the default public authority assigned to the object. Although private authorities are needed and desirable in many situations, if the use of private authorities is reduced in favor of the use of primary group authorities, the majority of the users in an application work group may be serviced without granting all authorities to everyone to sustain performance.

The assignment to objects of a primary group designation is accomplished by the use of the Change Object Primary Group (CHGOBJPGP) command shown in Figure 13.6. The group authority type of *PGP identifies that all users who possess the object's primary group name as one of their supplementary groups or as their main group profile will share the object's primary group authority designated in the object. In the ABC Inc. example in Figure 13.7, all objects in the APDATA library are assigned to the primary group of AP with *CHANGE authority. This will allow all users in the AP application group to conduct normal business transactions against the Accounts Payable database. Public authority to the APDATA library is changed from its default value to the *EXCLUDE authority. This will prevent all other users, who are without the *ALLOBJ special authority, from accessing the data kept in the APDATA library. The objects in the APOBJ library are, however, not associated with any primary group, but simply given a default public authority of *USE. This is because the APOBJ library only contains executable objects, and the default public authority of *USE is sufficient for all users to execute programs residing in that library. If the other application groups (AR, GL, TM, etc.) are also configured similarly, then all application group users

DESIGNING PROFILES 161

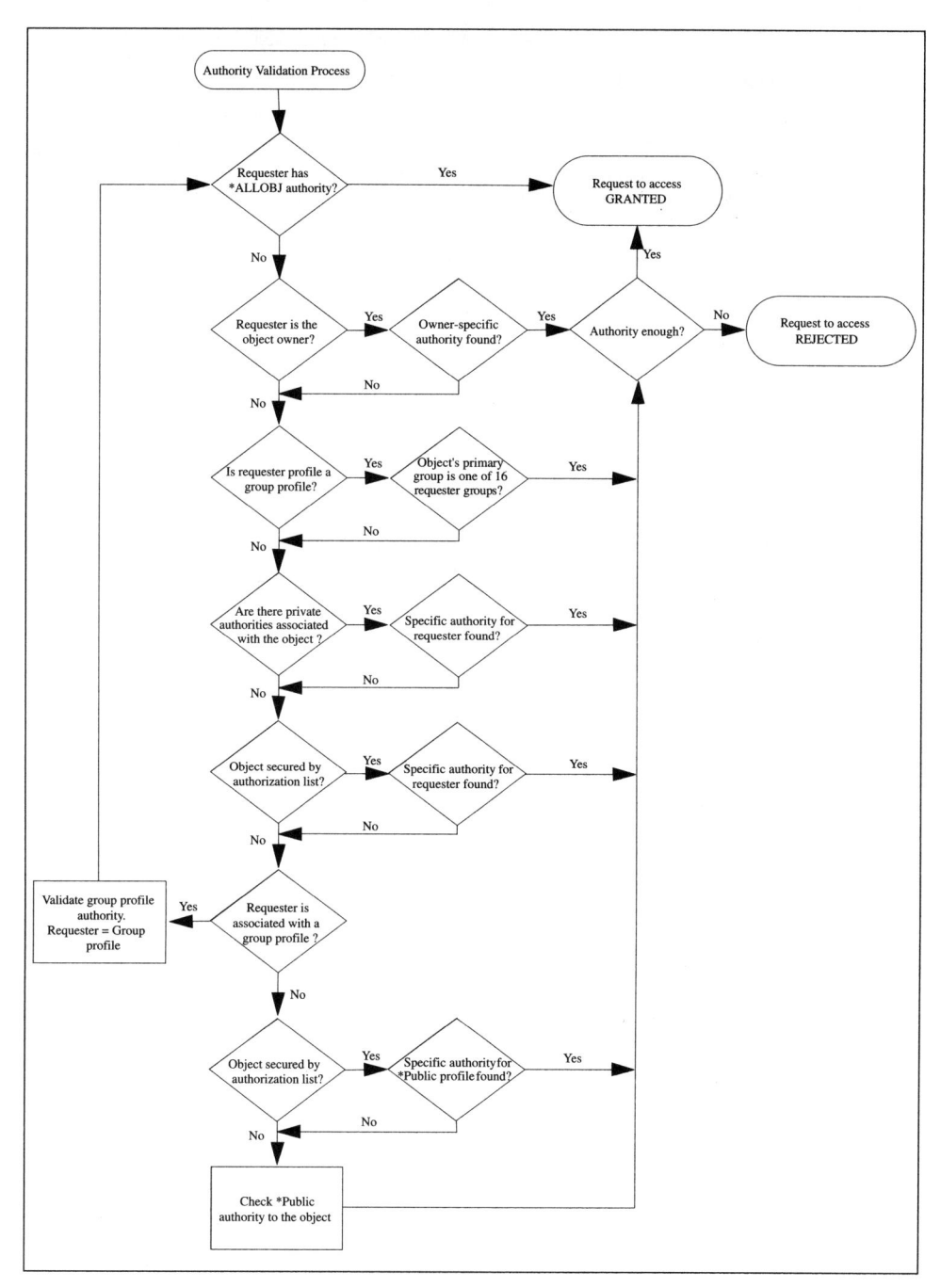

Figure 13.5 Authority validation procedure.

162 IMPLEMENTATION

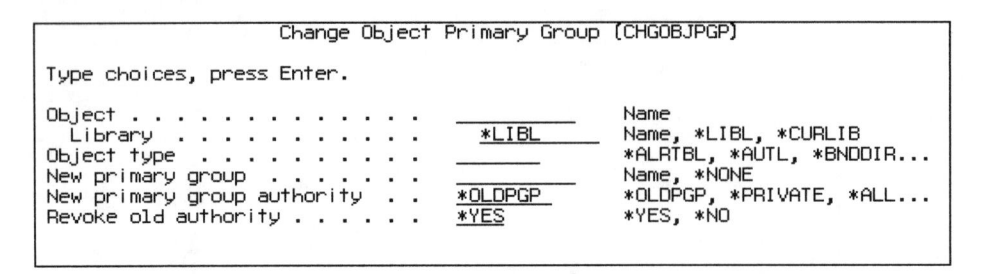

```
                    Change Object Primary Group (CHGOBJPGP)
Type choices, press Enter.

Object . . . . . . . . . . . . . .   _____    Name
  Library  . . . . . . . . . . .    *LIBL         Name, *LIBL, *CURLIB
Object type . . . . . . . . . .    _____      *ALRTBL, *AUTL, *BNDDIR...
New primary group . . . . . . .    _____    Name, *NONE
New primary group authority . .    *OLDPGP       *OLDPGP, *PRIVATE, *ALL...
Revoke old authority . . . . .     *YES          *YES, *NO
```

Figure 13.6 Object primary group assignment.

will be authorized only to their respective datasets, with public authority to use any executable objects in other application groups.

All this has been accomplished thus far without assigning any private authorities to objects. The authority model just constructed is seldom usable without applying a few exceptions, however. This is because there may exist programs that should be excluded from certain users or, more likely, application group users who may need access to more than their own dataset from time to time. Nevertheless, the authority model pre-

ABC Inc.

Accounts Payable
Group: AP
Mgr.: Karen
Jackie
Debbie
Donna
Stephanie

*CHANGE *USE

Accounts Payable
Primary Group: AP
Authority: *CHANGE
Pub.Auth.: *EXCLUDE
APDATA

Accounts Payable
Primary Group: *NONE
Pub.Auth.: *USE
APOBJ

*EXCLUDE *USE

Accounts Receivable
or other application
groups and users.

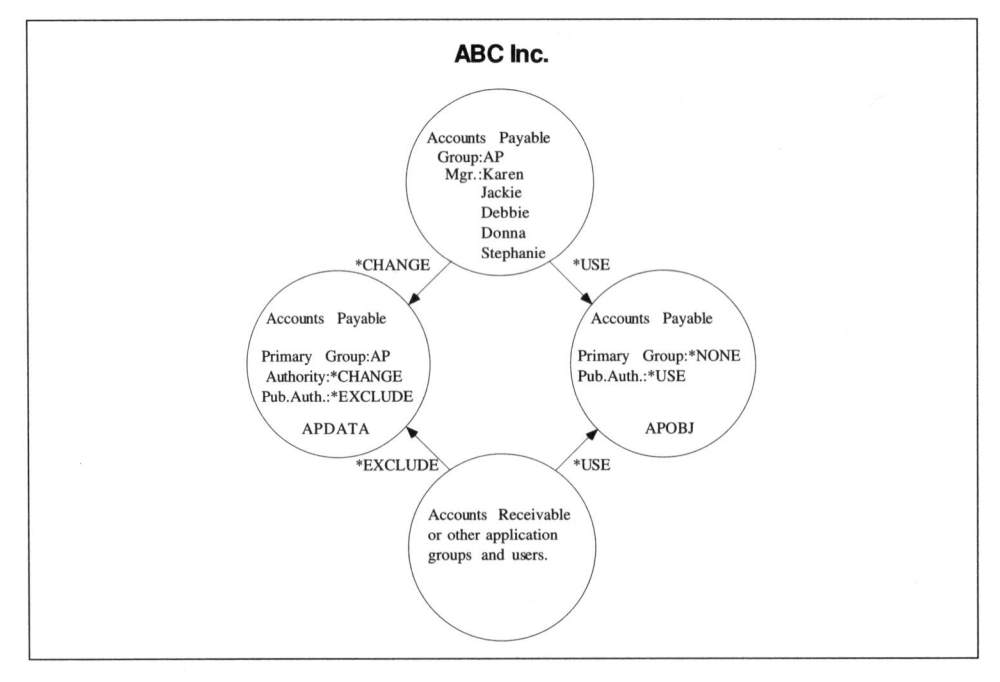

Figure 13.7 Primary group usage.

sented is an excellent base from which to mold customer site-specific user authorities.

Exception Management

There are basically two schools of thought in approaching exception management. The first approach restricts all authorities to all objects as a rule, then grants authorities to users on a case-by-case basis. The second grants enough authorities to all objects so that they may be used, then restricts those profiles that should be excluded from that privilege. The authority model discussed in the preceding sections uses both of these principles. The dataset is restricted as a default, and the use of programs is granted as a default. In the case where an AP user requires access to the General Ledger dataset, individual authority may be granted to the GL dataset by designating the GL application group as a supplemental group to that user's profile. This will allow the entire GL dataset to be available only to that individual and not to the group to which that person belongs. Figure 13.8 illustrates the use of supplemental group profiles. The use of supplemental groups and the order in which they are specified in the user profile should be carefully streamlined, for only 15 supplemental groups may be specified, and the authority validation process will check for the necessary authority in the order in which the supplemental groups are listed.

The use of supplemental groups is ideal when granting blanket authority to the entire application dataset, but may not be appropriate if only certain objects are needed. A determination as to what represents a minority portion of the application group's dataset in comparison to the requested objects will have to be considered. Generally, the majority will rule the use of the supplemental groups. For example, if Karen, the AP supervisor, requires all authority to the GL dataset except for the GL Journal Entry master file, then the use of the GL supplemental group is warranted provided private object authority is used to enforce the defined restrictions. Conversely, designation of a supplemental group is not necessary, nor is it desirable if she requires only one file in the General Ledger application group. In that case, private object authority should be used to grant access to the GL Journal Entry master file. Figure 13.9 illustrates the private object authority concept.

164 IMPLEMENTATION

```
                              ABC Inc.
                         Accounts Payable
                         Group:AP
                         Mgr.:Karen          →  Supplemental Groups:GL
                         Jackie
                         Debbie
                         Donna
                         Stephanie
         *CHANGE      *CHANGE        *USE          *USE

  General Ledger    Accounts Payable   Accounts Payable    General Ledger
  Primary Group:GL  Primary Group:AP   Primary Group:*NONE Primary Group:*NONE
  Authority:*CHANGE Authority:*CHANGE  Pub.Auth.:*USE      Pub.Auth.:*USE
  Pub.Auth.:*EXCLUDE Pub.Auth.:*EXCLUDE
  GLDATA            APDATA             APOBJ               GLOBJ

       *EXCLUDE       *EXCLUDE         *USE            *USE
                         Accounts Receivable
                         or other application
                         groups and users.
```

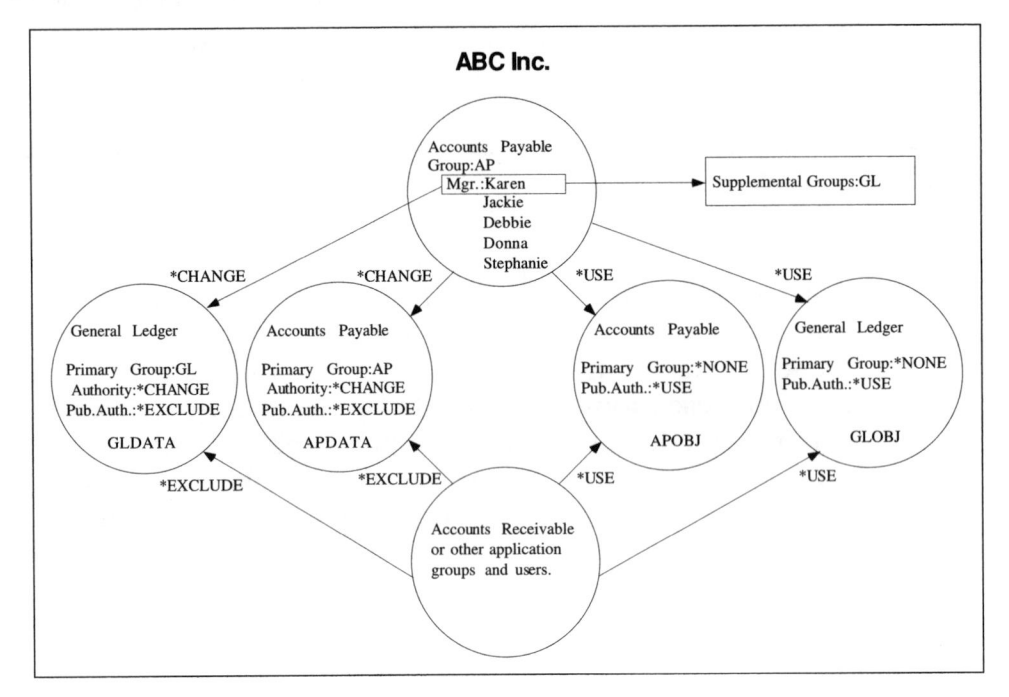

Figure 13.8 Supplemental group usage.

Unfortunately, as we have suggested previously, some software vendors lump all their applications into a single library. This makes the assignment of an object's primary groups more difficult, although not impossible. In such a case, the library (FINANCIALS) should be designated with a public authority of *USE, all database objects should be set to *EXCLUDE for public access, and all executable objects should be available to the public via the *USE authority. The difficult part is that the security administrator will need to identify the primary functions of each database, one at a time. Once the definitions have been established, the process of assigning the object's primary group is the same as previously discussed.

The use of executable objects should also be managed by exception. Since there may be programs that adopt supervisor's authority such as MAKEMEGOD, which is seldom required by everyone, these privileged programs should be excluded from the public domain. The exclusion may be accomplished either by using private object authority or by using the public object authority value, based on the majority rules principle discussed previously. If the majority of users do not require such a program,

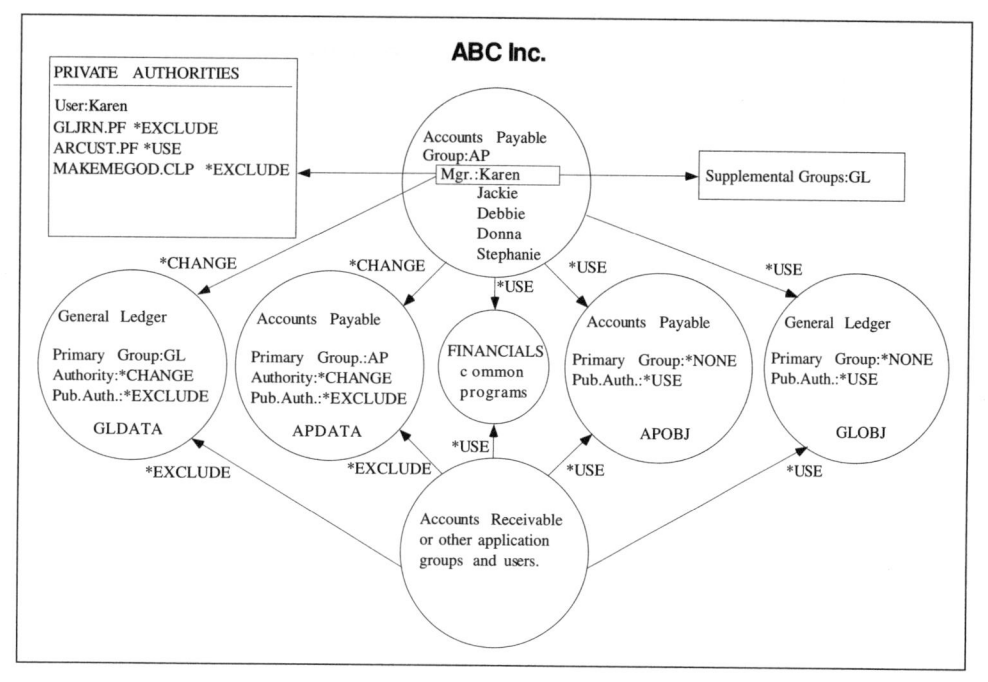

Figure 13.9 Private authority usage.

then the best way to secure such an object would be to change the program's public authority to *EXCLUDE; otherwise, private object authority may best suit the purpose. Figure 13.10 illustrates how private authorities may be associated with user profiles.

Finally, grant special authorities to those who require job controls (*JOBCTL), spool controls (*SPLCTL), and other privileges. These special authorities should be specified within the individual user profile rather than the user's group profile. This will allow specific representatives from each application work group to be accountable in using these special privileges, while providing users with some flexibility and a degree of independence.

Technical Profiles

Creating and maintaining a technical staff's profiles is an exercise in risk management. The security administrator must carefully weigh the re-

166 IMPLEMENTATION

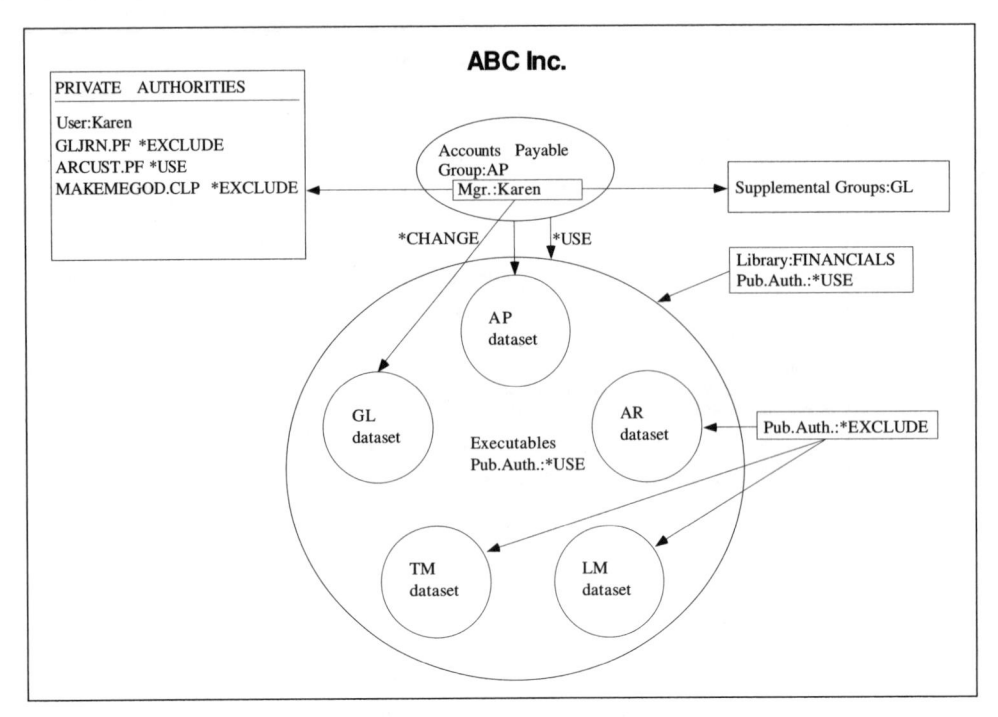

```
                              ABC Inc.
 ┌─────────────────────────┐
 │ PRIVATE  AUTHORITIES    │
 │ User:Karen              │
 │ GLJRN.PF  *EXCLUDE      │        Accounts  Payable
 │ ARCUST.PF *USE          │ ◄──    Group:AP              ──►  Supplemental Groups:GL
 │ MAKEMEGOD.CLP *EXCLUDE  │        Mgr.:Karen
 └─────────────────────────┘
                   *CHANGE       *USE
                                                          Library:FINANCIALS
                                                          Pub.Auth.:*USE
                              AP
                           dataset

                  GL                    AR
                dataset                dataset          Pub.Auth.:*EXCLUDE
                         Executables
                         Pub.Auth.:*USE

                       TM         LM
                    dataset     dataset
```

Figure 13.10 Primary group usage in a centralized database.

sponsibilities of the staff members in relation to their designated authorities and privileges. Just as a responsible person would not give a loaded gun to a child, the security administrator must not blindly distribute privileges without justification. On the other hand, it is just as irresponsible to withhold authorities from a person who needs them simply because of the fear of abuse. Those receiving the responsibility must be given chance to be accountable for their actions. Lack of management experience in this area may lead to the creation of a suite of program routines that adopt the security officer's authority at runtime. Although there are a few instances where such a program may be acceptable, the vast majority of circumstances do not warrant such intentional security breaches. From a hacker's point of view, it is far safer to hide among trees of the same color than to stand alone in a desert! If authority adoption routines are prevalent in the system, the chances of identifying a back door diminish considerably. Before creating any technical profiles, take a few minutes to ensure that all default system profiles' passwords are changed. Although IBM promised to remove all default passwords (except for the password for the QSECOFR profile) prior to shipping new systems, starting with the OS/400 version 3 release 1, it is worth the trouble to display all profiles (DSPAUTUSR) to verify that they were indeed removed.

Although the concept of separation by functional work groups applies to technical profiles as it has in the nontechnical staff's roles, the technical staff's application group is seldom confined to a single definable entity such as Accounts Payable. For example, in a large AS/400 shop, a management information systems department may be divided into several smaller groups, such as Data Processing Operations, Network Administration, Security Management, Application Development, and Customer Support. Many of these groups will need to access data across multiple application boundaries for a variety of purposes.

Data Processing Operations

The Data Processing Operations department is mainly concerned with system backups, restorations, scheduled batch job executions, and overall smooth running of daily operations. The operations group profile should be created as a system operator (*SYSOPR) class profile. The *SYSOPR class profile will assign two special authorities as default authorities, the job controls (*JOBCTL) authority and the save systems (*SAVSYS) authority. The job controls authority will allow operations group users to control the initiation and termination of the system, user jobs, priorities, writers, and other job-related functions and environments. The save systems special authority grants a unique privilege to save and restore objects regardless of the requester's private authorities. Users with this special authority may save or restore objects for which they do not have explicit or default authority. The *SAVSYS special authority eliminates the need to grant specific authorities to all objects on the system in order for the operator to save the system, but at the same time, the *SAVSYS special authority prevents the operator from deleting, changing, or browsing the contents of sensitive files for which he or she does not have explicit authority. Depending on the size of the operational staff, the OS/400 default system operator profile (QSYSOPR) may be used as a user profile (if only one operator), or used as a template to create an operational group profile. The members in this group profile should be configured as *USER class profiles with or without command line interface capabilities (LMTCBP), based on their needs.

Application Development

Ideally, application developers should be restricted to a world of their own, even using their own development machine. Any necessary access to the production machine should be carefully controlled and only gained by user class profiles. Programmers may be allowed to sign on to a production machine as guests with the same sphere of authority as the user that the programmers are emulating, in order to determine problem situations or to verify that which could not be simulated in their own system. If such external development systems are utilized, it is best to remove all compilers from the production machines. Separating the development staff from the production system essentially establishes a parallel relationship, like that of a software vendor to a customer. This practice necessarily isolates the production system from accidental destruction of data, untested releases of software, and periodic whims and experiments conducted by the development staff. Under this scenario, the development staff may only utilize a copy of data from the production system given to them by a security administrator, so the release of data is controlled. Also, the option to install new programs—both bug fixes and enhancements—onto the production machine, remains with the security administrator. In addition, if the necessary quality assurance tests and documentation do not meet the standards required, production systems users will have the final say as to the fate of such software.

This does not necessarily mean that development machines are free from standards and security guidelines. Software engineers' profiles are generally created under a group profile that reflects the organization's name, such as ABC for ABC Inc., with the objects that have been created by the members owned by the group profile rather than by the individual member. This configuration essentially eliminates all private authorities in favor of implicit object ownership authority granted to all programmers within the development group. As in the operations staff profile configurations, only the group profile is identified as a *PGMR class user with special authorities; individual programmer profiles are identified as *USER class profiles with no special authorities. Exceptions to this rule are handled by granting specific special authorities to individual profiles as needed.

This scenario can work well for many software companies and internal application development groups. However, it does grant to all programmers the authority to destroy all objects within their own development world. This may or may not be an issue, based on what other development may be going on simultaneously and on the sensitivity of individual projects. If multiple application development projects are active, or there exists a need to separate programmers working on one project from those working on another within a single machine environment, then the work group concept previously discussed will be most effective. For example, a group profile AP may be created as a *PGMR class profile with a group member AP#PGMR *USER class profile. An application library, APLIB, is created with public access to the library excluded, but all objects, including the library object itself, belonging to the AP primary object group with primary group authority of *ALL. If each project is set up in a similar fashion, only those programmers belonging to the respective project groups will be authorized to access the data of those project groups, thus securing each project separately yet maintaining the flexibility to disassociate programmers from and associate them to projects without transferring a maze of private authorities held by each programmer. The standard profile for a programming group enjoys job control and save system special authorities. Save system special authority may not be needed for all programmers, and depending upon the application being created, some programmers may require other special authorities to ensure that their programs work properly. For instance, a security auditing application may require the use of *AUDIT special authority, normally not given to programmers, in order to configure and monitor for abnormal situations. A programmer who is tasked to create such an application will require more than the normal set of special authorities for the duration of his or her project. In such instances, modify the individual programmer's profiles to include the necessary special authorities.

Network Administration

Network and communication specialists, provide answers to the often convoluted questions surrounding connectivity. Although this role was not as well established in the past within the corporate information technology structure, it has become one of the most visible areas in recent years. The area of network administration not only covers the topology design issues of wide and local area networks, but also the details of protocols, servers, repeaters, gateways, and so on. In recognizing the special needs of this group of professionals, the OS/400 version 3 release 1 provides a new special authority specifically designed to address the needs of network configuration. The *IOSYSCFG special authority allows users to work with communication devices, controllers, and other essential objects in order to perform their duties without the hindrance of authority violations. The network administrator's group profile should be created under the *SYSOPR class user profile with the *IOSYSCFG special authority in addition to the default special authorities granted by the profile class designation. If the network administrator requires access to other special authorities, such as security administration (*SECADM), they should be added to the individual profiles as needed.

Security Management

The members of security management group should generally be divided into two major categories: those who administer, enforce, and audit corporate security policies, and the others, who seek and exploit the weaknesses of the exisitng security policies. The administration arm of the security management group deals primarily with implementation of security policies and identification of situations where the security policies are being challenged. Tasks such as creating new users or removing terminated employee's profiles are handled by this group. In addition, this group is responsible for investigating system integrity violations and ensuring that users are only authorized to an appropriate set of objects. These security administrators are collectively responsible for safeguarding the system from internal and external threats. The other, lesser known segment of a security management group is frequently nicknamed the "Tiger Team." This group's sole purpose is to find and exploit any security weakness and develop procedures to counter any such identified exposures. Tiger Team members should think of themselves as hackers, in every sense of the word, defending their systems against other would-be intruders. Although many AS/400 shops use a security officer or other equivalent user profile to conduct both of these duties, only security administrator profiles should be allowed to possess the authorities associated with a security officer class user. Profiles belonging to members of the Tiger Team should be created as users with no special authorities and restricted from command line access.

Customer Support

The most significant difference between customer support profiles and nontechnical user profiles is that customer support representatives may need to access all user applications in order to provide service to their clients. This may be accomplished by using guest profiles associated with each work group or by using a group profile with a list of supplementary groups. The guest profile is simply another application work group profile that may be used only by customer support representatives. The group profile method, on the other hand, utilizes a single profile with a list of application groups specified as supplementary groups. In the latter method, all members of the customer support group would be allowed to access applications listed in the supplemental group list of their master profile.

CHAPTER FOURTEEN

Authority Management

Implementing object authority involves more than simply matching users' needs with the appropriate authorities. The security administrator not only must consider the impact of special authorities, public authorities, and user-to-object relationships, but must also prevent those who may purposely misuse the authorities granted to them from exploiting the weaknesses in the OS/400 operating system. User-to-object authority relationships have been previously discussed; this chapter exposes some of OS/400's design specifications that allow for potential security exposures. This chapter also recommends, where possible, policies and procedures to secure a system from any known potential threats.

Objects

All object authorities except *EXCLUDE (*ALL, *CHANGE, *USE) may be further defined using three additional authority categories: Operational, Management, and Existence special authorities as illustrated in Figure 14.1. Operational special authority allows the requester to view object information, but not necessarily the object's content. For example,

174 IMPLEMENTATION

	Object Authorities						
	OBJECT			DATA			
	OPER	MGMT	EXIST	Read	Add	Delete	Update	Execute
*ALL	X	X	X	X	X	X	X	X
*CHANGE	X			X	X	X	X	X
*USE	X			X				X
*USER DEF		X						

Figure 14.1 Object authorities.

with operational authority, a user may view an object's size, description, creation date, and the date when it was last used, but may not be able to view the inventory records residing within the object. Operational special authority simply allows a user to reference and view the "surface" information of an object. Management special authority grants the user the ability to rename, move, duplicate, and grant object authorities to other users. Existence special authority permits object deletion, restoration, saving, and transferring of ownership. Operational special authority is automatically granted to a user when the *USE authority to an object is permitted. If the object contains data, the operational authority associated with the *USE object authority allows the user to read the contents of the object, but prevents the user from adding, deleting, or updating its contents. If the object is an executable program, operational special authority allows the user to execute the program. If, however, the operational authority is accompanied by *CHANGE object authority, the user will be allowed to read, add, delete, and update the content of the object. Operational, management, and existence special authorities to an object are automatically implied by the assignment of *ALL object authority to any user. Under *ALL object authority, all data authorities, such as read, add, delete, and update authorities, are also granted.

To grant a user object management authority but prevent that user from adding, deleting, or updating a database file, use the Edit Object Authorities (EDTOBJAUT) command (Figure 14.2). Review and modify the authority details to reflect the desired change. The object authority designation may change from its original setting to reflect a USER DEF designation after the modification.

```
                       Edit Object Authority
Object . . . . . . . :   APFILE        Object type . . . . :  *FILE
  Library . . . . . :   AP              Owner . . . . . . . :  QSAI
Type changes to current authorities, press Enter.
  Object secured by authorization list . . . . . . . . . . .   *NONE

                 Object     ----Object-----   ----------Data----------
User             Authority  Opr  Mgt  Exist   Read  Add  Update  Delete
QUSER            USER DEF    _    X     _      _     _     _       _
*PUBLIC          *EXCLUDE    _    _     _      _     _     _       _
```

Figure 14.2 Edit object authority.

Libraries

Objects may be grouped together into a library, and the authority to the library may be revoked from everyone, thus securing all objects within the library. This is an easy method for securing a group of objects, but it alone may not be effective enough to address all security needs in a practical manner. Even within an Accounts Payable staff, some clerks may require more authority than others. For example, a clerk who is responsible for reconciling returned checks may require access to the paid items file, whereas a clerk whose job is to enter invoices may have no need for that particular file. Although this type of access control is often controlled by application function or menu security, it can also be accomplished by restricting individual database files and program objects. In general, access to libraries, especially data libraries, should only be granted to those users who need to access their contents. Furthermore, each individual user's authorities to objects should be augmented accordingly to allow or disallow access within the library as needed, using authorization lists or private authorities.

Be aware of library lists. Don't hesitate to use them—simply be on the lookout for programs that employ special libraries in production systems. The OS/400 uses library lists as a means to search for user-requested objects. The system library list portion is searched first, followed by product libraries, the current library, and finally the user library list. The operating system terminates the search as soon as it locates an object with the same name and type. In many instances, application security could be breached by introducing another program with the same name but higher in the library list than the original program. When an application security requesting program calls the validation program, the new validation program found higher in the library list is invoked rather than the original program. The impostor program then calls the original security program, stating both the library and the program names. When it returns from the original validation program, the creator of the fake program can analyze and return a valid security code even if the original program had previously reported a security failure.

Job Descriptions

Although many people have kept the secret for a long time, job description objects have been used to gain security officer class user authorities on both the System/38 and the AS/400 machines since the machines have been in use. This security exposure was not precipitated by some ingenious programming, but rather took advantage of an oversight by OS/400 developers. When an OS/400 job description object is created, the USER parameter of the job description defaults to the *REQUESTER. If this parameter is changed to host a privileged user's profile name rather than the value *REQUESTER, any users who have enough authority to use the job description may submit a job to execute using the profile specified in the job description rather than their own. The submitted job will then execute under the authority of the privileged user found in the job description's USER parameter location. Because of the nature of job description object usage by the OS/400 operating system, this security exposure is not limited to submitted jobs, but may also be applied to interactive jobs. For example, if a job description with a specific profile name is associated with a workstation entry in a subsystem, anyone can simply press the Enter key to gain access to the AS/400 without specifying a profile and a password. This is because the abovementioned job description may be used to provide a default user profile for the operating system during the sign on process.

This security exposure was never addressed until the arrival of the QSECURITY system value of 40. Even today, all AS/400s operating under security level 30 or below are subject to this type of security breach. All

```
                    Display Job Description
                                                   System:   GONZO
Job description:   QHOSTPRT      Library:    QGPL

User profile . . . . . . . . . . . . . . . . . :   QPGMR
CL syntax check  . . . . . . . . . . . . . . . :   *NOCHK
Hold on job queue  . . . . . . . . . . . . . . :   *NO
End severity . . . . . . . . . . . . . . . . . :   30
Job date . . . . . . . . . . . . . . . . . . . :   *SYSVAL
Job switches . . . . . . . . . . . . . . . . . :   00000000
Inquiry message reply  . . . . . . . . . . . . :   *RQD
Job priority (on job queue)  . . . . . . . . . :   5
Job queue  . . . . . . . . . . . . . . . . . . :   QBATCH
   Library . . . . . . . . . . . . . . . . . . :      QGPL
Output priority (on output queue)  . . . . . . :   5
Printer device . . . . . . . . . . . . . . . . :   *USRPRF
Output queue . . . . . . . . . . . . . . . . . :   *USRPRF
   Library . . . . . . . . . . . . . . . . . . :
```

Figure 14.3 Job description object.

that is required by nonprivileged users is to find a job description that has a specific profile whose authority is higher than theirs, and for which public authority to the job description is at least *USE. OS/400 provides such a job description. The QHOSTPRT job description shown in Figure 14.3 may be used by anyone to submit jobs that will execute under a QPGMR class user authority. This loophole could be exploited by a user class profile to gain the same authority to objects that programmers enjoy. Furthermore, if a programmer class user has management authority to PC Support or the DDM access user exit programs, or authority to the database from which PC Support or DDM access is determined, the intruder may be able to replace the PC Support and DDM access programs or add the necessary records to the user exit database file by creating a simple program. The end result is that the intruder could upload more insidious programs or download confidential data thanks to the help of the QHOSTPRT job description and the security level value of 30. Obviously there are many more possibilities, perhaps even the possibility of using the QHOSTPRT job description to sign on without specifying a profile and a password.

The fundamental security breach, in this case, is caused by a low security level value. If security level 40 is used, the same job description would not pose a threat, since under security level 40, the OS/400 verifies that the user of the submitted job has the authority to use the profile specified in the job description in addition to the job description object itself. Readers who are still using a security level value of 30 should seriously consider raising the system security value to 40.

Saved Objects

All objects may be saved by a user with a special authority of *SAVSYS, even if the user does not have the authority to access the object. This allows an operations staff to back up the system without necessarily having the ability to view or alter the company's confidential information. However, this feature does come at a price. Users with a *SAVSYS special authority may save objects from a library for which they are not authorized and restore them into a library to which they are authorized. This process allows users with *SAVSYS special authority to view, add, change, and update any records in a database file that they have restored. Furthermore, the altered database may then be saved and restored over the existing original database, thus destroying the original data. Although an authorization list may be used to prevent such a user from restoring the database into a different library and altering that database, the authorization list restriction only applies if the perpetrator restores the database on the same machine in a different library. If the restoration of the database is to be performed at another site where the restoring user is not restricted by an authorization list, there may be no effective means to prevent such a security exposure, other than by way of a physical security measure. Furthermore, system operators can overwrite operating system programs accidentally or on purpose, both of which may render the AS/400 unusable. Situations like these may not have effective solutions. The operations staff must be educated to ensure that such events are avoided at all cost. At the same time, restricting the use of the Dump Tape (DMPTAP) command may be an effective way to prevent the operators from viewing the company's payroll records by saving the file onto a tape and dumping the contents of the tape on to a printer.

Restored Objects

The ability to restore objects and libraries is given to all users on the system by default. This also implies that both local and remote users may restore objects onto the system. Local and remote terminals cannot restore objects, since they do not possess the capability to use magnetic storage media, but in today's client/server environment, most personal computers are capable of uploading and downloading data as well as executable objects. This can be a huge security exposure if not managed properly. If PC support and DDM access user exits are not used to control who may perform what types of remote functions, anyone may upload programs that could undermine operating system security. For instance, an intruder can save an entire library of objects into a savefile on his or her own AS/400, transfer the contents of the savefile to a database file, download the database file to PC diskettes using PC Support functions, establish a connection to the target AS/400, create a source file via remote command, upload a simple REXX procedure to the source file, and submit remote commands to execute. The remote commands will create a database file on the target AS/400, upload the savefile data kept in the PC diskettes to the target system's database file, create a temporary savefile, initiate the REXX procedure to transfer the database records to the savefile object, and restore the savefile contents into a library. If user exit programs are used to discriminate among transfer abilities based on profiles, this type of security exposure may be lessened. However, if anyone can upload or download data using the default object authorization mechanism, a simple REXX procedure may be sufficient to transfer a whole library of undesirable programs onto an unsuspecting AS/400. Although it has been said that REXX procedures could not be used to access database records, that theory has been proven to be erroneous. (For example, the REXX procedure in the appendix, in conjunction with a PC batch file, was quite successful in copying database file contents to a savefile.) This means that if one can connect with an AS/400 and has the ability to create programs that undermine the operating system's security, any AS/400 that does not scrutinize a remote user's ability to up- and download data may be compromised in the future.

System Objects

It is worthwhile noting that many OS/400 programs are used by the operating system according to their address or location. These addresses are kept in an object, QINSEPT, that serves as a lookup table. During the installation of the operating system, this object and others like it are built by the installation process. Once the operating system is activated, the system assumes that the addresses found in these tables reference the actual objects. Therefore, the operating system no longer needs to locate an object by its type, subtype, name, and library designation, a process that requires a great deal of time in comparison to a lookup operation. The existence of addresses in these tables allows the operating system to perform its duties much more efficiently than if it had to look for every program that it requires at each program invocation. This is the reason why so many systems programmers are befuddled when the operating system locates and uses an original OS/400 program even if another identically named program is listed higher in the system portion of the library list. Even if the user renames and moves an operating system program from the QSYS library to another library, the operating system seems to mysteriously track it down. Although not all OS/400 programs are registered in the table, the most commonly used programs are protected this way.

Security administrators should be aware of IBM's employment of this built-in protection mechanism in the OS/400, because the same design can also lend itself to problems. If an address in the QINSEPT table does not coincide with the actual object in a given library, the operating system has no alternative but to abandon the attempt to use it. If the mismatched address of the object is a workstation put or get program, the usefulness of the OS/400 would be severely impaired if not irreparably damaged. Surprisingly, it is very simple to destroy the OS/400 operating system in this way either accidentally or purposely. It can happen to an operator or to an experienced techie; all that is required to disable OS/400 in this way is the ability to restore the same operating system programs, untouched and unmodified, back to where they came from using the OS/400-provided restore commands. It does not matter whether or not the profile restoring the object has the ability to use the object. The restoration procedure simply marks the old program as deleted and the new program is added to the QSYS library. Missing, of course, is the new program's address in the address table on which OS/400 depends.

In many ways, AS/400 developers created their machine to be as secure as Fort Knox, but the majority of their security controls seems to be aimed at casual users. Once a user attains enough authority, by whatever means, such as through a stolen pointer via an MI program using blocked instructions, the AS/400 becomes as vulnerable as a newborn. There even exists a self-destruct mechanism that was published by IBM back in August of 1990.[1] Therefore, do not assume that the responsibility of safeguarding your AS/400 is IBM's, or is built into the operating system. It is absolutely vital to discriminate when granting special authorities to users, especially those authorities that allow access to all objects.

---

1. AS/400 System Support Installation Guide, IBM, SY31-0701, August 1990.

CHAPTER FIFTEEN

Backup and Recovery

Although, strictly speaking, backup and recovery actions fall more into the realm of the data processing operations department than in security management, there are some good reasons why a security administrator may be interested in system backup procedures. For instance, if the system requires a full reload of user and system data, it is important for the security administrator to know what the security officer's password is as well as what authorization lists and private authorities are associated with objects. Some security-related information is embedded within each object, such as public authority, owner profile, owner's authority, authorization list designation, object audit flag, and private and public authority existence values. Additionally, user profile objects also host security information relating to the individual's sign-on parameters, private and public authorities, and ownership authorities to objects. If these configurations are lost due to the lack of proper backup measures, it may take considerable effort to re-create the desired secured environment.

Saving Security Data

When security information is saved onto magnetic media, it must be formatted in a way that may take an inordinate amount of time, especially

```
                    Save Security Data (SAVSECDTA)

Type choices, press Enter.

Device . . . . . . . . . . . . . > TAP01         Name, *SAVF
              + for more values   _____
Volume identifier  . . . . . . .   *MOUNTED      Character value, *MOUNTED
              + for more values   _____
Sequence number  . . . . . . . .   *END          1-9999, *END
File expiration date . . . . . .   *PERM         Date, *PERM
End of tape option . . . . . . .   *REWIND       *REWIND, *LEAVE, *UNLOAD

                         Additional Parameters

Clear  . . . . . . . . . . . . .   *NONE         *NONE, *ALL, *AFTER
Object pre-check . . . . . . . .   *NO           *NO, *YES
Data compression . . . . . . . .   *DEV          *DEV, *NO, *YES
Data compaction  . . . . . . . .   *DEV          *DEV, *NO
Output . . . . . . . . . . . . .   *NONE         *NONE, *PRINT, *OUTFILE
```

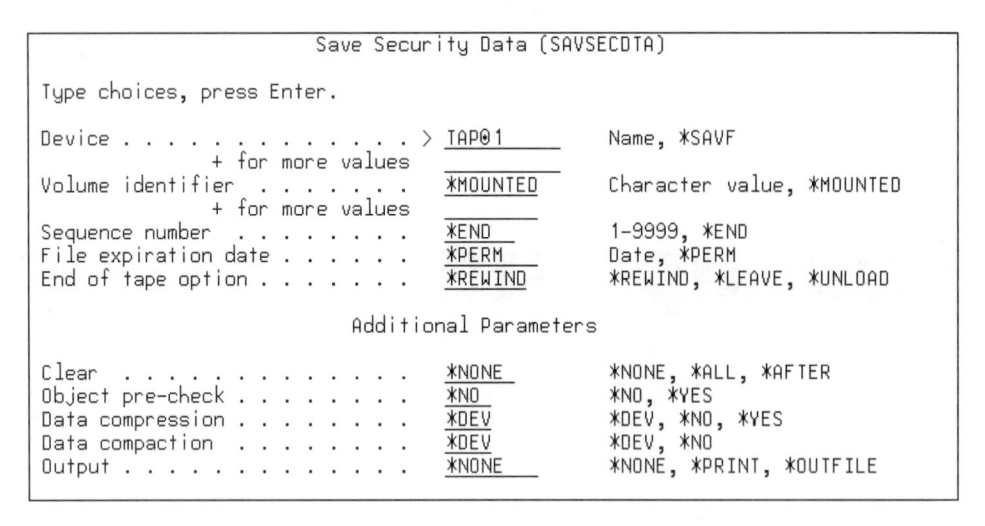

Figure 15.1 Save Security Data.

if there are many private authorities associated with objects. Each object's security information is saved, followed by its authorization list data, user profile information, and the security information associated with each profile. The Save Security Data (SAVSECDTA) is used to save security related information onto magnetic media, as illustrated in Figure 15.1.

Recovering Security Data

A complete restoration of security information saved on magnetic media is possible using the Restore User Profiles (RSTUSRPRF) command (Figure 15.2) followed by the Restore Library (RSTLIB) (Figure 15.3), Restore Object (RSTOBJ), Restore Configuration (RSTCFG), and Restore Authorities (RSTAUT) commands. The Restore User Profiles command will automatically verify and reset any parameters referencing objects or profiles that no longer exist on the system. Also, if the profile being restored already exists on the system, the restoration process will not overwrite its password, document password, and group profile designations. However, if all user profiles are being restored from magnetic media, then no such editing is performed. All parameters associated with user profiles are restored from the magnetic media as they were stored on the media without alterations; it is important to keep track of passwords of sensitive

BACKUP AND RECOVERY 185

```
                    Restore User Profiles (RSTUSRPRF)

Type choices, press Enter.

Device . . . . . . . . . . . . . >   TAP01        Name, *SAVF
              + for more values
User profile . . . . . . . . . .     *ALL         Name, generic*, *ALL
              + for more values
Volume identifier  . . . . . . .     *MOUNTED     Character value, *MOUNTED
              + for more values
Sequence number  . . . . . . . .     *SEARCH      1-9999, *SEARCH
End of tape option . . . . . . .     *REWIND      *REWIND, *LEAVE, *UNLOAD
```

Figure 15.2 Restore User Profiles.

profiles for just that reason. If the user profile table being restored is from another system, with a different machine serial number on the magnetic media than on the system, *ALLOBJ special authority is removed from all user profiles except QSYS, QSECOFR, QLPAUTO, and QLPINSTALL IBM profiles (this occurs at security level 30 or higher).

Restoring Objects

An object is restored onto a system with its proper owner profile designation if the owner's profile exists on the system. If the owner of the object is not on the system, the object is assigned to a new default owner, QDFTOWN. If the object's owner on the system is different than the

```
                         Restore Library (RSTLIB)

Type choices, press Enter.

Saved library  . . . . . . . . . >   *NONSYS      Name, *NONSYS, *ALLUSR, *IBM
Device . . . . . . . . . . . . . >   TAP01        Name, *SAVF
              + for more values
Volume identifier  . . . . . . .     *MOUNTED     Character value, *MOUNTED...
              + for more values
Sequence number  . . . . . . . .     *SEARCH      1-9999, *SEARCH
Label  . . . . . . . . . . . . .     *SAVLIB
End of tape option . . . . . . .     *REWIND      *REWIND, *LEAVE, *UNLOAD
Starting library . . . . . . . .     *FIRST       Name, *FIRST
Library to omit  . . . . . . . .     *NONE        Name, *NONE
              + for more values
```

Figure 15.3 Restore Library.

186 IMPLEMENTATION

```
                    Restore Object (RSTOBJ)

Type choices, press Enter.

Objects  . . . . . . . . . . . . > MYFILE       Name, generic*, *ALL
             + for more values
Saved library  . . . . . . . . > MYLIB         Name
Device . . . . . . . . . . . . > TAP01         Name, *SAVF
             + for more values
Object types . . . . . . . . .   *ALL          *ALL, *ALRTBL, *BNDDIR...
             + for more values
Volume identifier  . . . . . .   *MOUNTED      Character value, *MOUNTED...
             + for more values
Sequence number  . . . . . . .   *SEARCH       1-9999, *SEARCH
Label  . . . . . . . . . . . .   *SAVLIB
End of tape option . . . . . .   *REWIND       *REWIND, *LEAVE, *UNLOAD
```

Figure 15.4 Restore Object.

owner as designated on the object being restored from the media, then the object is not restored unless specifically overridden with an Allow Object Difference (ALWOBJDIF) parameter in the Restore Object (RSTOBJ) command illustrated in Figure 15.4. The public authority of the existing object on the system prevails over that of the same named object being restored, unless the restored object does not exist on the system. Any object secured by an authorization list will automatically be associated with the same authorization list when restored back onto the system. If the object's authorization list no longer exists, then public authority to the object is changed to *EXCLUDE prior to restoration.

Starting from OS/400 v2r3, users have the option to restrict the placement of user domain objects into particular libraries during the restore process. Although this process restricts restoration of user domain objects into specific libraries, it does not prevent any existing objects from becoming user domain objects once they have been restored. Some software vendors have used this loophole to access system domain objects directly by altering the object's domain into the user domain. This process is explained in more detail in Chapter 7.

Restoring Programs

During program restoration, the program validation value is calculated and compared against the stored validation value within the object. If the calculated value does not match the stored value, then it is considered to have been altered and may not be restored unless it is specifically overridden with an Allow Object Difference (ALWOBJDIF) parameter in the Restore Object (RSTOBJ) command. None of the programs created prior to version 1 release 3 of OS/400 contain program validation values. Therefore, the Allow Object Difference parameter may be needed in order to restore those objects. In that case, it is strongly recommended that they be re-created as soon as possible. Fortunately, if program observability exists within the object, the system will automatically re-encapsulate the program during the restore operation, and if the re-encapsulation is completed successfully, a new program validation value will be given to the program.

PART THREE

Auditing

The chapters in this section encourage readers to find operating system utilities that will spotlight weaknesses in security or detect intrusions by others. It is designed to explore hacker-like thinking and probe means of exposing and exterminating suspicious programs and activities. It is this section that illuminates most of the operating systems' weaknesses. The auditing section assumes that the recommended security implementation has been established. It does, however, report all the residual consequences associated with implementing these measures. In addition, these chapters educate readers as to what controls they may have when dealing with objects that are not indigenous to their own AS/400. The existence and creation of viruses, worms, and Trojan horses are discussed, as well as suggestions on how to lessen the chance of becoming infected by such creations.

Developing a system auditing procedure is a tedious, seemingly endless process. The auditing strategy must consider the possibility not only of external assaults, but also of internal changes and unintentional mishaps that may occur from time to time in a normal business environment. Although one might associate system security with computers and attached peripheral equipment, the truth is that hardware itself doesn't cause problems—people do. Computer system security administrators must consider the security of data not only from the standpoint of accidental deletion, but also from the standpoint of those intent on doing harm. Therefore, developing a comprehensive system auditing procedure should, first and foremost, focus on the people who have access to the system. It follows, then, that as people and work environments change, security auditing procedures should reflect such changes. Some of the changes, such as implementation of call-back units, may involve hardware. This may cause a fundamental change in the way the auditing reports are to be generated; the information that a security administrator is interested in tracking may expand. On the other hand, operating system enhancements may require minor adjustments to an existing security auditing policy, such as creation and utilization of significant new features that were unavailable on prior operating system releases. Additionally, all business entities experience staff turnovers from time to time. It is imperative to have a plan that will address the addition or deletion of an individual user profile without delay, since disgruntled employees seldom give notice of their intent to do harm. Most of all, it should be understood that there is no single master outline dictating what should be and should not be included in developing security auditing procedures. There are suggestions and recommendations, but they seldom address the uniqueness of each customer's environment. A good security auditing plan should incorporate within its policy the encouragement to defeat its own security measures; this will ensure that security auditing practices will stay abreast of changing technologies and overcome the natural tendency to become outdated.

CHAPTER SIXTEEN

System Values

The System values table represents a focal point for most default data required to manage operating system functions. The manner in which the table is configured is of prime importance to a hacker; although the system values can only be changed by authorized users, they can be printed by anyone. An intruder would most likely try to get as much information about his or her target as possible without being noticed. Such an individual would avoid generating authority violation messages, lest the security administrator take notice and take appropriate actions. Providing system configuration information to anyone who can sign on to the system may not be the most secure means of reducing potential risks. It would be worthwhile to secure the Work with and Display System Values (WRKSYSVAL DSPSYSVAL) commands from the public domain, if possible.

System values should be printed and reviewed periodically using the Work with System Values (WRKSYSVAL) command (Figure 16.1). Although these values are seldom changed, and usually only by the security officer or the security administrator, if further scrutiny is necessary as to how and when the system values were changed, the audit level can be configured to include the *SECURITY parameter. The *SECURITY parameter will log, among other things, all changes made to the system values table.

192 AUDITING

```
                    Work with System Value (WRKSYSVAL)

  Type choices, press Enter.

  System value . . . . . . . . .    *ALL          Name, generic*, *ALL, *ALC...
  Output . . . . . . . . . . . .    *print        *, *PRINT
```

```
                                   System Values                                             Page    1
5738SS1 V2R3M0  931217                                              GONZO          09/01/94  14:11:44
                Current              Shipped
Name            value                value          Description
QABNORMSW       0                    0              Previous end of system indicator
QACGLVL     >   *JOB *PRINT          *NONE          Accounting level
QACTJOB     >   50                   20             Initial number of active jobs
QADLACTJ    >   20                   10             Additional number of active jobs
QADLSPLA        2048                 2048           Spooling control block additional storage
QADLTOTJ        10                   10             Additional number of total jobs
QALWUSRDMN      *ALL                 *ALL           Allow user domain objects in libraries
QASTLVL     >   *ADVANCED            *BASIC         User assistance level
QATNPGM     >   QSYS/QUSCMDLN        *ASSIST        Attention program
QAUDCTL     >   *AUDLVL              *NONE          Auditing control
QAUDENDACN      *NOTIFY              *NOTIFY        Auditing end action
QAUDFRCLVL      *SYS                 *SYS           Force auditing data
QAUDLVL     >   *AUTFAIL             *NONE          Security auditing level
                *OFCSRV              ' '
                *PGMADP              ' '
                                                                                              More...
```

Figure 16.1 Work with System Values.

Security Audit Journals

Once the *SECURITY audit level value has been inserted, readers may use the Print Security Journal (PRTSECJRN) command provided with this book to report the history of system value changes (Figure 16.2). This command provides the option to list system value changes by job or by program. The *JOBS option will sort the history by names of jobs that had changed the system values, and the *PGM option will sort the report by the program that was used to change the system values. The job name option is most often used to identify the user profile that had changed a particular system value.

The Print Security Journal command assumes that the QAUDCTL and QAUDLVL system values have been properly configured, and that the system audit journal and receiver have been created. If this is not the case, review and execute the Change Security Values (CHGSECVAL) command documented in the appendix. The Change Security Values command will create the necessary journals and journal receivers to accommodate the use of the Print Security Journal function. The reports generated by the PRTSECJRN command may be used to identify programs that will not function at security levels above security level 30. The Authority Failure report, available through the PRTSECJRN command, will list any programs using blocked MI instructions, unsupported application program

```
                    SECURITY JOURNAL ANALYSIS (PRTSECJRN)
        Type choices, press Enter.
        Journal Entry Type  . . . .( 2)    SV         *ALL, AF, CP, OW, SV
        Report Sort Order   . . . . . .    *JOB       *OBJ, *JOB, *PGM, *ALL

9/01/94 15:10:47                                              PRINT AUDIT JOURNAL
SV (Changes to System Values)
Sorted by Job
------------ JOB ------------  Sequence
Job         User     Program    Number   Date     Time     SYS Value   Value Before...              Val
DSP010002   JPARK    GIPEXEC0        5   09/01/94 15:04:17 QAUTOCFG    1                              0
DSP010002   JPARK    GIPEXEC0        5   09/01/94 15:05:35 QAUTOCFG    0                              1
DSP010002   JPARK    MCPCMDL2        7   09/01/94 15:10:29 QAUTOCFG    1                              0
------------
    3 Entries
                                                                     ***** END OF REPORT *****
```

Figure 16.2 Print Security Journal.

interfaces, and state/domain violations. These actions are classified by IBM as system integrity violations and are restricted from execution under system security level 40. The authority violations report lists users, programs, and objects that may have been involved in compromising system integrity. If all AS/400s were to run under security level 40 or if IBM were to enforce security level 40 as a default for all AS/400s, any programs that violated operating system integrity under security level 30 would not run at all under security level 40 or above. Any program registering a *DOMAIN failure, use of *UNSUPPORTED access, use of *BLOCKED instructions, or restoration of *ALTERED programs would constitute a system integrity violation. The system security audit journal is the operating system's main defense mechanism that alerts users to these kinds of violations.

The security journal should remain active for at least one full week of typical business days. It should capture as much data from all applications as possible. If there are applications that are only used at a particular time, consider activating those applications in order to perform a test function. The security audit journal can only log information based on the activity level of the programs that are active at the time. Therefore, it is best to try to utilize as many programs as possible.

Resource Accounting Journals

In addition to the system audit journal, the resource accounting journal provides valuable information about a particular individual or a group

```
                   GRAPH RESOURCE ACCOUNTING DATA (GPHRSCDTA)

       Type choices, press Enter.

       Department or User name  . . . .   *ALL
       Type of Inquiry  . . . . . . . .   *USER     *USER, *DEPT
       Inquiry by Period  . . . . . . .   *DAILY    *DAILY, *MONTHLY, *YEARLY
       Data to Graph  . . . . . . . . .   *CPU      *CPU, *IO, *SPL
       Skip Weekends  . . . . . . . . .   *NO       *YES, *NO

GPHRSCDTA1  GPHRSCD2                                        INFORMATION RESOURCE ACCOUNTING
  9/01/94   18:06:46                                                        QSAI
   %
 100
  98
  96
  24
  22 #####
  20 #####
  18 #####                       #####      #####
  16 #####                       #####      ##### #####
  14 #####         #####         #####      ##### #####
  12 #####         #####         #####      ##### #####
  10 ##### ##### #####           #####      ##### #####
   8 ##### ##### #####           #####      ##### #####
   6 ##### ##### ##### ##### #####          ##### #####
   4 ##### ##### ##### ##### ##### ##### ##### #####
   2
   %
```

Figure 16.3 Resource accounting graph.

of individuals (Figure 16.3). The resource accounting journal report may be used to establish a pattern of unusual activity associated with a specific user. It is capable of reporting on aggregate processing time (*CPU), database access (*IO), or reports (*SPL) in either *DAILY, *MONTHLY, or *YEARLY intervals. To track a particular user, enter the user name and specify that the system resource usage information be graphed in daily format without skipping weekends. This will generate a bar graph with peaks and valleys based upon the individual's activities. Months and dates are also reported, along with a percentage of the total system resource dedicated to that individual. The dates may be of particular importance, if there exists a recurring cycle of unexplained remote user activity—as in every seventh day.

CHAPTER SEVENTEEN

User Profiles

Auditing user profiles may be helped along by the use of the Print Profile Management (PRTPRFMGT) command. This function provides a comprehensive set of reports, each of which is designed to interrogate a specific value or values for each OS/400 user profile. These reports are designed to catch the "impossible" and the "improbable" as well as the "unlikely." Printing these reports is simple. Understanding what to look for, where to look, and how to fix the problems encountered are the key issues.

Indefinite Password Duration

There are seven reports produced by the Print Profile Management analysis. The first of these reports contains a listing of current system values. The system values report is needed as a reference in understanding some of the data presented in the profile management reports. The second report lists all user profiles that have no password expiration duration (Figure 17.1). If a system value is used to control the password expiration interval, verify that the QPWDEXPITV system value is not greater than

```
09/02/94  10:56:11                    PROFILE MANAGEMENT ANALYSIS                      PAGE    1
   User         User      Password Password User    Password System  Text
                Class     Last     Last     Profile of *NONE
                          Changed  Used Date Damaged
   QSAI         *SECOFR   94/08/26 94/09/02          *NO     GONZO   Software Architects International Inc. -Master
   QSECOFR      *SECOFR   94/08/25 94/08/25          *NO     GONZO   Security Officer
   QSYSOPR      *SYSOPR   93/12/04 92/07/03          *YES    GONZO   System Operator
   RHARVEY      *SECOFR   92/08/09 94/06/28          *NO     GONZO   R. Harvey
   SRICHARDS    *SECOFR   94/06/30 94/03/12          *YES    GONZO   S. Richardson
Total Users
COUNT  5
*** END OF REPORT ***
```

Figure 17.1 Indefinite password duration report.

30. Any explicit override of password expiration interval values associated with individual user profiles should be checked to ensure that it does not exceed the recommended default of 30 days.

User profiles that contain passwords should be checked to ensure that their passwords have been changed within the last 30 days. If not, the appropriate users should be notified that they will need to change their passwords the next time they sign on. The security administrator should make certain the password expiration interval system value is set to 30 days or fewer and the individual profile that needs the password changed should be updated to require a new password on the next sign-on.

Invalid Sign-on Attempts

This report lists user profiles with one or more invalid sign-on attempts (Figure 17.2). It also specifies the last time the user signed on to the system and the date of the last password change. In general, if a user has not signed on to the system for over six months, the profile should be considered for deactivation or deletion. If a profile has many invalid sign-on attempts, but is frequently used, the user should be contacted to verify that he or she is having problems signing on. If a profile contains many invalid sign-on attempts but has not successfully signed on for over 30 days, consider deactivating the profile and contacting the user for

```
09/02/94  10:36:20                    PROFILE MANAGEMENT ANALYSIS                      PAGE    1
   User         User      Invalid  Password Password Password System  Text
                Class     Signon   Last     Last     of *NONE
                          Attempts Changed  Used Date
   QSYSOPR      *SYSOPR      1     93/12/04 92/07/03  *YES    GONZO   System Operator
Total Users
COUNT  1
*** END OF REPORT ***
```

Figure 17.2 Invalid sign-on attempts report.

verification of sign-on attempts. Any profile that has been damaged should be deactivated or deleted, and any profile the password of which has not been changed for over 30 days should have its password expired, and a new password should be assigned.

System Profiles with Passwords

The default passwords for the profiles listed in this report should be used to sign on to the system. If default passwords have not been changed since the installation of the machine, anyone may sign on as a system service representative or a security officer. If access is granted using the default passwords (which correspond to profile names [e.g., QSRV = QSRV]), the passwords should be changed immediately. In addition, this report should *not* contain any of the following system user profiles: QDBSHR, QDFTOWN, QDOC, QDSNX, QFNC, QGATE, QLPAUTO, QLPINSTALL, QSNADS, QSPL, QSPLJOB, QSYS, and QTSTRQS. The OS/400 will not allow anyone to enter passwords for these profiles. Therefore, if any one of these profiles is listed in the report, someone has purposely patched the profile to host a password. This is a serious security breach. The current release of the operating system will not allow users to correct this type of problem, since it cannot happen through normal use of the operating system.

Figure 17.3 illustrates a system profile, QSYS, with a password. This report may be verified by using the Display Authorized User (DSPAUTUSR) OS/400 command (Figure 17.4). If the Display Authorized User command reports that there exists a password for any of the restricted profiles previously mentioned, contact your IBM support representative immediately for further instructions.

```
09/02/94  11:02:55                           PROFILE MANAGEMENT ANALYSIS                                  PAGE    1
        User       User        Invalid   Password Password User    System  Text
                   Class       Signon    Last     Last     Profile
                               Attempts  Changed  Used Date Damaged
        QOPS       *SYSOPR        0      94/08/28 94/08/28          GONZO
        QSAI       *SECOFR        0      94/08/26 94/09/02          GONZO   Software Architects International Inc. -Master
        QSECOFR    *SECOFR        0      94/08/25 94/08/25          GONZO   Security Officer
        QSYS       *SECOFR        0      94/08/13 94/09/01          GONZO   Internal System User Profile
        QUSER      *USER          0      94/08/31 94/08/31          GONZO   Work Station User
Total Users
COUNT  5
*** END OF REPORT ***
```

Figure 17.3 System Profiles with Passwords report.

```
                     Display Authorized Users

                        Password
User        Group       Last        No
Profile     Profile     Changed     Password   Text
QSAI                    08/26/94               Software Architects International
QSAIRMT                 12/16/93    X          Software Architects International
QSECOFR                 08/25/94               Security Officer
QSNADS                  02/04/92    X          Internal SNADS User Profile
QSPL                    02/04/92    X          Internal Spool User Profile
QSPLJOB                 02/04/92    X          Internal Spool User Profile
QSRV                    12/04/93    X          Service User Profile
QSRVBAS                 12/04/93    X          Basic Service User Profile
QSYS                    08/13/94               Internal System User Profile
QSYSOPR                 12/04/93    X          System Operator
QTSTRQS                 02/04/92    X          Test Request User Profile
QUSER                   08/31/94               Work Station User
QX400                   02/05/92    X
```

Figure 17.4 Display Authorized Users.

Privileged Users with Unlimited Access

This report lists any security officers or security administrator class users and any users with *ALLOBJ, *SERVICE, *AUDIT, and *SECADM special authorities (Figure 17.5). The purpose of the report is to identify supervisory users who are able to use any device to access the system. In most instances the limitation is based on the system value, in which case the system value (QLMTSECOFR) should be verified and set to value 1. This change will eliminate the possibility of someone using a stolen supervisor class user password from a remote workstation. The physical workstation location will dictate whether the use of a supervisory class profile is allowed. These privileged user profiles with unlimited access capabilities should be changed to sign on only through the specified devices. To

```
09/02/94  10:36:27                          PROFILE MANAGEMENT ANALYSIS                              PAGE    1
         User       User        Invalid   Password  Password            Limit  Text
                    Class       Signon    Last      Last      Password  Device
                                Attempts  Changed   Used Date *NONE     Session
         JPARK      *SECOFR     0         94/08/25  94/09/02  *NO       *NO     J. Park
         QLPAUTO    *SYSOPR     0         92/02/04    /  /    *YES      *SYSVAL QLPAUTO User Profile
         QLPINSTALL *SYSOPR     0         92/02/04    /  /    *YES      *SYSVAL QLPINSTALL User Profile
         QSAI       *SECOFR     0         94/08/26  94/09/02  *NO       *NO     Software Architects International Inc. -Master
         QSECOFR    *SECOFR     0         94/08/25  94/08/25  *NO       *SYSVAL Security Officer
         QSRV       *PGMR       0         93/12/04    /  /    *YES      *SYSVAL Service User Profile
         QSYS       *SECOFR     0         94/08/13  94/09/01  *NO       *SYSVAL Internal System User Profile
         RHARVEY    *SECOFR     0         92/08/09  94/06/28  *NO       *NO     R. Harvey
         SRICHARDS  *SECOFR     0         94/06/30  94/03/12  *YES      *NO     S. Richardson
Total Users
COUNT   9
***  END OF REPORT  ***
```

Figure 17.5 Privileged Users with Unlimited Access.

```
09/02/94  10:52:21                          PROFILE MANAGEMENT ANALYSIS                        PAGE    1
         User         User      Password Password Password Password Group        Text
                      Class     Last     Last     Last     of *NONE Profile
                                Changed  Used Date Used Time
         QUSER        *USER     94/08/31 94/08/31 21:20:56  *NO     QSYS         Work Station User
Total Users
COUNT 1
*** END OF REPORT ***
```

Figure 17.6 Patched User Profiles report.

implement this procedure, identify the physical device names that will be used by the privileged users; grant *CHANGE authority to those devices for the specified privileged user, change the QLMTSECOFR system value to 1 and change all user profiles' Limit Device Sessions (LMTDEVSSN) parameters to *SYSVAL.

Patched User Profiles

This report lists any OS/400 user profiles that may have been altered to adopt operating system profiles (Figure 17.6). Normally this report will list no profiles. However, if profile QUSER, for example, has been patched to be in QSYS's group—or in that of any other restricted system profile—this report will list the violation. This type of alteration is not allowed by the OS/400, but may be accomplished by patching objects at a low level, which bypasses the intended OS/400 editing rules. If this report lists any profile, it indicates that someone or something has seriously compromised the system. This type of violation should be brought to IBM's attention immediately.

Group Profile Audit

This report lists each user profile that serves as the head of a group (Figure 17.7). If a listed profile is a supervisor class profile, or has special authorities (*ALLOBJ, *SECADM, *AUDIT and *SERVICE), a complete report of the user's profile definition, authorized commands, authorized devices, authorized objects, owned objects, and members of the group is printed. It is important to realize that each member of the group has implied authority to any object to which the head of the group is authorized,

200 AUDITING

```
09/02/94  10:36:33                        PROFILE MANAGEMENT ANALYSIS                                    PAGE    1
        User      User       Password Password Limit    Password Special
                  Class      Last     Last     Device   of *NONE Authorities
                             Changed  Used Date Sessions
        QDIST     *USER      93/12/04    /  /  *SYSVAL  *YES    *NONE
        QOPS      *SYSOPR    94/08/28 94/08/28 *SYSVAL  *NO     *JOBCTL  *SAVSYS
        QPGMR     *PGMR      93/12/04    /  /  *SYSVAL  *YES    *JOBCTL  *SAVSYS
        QRJE      *PGMR      94/08/13 94/08/13 *SYSVAL  *YES    *JOBCTL
        QSAI      *SECOFR    94/08/26 94/09/02 *NO      *NO     *ALLOBJ  *JOBCTL  *SAVSYS  *SECADM  *SERVICE *SPLCTL
        QSAIRMT   *USER      93/12/16    /  /  *SYSVAL  *YES    *NONE
        QSECOFR   *SECOFR    94/08/25 94/08/25 *SYSVAL  *NO     *ALLOBJ  *AUDIT   *JOBCTL  *SAVSYS  *SECADM  *SERVICE
        QSYSOPR   *SYSOPR    93/12/04 92/07/03 *SYSVAL  *YES    *JOBCTL  *SAVSYS
        QUSER     *USER      94/08/31 94/08/31 *SYSVAL  *NO     *NONE
        QX400     *SYSOPR    92/02/05    /  /  *SYSVAL  *YES    *JOBCTL  *SAVSYS
Total Users
COUNT 10
* * *  E N D   O F   R E P O R T  * * *

User Profile . . . . . . . . . . . . . . . :  QSAI
Previous sign-on . . . . . . . . . . . . . :  09/02/94  09:47:10
Sign-on attempts not valid . . . . . . . . :  0
Status . . . . . . . . . . . . . . . . . . :  *ENABLED
Date password last changed . . . . . . . . :  08/26/94
Password expiration interval . . . . . . . :  *NOMAX
Set password to expired  . . . . . . . . . :  *NO
User class . . . . . . . . . . . . . . . . :  *SECOFR
Special authority  . . . . . . . . . . . . :  *ALLOBJ
                                              *JOBCTL
                                              *SAVSYS
                                              *SECADM
                                              *SERVICE
                                              *SPLCTL

User Profile . . . . . . . . . . . . . . . :  QSAI
    GONZO                      RHARVEY
    JPARK                      SRICHARDS
                                * * * * *  E N D   O F   L I S T I N G  * * * * *
```

Figure 17.7 Group Profile Audit report.

unless the authority is specifically revoked. Therefore, each member of the group should be reviewed to be certain that all users listed should have the privileges implied by the group profile.

CHAPTER EIGHTEEN

Resource Usage Audit

System resource usage should be controlled and verified regularly in order to ensure that objects and data are being used by those who are authorized to them. Although the owners of data are often asked to validate the authorities required to access their data, that process is often overwhelming due to the use of group profile ownership of objects. Furthermore, a group profile generally reflects a conceptual user and not a specific user. Enforcing ownership-regulated authority validation is difficult and ambiguous at best. The concept of verifying required object authorities in order to gain access to information is absolutely essential, however. But the procedures used to accomplish this task should be re-focused to reflect the concerns of a security administrator, using automated means to report any exceptions to preset guidelines. The most time-consuming process involves the establishment of the initial secured environment. Once the environment has been established, security information may be saved in database files so that it may be compared against subsequently generated information. Using this approach, the public authorities of sensitive objects may be verified periodically by using the Display Object Authorities (DSPOBJAUT) command. The public authority of all user profiles as well as any Job Description objects that contain

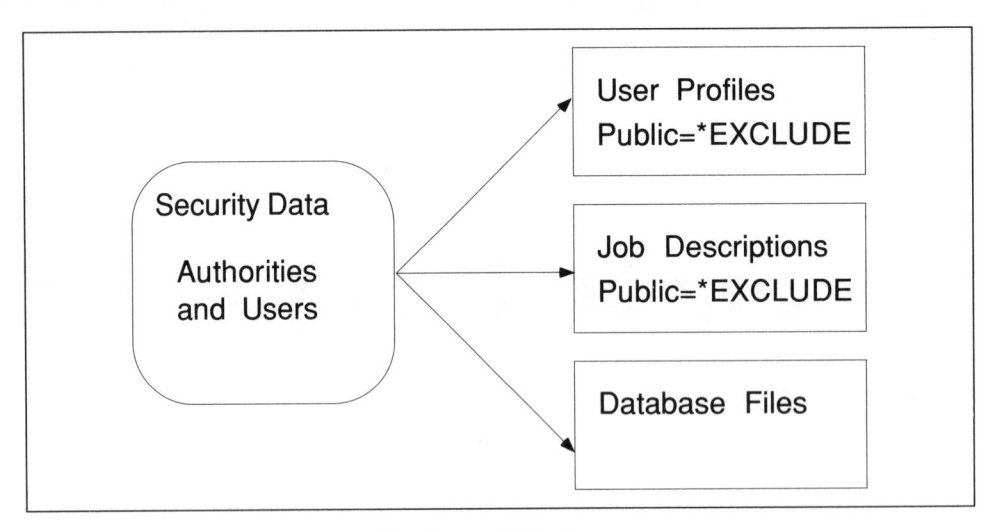

Figure 18.1 Automated authority validation.

specific user profiles may be automatically set to *EXCLUDE. Figure 18.1 illustrates an example of the outfile-driven authority validation procedure. This type of procedure may best be handled by a job scheduler in a cyclical rotation that will identify any exceptions found during its validation process.

Establishing Security Journals

System security audit journals are not automatically created and initiated by the system. The necessary objects must be created and the scope of security data to collect must be defined and configured. There are two objects needed to store security data: a journal and a journal receiver. The journal receiver must be created before creation of the journal takes place. Although the journal receiver may reside anywhere in the system, the journal must be created in the QSYS library. The Change Security Values (CHGSECVAL) command provided in the appendix automatically creates the necessary objects and assigns the recommended security audit values. However, if not all security values need to be changed, the following directions demonstrate how to create and configure the security journal receiver, the security journal, and audit-related system value parameters.

```
CRTJRNRCV  JRNRCV(QUSRSYS/QAUDJRN001) AUT(*EXCLUDE)
CRTJRN     JRN(QSYS/QAUDJRN) JRNRCV(QUSRSYS/QAUDJRN001) AUT(*EXCLUDE)
CHGSYSVAL  SYSVAL(QAUDCTL)     VALUE('*AUDLVL')
CHGSYSVAL  SYSVAL(QAUDENDACN)  VALUE('*NOTIFY')
CHGSYSVAL  SYSVAL(QAUDFRCLVL)  VALUE('*SYS')
CHGSYSVAL  SYSVAL(QAUDLVL)     VALUE('*AUTFAIL *OFCSRV *PGMADP +
                                     *PGMFAIL *SAVRST *SERVICE')
```

It is recommended that the Audit Control (QAUDCTL) system value initially be set to *AUDLVL. Once the audit journals indicate that a specific object or user should be examined more closely, then the Audit Control system value should be set to *OBJAUD and the Change User Audit (CHGUSRAUD) command should be used to specify the particular actions that will be examined for the user in question (Figure 18.2). In order to work with security audit journal data, the user must possess the *AUDIT special authority.

The security audit journal receiver will grow in size rapidly unless it is monitored regularly and replaced with a new receiver. Even the automated clean-up features of the Operational Assistant do not remove security audit journal receivers. In addition to the wasted disk space, a large security journal receiver will result in slower system performance. The process of detaching the old receiver and attaching a new journal receiver is accomplished using the Change Journal (CHGJRN) command. However, the security journal receiver data should first be imported into a database for the purposes of security audit reporting. Once the security

```
                    Change User Auditing (CHGUSRAUD)

 Type choices, press Enter.

 User profile . . . . . . . . . . > SRICHARDS      Name
             + for more values
 Object auditing value  . . . . . > *ALL           *SAME, *NONE, *CHANGE, *ALL
 User action auditing . . . . . . > *PGMADP        *SAME, *NONE, *CMD...
                                  > *SERVICE
                                  > *SECURITY
             + for more values   > *OFCSRV
```

Figure 18.2 Change User Auditing.

204 AUDITING

```
                     Change Journal (CHGJRN)

 Type choices, press Enter.

 Journal  . . . . . . . . . . . . >  QAUDJRN      Name
    Library  . . . . . . . . . . >  QSYS         Name, *LIBL, *CURLIB
 Journal receiver:
    Journal receiver . . . . . . .   *gen         Name, *SAME, *GEN
       Library . . . . . . . . . .                Name, *LIBL, *CURLIB
    Journal receiver . . . . . . .                Name, *GEN
       Library . . . . . . . . . .                Name, *LIBL, *CURLIB
 Sequence option  . . . . . . . .   *reset       *RESET, *CONT
 Journal threshold msgq . . . . .   QSYSOPR      Name, *SAME
    Library . . . . . . . . . . .   *LIBL        Name, *LIBL, *CURLIB
 Text 'description' . . . . . . .   'Security Audit Journal'
```

Figure 18.3 Change Journal.

journal data has been processed and is detached, it may be saved and deleted or simply deleted in order to recoup disk space. This process may be automated using the Print Security Journals (PRTSECJRN) and Delete Old Journal Receivers (DLTOLDRCV) commands provided in the appendix. Alternatively, there may exist a command Display Audit Logs (DSP-AUDLOG) in the library QUSRSYS that will assist users in printing the security audit journal data. If security auditing is to be terminated, simply change the Audit Control (QAUDCTL) system value to *NONE, change the security journal to *RESET as illustrated in Figure 18.3, and remove any security journal receivers previously detached.

System Audit Journals

System security audit journal entries provide a wealth of information regarding the effectiveness of system security. The information in these journals ranges from authority violations to the incidence of e-mail tampering. It is recommended that readers regularly print various types of journal entries and review authority failures, changes to distribution directories, adoption of authorities, program failures, save and restoration of objects, and use of system service tools by unauthorized individuals, among others. Table 18.1 lists some journal entry types, message identifiers, and their respective message text.

Table 18.1 Security Journal Entries

Authority Failure	AF	A	CPI2246	Unauthorized access or operation.
		J	CPI2248	Unauthorized use of a job description object profile.
		P	CPI2270	Unauthorized use of profile handle.
		S	CPI2249	Profile and/or password not specified during sign-on.
	PW	P	CPI2251	Incorrect password entered.
		U	CPI2252	Incorrect user ID entered.
		A	CPI2292	APPC Bind failure.
Object Management	OM	M	CPI2281	Object was moved to a different library.
		R	CPI2282	Object was renamed.
Office Services	ML	O	CPI2289	Mail log was opened.
		S	CPI2293	System directory entry was changed.
Program Adopt	AP	S	CPI2287	A program started that adopts owner's authority.
		E	CPI2287	A program ended that adopts owner's authority.
Program Failure	AF	B	CPI2268	Program used restricted MI instructions.
		C	CPI2250	Program was restored that failed validation check.
		D	CPI2247	Program used unsupported interface to access system object.
		R	CPI2274	Attempt was made to update read-only object.
Print Data	PO	D	CPI2290	Output was printed directly to a printer.
		S	CPI2290	Output was spooled and printed.
Save/Restore	OR	E	CPI2280	An object was restore that replaced an existing object.
	RA	A	CPI2261	System changed the authority to the object that was restored.
	RJ	A	CPI2259	A job description that contained a profile was restored.
	RO	A	CPI2260	Object owner was changed to QDFTOWN during restore.
	RP	A	CPI2258	Program that adopts owner's authority was restored.
	RU	A	CPI2262	Authority was restored by using the RSTAUT command.
Service Tools	ST	A	CPI228F	System service tool was used.

(continues)

Table 18.1 Security Journal Entries (*Continued*)

Security	AD	D	CPI2285	DLO auditing was changed with CHGDLOAUD command.
	CA	A	CPI2253	Changes were made to authorization list or object authority.
	CP	A	CPI2266	User profile was created, changed, or restored.
	DS	A	CPI2267	DST and QSECOFR passwords have been set back to the default.

Program Failure Journals

Program failure journal entries are automatically added to security audit journal receivers if the recommended system audit values have been implemented. These journal entries report users, programs, and objects that have been involved in compromising system integrity. If all AS/400s were to run under security level 40 or if IBM were to enforce security level 40 as a default on the next generation of AS/400s, any programs that violate operating system integrity would not run at all. Any program registering a *DOMAIN failure, use of *UNSUPPORTED access, use of *BLOCKED instructions, or restoration of *ALTERED programs would constitute a system integrity violation.

The system security audit journal is the operating system's main defense mechanism that alerts users to these kinds of violations. OS/400 version 3 release 1 provides one additional command, Check Object Integrity (CHKOBJITG), that will check for altered objects (Figure 18.4). This command may be used to look for objects that may have been altered in the system.

Authority Adoption Audit

The purpose of this function is to identify all objects owned by supervisory class users that will execute under the owner's authority (Figure 18.5). Although there are instances where such programs are necessary, the

```
                    Check Object Integrity (CHKOBJITG)
Type choices, press Enter.

User profile . . . . . . . . . . .                         Name, generic*, *ALL
File to receive output . . . . .                           Name
   Library . . . . . . . . . . .    *LIBL                  Name, *LIBL, *CURLIB
Output member options:
   Member to receive output . . .   *FIRST                 Name, *FIRST
   Replace or add records . . . .   *REPLACE               *REPLACE, *ADD
Check domain . . . . . . . . . . . *YES                    *YES, *NO
Check program and module . . . .   *YES                    *YES, *NO
```

Figure 18.4 Check Object Integrity.

number of these programs should be closely monitored so that they do not overwhelm the system. It is essential to maintain a proactive role in the management of these intentional security breaches. Consider the following guidelines in creating, managing, and standardizing programs that adopt supervisory authority:

- The absolute necessity of such programs should be considered, along with suitable alternatives.
- Adopt the object owner's authority rather than a security officer's authority.
- Keep a close count of the number of programs that adopt authority, and check this number once a week. Any fluctuation in this number should be immediately investigated.
- *Do not* allow any program with adopted authority to present a command line screen.
- Ask software vendors why supervisory adoption is necessary. Do not accept simple answers; ask for answers in writing before purchasing the software.

```
                    Display Program Adopt (DSPPGMADP)
Type choices, press Enter.

User profile . . . . . . . . . . .    qsecofr         Name
Object type  . . . . . . . . . . .    *ALL            *ALL, *PGM, *SQLPKG, *SRVPGM
             + for more values
Output . . . . . . . . . . . . . .    *print          *, *PRINT, *OUTFILE
```

Figure 18.5 Display program adoption.

- Keep in mind that many software vendors require that their software be owned by the security officer simply to avoid "potential" authority problems, and not because it is necessary. In many cases, the software vendor is simply unwilling or unable to address security issues.

CHAPTER NINETEEN

Soul of a Hacker

Not all hackers and phone phreaks are obsessed with doing harm; often it is the intellectual challenge that presents the greatest appeal. Because of the nature of such a challenge, accomplished hackers usually possess qualities similar to those of other successful professionals. Unlike the stereotypical "computer nerd," these cream-of-the-crop cyberpunks are first and foremost driven by persistence, like mountain climbers. The tougher the challenge, the greater the thrill and level of peer recognition. These cyberpunks also seem to have the unique ability to familiarize themselves with the environments of their targets. But most of all, they realized long ago that the weakest link in any security system chain lies in the people who are charged with its maintenance. Thus, the art of social engineering plays a big part in their strategy.

Hacking is not limited to the work of incorrigible computer nerds or phone phreaks. For example, students at MIT have created well-publicized programs such as Fido, Spy, and J. Edgar Hoover. Fido's job was to alert its "master" when a particular user logged on to the system. The Spy program allowed users to view other peoples' reports throughout the system, until the voyeur was caught by the J. Edgar Hoover program, which terminated the Spy user with extreme prejudice. Even governments are involved in hacking for the purposes of espionage, as exemplified by the famous case involving Clifford Stoll, an astronomer at Lawrence Berkeley Laboratory, who eventually helped bring KGB-backed assailants to justice in the mid-1980s.

This chapter exposes some of the weaknesses intrinsic to the OS/400 operating system. The reader should bear in mind, however, that the opportunity to exploit the operating system must first present itself to the assailant before it can be taken advantage of. If the security system is regularly audited and tested for its effectiveness, the chances of assault may be minimal. On the other hand, accept that there is no such thing as absolute security. One can only minimize the risks.

Cold Calls

This type of frontal attack is very rarely attempted on the AS/400, because it is seldom successful. If proper precautions are taken to validate communication sessions, a cold caller with no prior knowledge of the system will almost certainly fail to connect with the system. Even if a communication session is successfully established (usually, this would be due to the overuse of defaults and configuration for simplicity's sake), the profile-naming conventions and password controls recommended in previous chapters make the probability of reaching beyond a sign-on screen very unlikely. Nevertheless, if we assume for a moment that a cold caller has enough finesse to reach the sign-on prompt, what would such a person likely do with the opportunity? A report issued by an insurance brokerage firm, Hogg Robinson, suggests that the assailant may experiment with passwords like spouse names, pet names, "GOD", "HACKER", "GENIUS", and "PASS". The same report tells us that the most popular passwords among Americans are "LOVE" and "SEX", whereas the British prefer a more conventional approach, using names like "FRED". Routine attempts to sign on using these passwords have yielded success rates as high as 20 percent, according to Hogg Robinson. Fortunately, AS/400s use a qualifier in addition to the password—a profile name. These user identifiers can be colorful, like the CB "handles" of the 1970s, or more conservative—a first initial followed by the last name of the user, for example. The probability of an outsider with no prior knowledge guessing both the profile name and the password within three tries is extremely small, if not nonexistent. In this type of attack, even a routine AS/400 security policy would present formidable barriers to an outsider. But not all hackers are so naive, and not all intruders are hackers.

Curious Staff

The curiosity of internal staff may be categorized according to whether staff is nontechnical or technical. Although there are many levels of technical knowledge within the latter group, they all share some degree of independence and may not be limited to the menus given to them at sign-on time. The securing of the nontechnical staff is directly related to the amount of security planning one has implemented. The practice of the principles involved in user profile management, resource management, and application management has a direct impact on how well nontechnical users are able to perform the jobs assigned to them. The same guidelines are also responsible for keeping users within the sphere of their primary responsibility and preventing them from accessing arbitrary data files at their discretion. Generally, nontechnical users are clerks who enter invoices and process accounting functions from day to day. They are almost always completely dependent upon the technical staff for computer assistance. Short of using their knowledge of the Accounts Payable or Payroll systems to produce large checks addressed to themselves, or purposely deleting records for which they have working authorities, they represent as much threat as a cold caller. However, a little knowledge combined with a loose tongue can have a devastating effect if delivered into the hands of a skilled hacker.

Members of the technical staff, on the other hand, have a suite of techniques at their disposal that could help them defeat the security policy implemented by the company. These range from using an adopted authority program to stealing the security officer's password via the password validation program. However, in most instances, the internal technical staff's ability to overcome security is usually based on knowledge of the specific work environment of the company. This is because most members of a programming staff do not possess the ability to gain the security officer's authority if they have to rely only on their technical skills. An opportunity to create a back door must present itself, along with the lack of accountability for programs that adopt privileged users' authority in order to successfully implant a permanent back door. A single chance is all one needs in order to create a suite of programs designed specifically to defeat corporate security plans. In some instances, the technician may not need to create programs. A brief encounter with an unattended security officer's terminal that is left signed on is all that an assailant needs to grant everyone authority to the security officer's profile. Anyone may then use the security officer's profile to submit jobs that in turn may defeat the best laid corporate security plans.

Parlor Tricks

Some members of any given technical staff will always be more technically proficient than others. Someone within that elite group of technicians could perform a simple trick, coupled with elaborate delivery mechanisms, and make it appear as if he or she had performed a miracle. For example, a simple break message handler associated with any message queue may be used in conjunction with a privileged user's authority to execute commands rather than deliver messages. This neat little process could be used to sign off another person's job or to compile a program interactively at the expense of someone else who waits without a clue. Additionally, the more astute technicians are usually aware of the operating system message file, QCPFMSG, which contains commands that control many of the operating system menus. Among the message constants that are changed on a regular basis, as soon as the operating system is installed or upgraded, is a popular message identifier, CPX2313. This particular message constant is used in the system request menu. In that menu, the Display Jobs (DSPJOB) option is often altered to the Work with Jobs (WRKJOB) option in order to access the system command line interface. Undoubtedly there are several other targets of opportunity in such a message file.

Some of these parlor tricks are not necessarily meant to defeat security, but discovering and mastering these techniques is a goal consistent with the drive that a hacker possesses. For instance, these techies are inclined to use nontraditional techniques to retrieve information about system hardware attributes, resource allocations, and device-dependent information through 5250 data stream commands. The tool that these systems programmers rely on to perform these miracles, for the most part, is the Machine Interface language. Using MI, they can provide highly efficient recursive programs that can be used to activate action bars from every application program. MI may also be used to create a duplicate display file in the QTEMP library and patch the copied display file to protect or hide a particular field, thus achieving one form of coveted field level security at runtime.

The technicians who perform these tasks are sometimes regarded as unsecurable, because they create programs that many security administrators do not themselves understand. However, it is not always necessary for security administrators to understand technical details in order to implement sound security guidelines. Designing and implementing security is separate from and independent of the technical explorations and abilities of programming staff. The OS/400 operating system delivers, by and large, excellent security controls, but these security values and options must be utilized and audited in order to maintain a safe, up-to-date environment.

Gift Horses

These programs work a little differently than those created in-house, and represent a much more serious attempt to undermine the integrity of the operating system. Readers should first understand that it is, beyond the shadow of doubt, possible to create a virus that can go undetected by the best AS/400 security measures as evidenced by Chapter 9. Even at security level 50 with the system state program restoration restriction in effect, one can still restore a patched user state program that will execute in system state and simply go about its business. Unless there will never be another piece of software installed in addition to the operating system, there is always a chance that a virus could be introduced to the system—even by your favorite software vendor. It is, however, much more difficult to overcome security at level 40 without notice than it is at lower security levels.

One popular target of opportunity for hackers is the System Entry Point Table (QINSEPT). By using this system data area object, a hacker can intercept most operating system operations. The purpose of operating system program interception may be completely benign—collecting program usage statistics, for example. But interception can also involve proliferation of a virus throughout the system until the system is completely disabled.

Detection of viruses is most often accomplished by inspecting every executable object on a system for specific viral "signatures." These viral signatures are collected as they are recognized, inspected, and defeated. The collection is then used as a database from which antivirus software may be created encompassing known diseases and their respective cures. Although there are exceptions to every rule, because most antivirus software packages rely on known symptoms, as in the case of real diseases, it is much more difficult to detect the unknown.

On the AS/400, the difficult task of collecting and searching for potentially harmful programs is magnified even further, since there are not enough publicized virus signatures, and the OS/400 operating system prevents programs from accessing the very places in which viruses would most likely be located. However, a little familiarity with the architecture of the OS/400 operating system makes it possible to take some precautions. The System Entry Point Table object (QINSEPT) may be printed at any time so that its contents can be inspected for nonoperating system programs. This method does not, however, prove the absence of a virus; rather, it is designed to identify any foreign nonoperating system programs in use at that particular time. The output of the QINSEPT object from the Dump System Object (DMPSYSOBJ) command may be processed by an application program. The search criteria may simply report all instance of program names that do not begin with the letter "Q", or may become more sophisticated, as desired. Figure 19.1 illustrates the Dump System Object (DMPSYSOBJ) command that may be used to print the System Entry Point Table object.

```
                    Dump System Object (DMPSYSOBJ)

  Type choices, press Enter.

  Object  . . . . . . . . . . . . .   qinsept
  Context or library  . . . . . . .   qsys
  Internal object type  . . . . . .   *ALL        *ALL, 01, 02, 04, 07, 08...
  Internal object subtype . . . .     *ALL        Character value, *ALL
  Object type . . . . . . . . . .                 *ALL, *ALRTBL, *AUTL...
  Hexadecimal offsets . . . . . .     *NONE       00000000-00FFFFFF, *NONE
              + for more values
  Area of space to dump:
    Hexadecimal offset  . . . . . .   *           00000000-00FFFFFF, *
    Hexadecimal length or * . . .                 00000001-00FFFFFF, *

                                                                          Bottom
  F3=Exit   F4=Prompt   F5=Refresh   F12=Cancel   F13=How to use this display
  F24=More keys
```

```
5738SS1 V2R3M0  931217           AS/400 DUMP            081290/QSAI/PCS116S1      11/28/94 20:48:53     PAGE    1
DMPSYSOBJ PARAMETERS
OBJ- QINSEPT                     CONTEXT- QSYS
TYPE- *ALL SUBTYPE-*ALL
OBJECT TYPE-        SPACE                                   *SEPT
NAME-       QINSEPT                     TYPE-      19  SUBTYPE-      C3
LIBRARY-    QSYS                        TYPE-      04  SUBTYPE-      01
CREATION-   07/01/94  08:42:12          SIZE-      000011E00
OWNER-      QSYS                        TYPE-      08  SUBTYPE-      01
ATTRIBUTES-         0800                ADDRESS-   004E5400  0000
SPACE ATTRIBUTES-
   000000   00FFFF00 00000000 19C3D8C9 D5E2C5D7   E3404040 40404040 40404040 40404040   *   - CQINSEPT            *
   000020   40404040 40404040 A0000000 00000000   00011D00 00040000 00000000 00000000   *   μ                      *
   000040   00000000 00000000 00030002 31000400   00000000 00000000 00000000 00000000   *                          *
SPACE-
   000000   00000000 00000011 025A011B 9200023F   00130000 0000FFFF 00FC005D E400023F   *     k            U ]U   *
   000020   00090000 00000000 00FC005D E100023F   00290000 00000000 00FC005D E800023F   *        U ]‡       U ]y  *
   000040   00000000 00000000 00FC005D CF00023F   000C0000 00000000 00FC005D EC00023F   *        U ]_       U ]ö  *
   000060   00460000 00000000 00FC005D ED00023F   00000000 00000000 00FC005D DE00023F   * !      U ]¶       U ]ú  *
.POINTERS-
   000000   SYP 02 01 QT3REQIO                     04 01 QSYS                 3F00      *PGM
   000010   SYP 02 01 QWSCLOSE                     04 01 QSYS                 3F00      *PGM
   000020   SYP 02 01 QSFGET                       04 01 QSYS                 3F00      *PGM
   000030   SYP 02 01 QWSOPEN                      04 01 QSYS                 3F00      *PGM
   000040   SYP 02 01 QWSPBOVR                     04 01 QSYS                 3F00      *PGM
   000050   SYP 02 01 QWSRST                       04 01 QSYS                 3F00      *PGM
   000060   SYP 02 01 QWSRTSFL                     04 01 QSYS                 3F00      *PGM
   000070   SYP 02 01 QSFCRT                       04 01 QSYS                 3F00      *PGM
   000080   SYP 02 01 QWSSPEND                     04 01 QSYS                 3F00      *PGM
```

Figure 19.1 System Entry Point Table.

Another likely target for viruses and Trojan horses is the System Work Control Block Table (QWCBT) object. This system data area contains information relating to each job on the system, and may for example, be altered to hide a job that deletes a random object at a set time interval. Although it may be more difficult to write a program that can analyze the QWCBT object than the QINSEPT object, it will probably take less time to identify the proper QWCBT entry formats. The System Work Control Block Table (QWCBT) may also be printed using the Dump System Objects (DMPSYSOBJ) command as illustrated in Figure 19.2.

The last, but most significant, preventive measure against Trojan horses and viruses lies in the regular use of the Check Object Integrity (CHKOB-

216 AUDITING

```
                    Dump System Object (DMPSYSOBJ)

 Type choices, press Enter.

 Object . . . . . . . . . . . . .   qwcbt
 Context or library . . . . . . .   qsys
 Internal object type . . . . . .   *ALL       *ALL, 01, 02, 04, 07, 08...
 Internal object subtype  . . . .   *ALL       Character value, *ALL
 Object type  . . . . . . . . . .              *ALL, *ALRTBL, *AUTL...
 Hexadecimal offsets  . . . . . .   *NONE      00000000-00FFFFFF, *NONE
              + for more values
 Area of space to dump:
   Hexadecimal offset  . . . . .    *          00000000-00FFFFFF, *
   Hexadecimal length or *  . . .              00000001-00FFFFFF, *




                                                                  Bottom
 F3=Exit   F4=Prompt   F5=Refresh   F12=Cancel   F13=How to use this display
 F24=More keys
```

```
5738SS1 V2R3M0  931217              AS/400 DUMP         081290/QSAI/PCS116S1        11/28/94 21:06:01      PAGE    1
DMPSYSOBJ PARAMETERS
OBJ- QWCBT                          CONTEXT- QSYS
TYPE- *ALL SUBTYPE-*ALL
OBJECT TYPE-           SPACE                                     *WCBT
NAME-       QWCBT                              TYPE-    19    SUBTYPE-      08
LIBRARY-    QSYS                               TYPE-    04    SUBTYPE-      01
CREATION-   02/04/92  15:20:37                 SIZE-    00001840
OWNER-      QSYS                               TYPE-    08    SUBTYPE-      01
ATTRIBUTES-           0800                     ADDRESS- 002E9C00    0000
SPACE ATTRIBUTES-
   000000  00FFFF00 00000000 19D0D8E6 C3C2E340  40404040 40404040 40404040 40404040   *       - }QWCBT                *
   000020  40404040 40404040 E0000000 00000000  00018300 00000000 00000000 00000000   * \                c             *
   000040  00000000 00000000 00030002 31000400  00000000 00000000 00000000 00000000   *                                *
SPACE-
   000000  00000000 00000011 02A4A001 AE000AFF  00000000 0000FF99 02A4A002 9B001A1F   *          up _         r up o  *
   000020  002D0000 00000000 00030010 D5000238  00220000 00000000 025A011B B9000238   *                N        !    ! *
   000040  00120000 00008B99 025A011B 1E000238  00000000 00000000 02A4A002 78000AFF   *  »r !                    up _ *
   000060  00000000 00000000 025A004E 54001900  00000000 00000000 00030034 1400193F   *  ! +ê                          *
.POINTERS-                                                                                                    PAGE   44
   000000  SYP 0A EF QWMJOBSQ                                                        FF00     *QTQ
   000010  SYP 1A EF QSYSARB     QSYS    081252                                      1F00     *QTPCS
   000020  SYP 02 01 QWTPIIPP                           04 01 QSYS                   3800     *PGM
   000030  SYP 02 01 QWTPITPP                           04 01 QSYS                   3800     *PGM
   000040  SYP 02 01 QMHPDEH                            04 01 QSYS                   3800     *PGM
   000050  SYP 0A EF QWCBTEQ                                                         FF00     *QTQ
   000060  SYP 19 C3 QINSEPT                            04 01 QSYS                   0000     *SEPT
```

Figure 19.2 Work Control Block Table.

JITG) command. This command should also be used against any new programs restored onto the system. Unfortunately, this command is only available to those who use the OS/400 version 3 release 1. An alternative solution for using earlier releases of the operating system would be to create a set of programs that saves and restores programs to ensure that program validation values are correct. Furthermore, if possible, any system state program that does not follow operating system naming conventions should be verified to ensure that it has been supplied by IBM. This may be accomplished by printing the questionable program using the System Service Tools. IBM-supplied programs nearly always contain a copyright string at the beginning of the program. Figures 19.3 to 19.5 show how to use the System Service Tools to print a program object.

```
                       System Service Tools (SST)
Select one of the following:

        1. Start a service tool
        2. Work with active service tools
        3. Work with disk units
        4. Work with diskette data recovery




Selection
     1
F3=Exit          F10=Command entry        F12=Cancel
```

Figure 19.3a Select option 1 to start a service tool.

```
                         Start a Service Tool
Warning: Incorrect use of this service tool can cause damage
to data in this system.  Contact your service representative
for assistance.

Select one of the following:

        1. Error log utility
        2. Trace Vertical Licensed Internal Code
        3. Work with communications trace
        4. Display/Alter/Dump
        5. Vertical Licensed Internal Code log
        6. Input/Output debug utility
        7. Print stand-alone dump
        8. Display hardware configuration



Selection
     4
F3=Exit          F12=Cancel         F16=SST menu
```

Figure 19.3b Select option 4 to Display/Alter/Dump objects.

218 AUDITING

```
                    Display/Alter/Dump Output Device
Select one of the following:

        1. Display/Alter storage
        2. Dump to printer
        3. Dump to diskette
        4. Dump to tape
        5. Print diskette dump file
        6. Print tape dump file
        7. Display dump status
        8. Display formatted dump




Selection
    2
F3=Exit    F12=Cancel
```

Figure 19.3c Select option 2 to direct output to a printer.

```
                            Select Data
Output device  . . . . . . :    Printer

Select one of the following:

        1. Machine Interface (MI) object
        2. Vertical Licensed Internal Code (VLIC) data
        3. VLIC module
        4. Tasks/Processes
        5. Starting address




Selection
    1
F3=Exit    F12=Cancel
```

Figure 19.4a Select option 1 to work with Machine Interface objects.

```
                        Select MI Object
Output device  . . . . . . :   Printer
Select one of the following:

     1. Access group (01)
     2. Program (02)
     3. Module (03)
     4. Permanent context (04)
     5. Temporary context (04)
     6. Byte string space (06)
     7. Journal space (07)
     8. User profile (08)
     9. Journal port (09)
    10. Queue (0A)
                                                          More...
Selection
     2

F3=Exit    F12=Cancel
```

Figure 19.4b Select option 2 to work with only program type objects.

```
                   Find By Object Name And Context Name
Output device  . . . . . . :   Printer
Type choices, press Enter.

  Object:
    Type . . . . . . . . . :   (02) - Program
    Name . . . . . . . . .     qliadopt
    Subtype  . . . . . . .     01    00-FF
  Context:
    Name . . . . . . . . .     qsys
    Subtype  . . . . . . .     01    00-FF




F3=Exit    F12=Cancel
```

Figure 19.4c Enter program and library name of the object you wish to dump to the printer.

220 *AUDITING*

```
                          Select Format
Output device  . . . . . . :   Printer

Select one of the following:

     1. Dump in hexadecimal
     2. Dump in hexadecimal (logical blocks)
     3. Format dis-assembled code




Selection
     3
F3=Exit    F12=Cancel
```

Figure 19.5a Select option 3 to print the object in dis-assembled code format.

```
                          Specify Dump Title
Output device  . . . . . . :   Printer

Type choices, press Enter.

   Dump title . . . . . . . . . . .   QSYS/QLIADOPT

   Perform seizes . . . . . . . . .   1            1=Yes, 2=No

   Partial print page numbers:
     From page . . . . . . . . . .          1      1-2147483647
     Through page  . . . . . . . .       9999      1-2147483647
```

Figure 19.5b Specify the title of the report.

```
    DISPLAY/ALTER/DUMP                              QSYS/QLIADOPT                                    11/28/94  21:42:17    PAGE
  MI PROGRAM              SUBTYPE:  01     NAME:  QLIADOPT                             ADDRESS:  0003  000DCB00  0000
  SEGMENT HEADER   (YYSGHDR)
    TYPE  01   FLAGS  81   SIZE  0003   EXT  0003   OBJ  000DCB00 0000   SPLOC  0000FF00 0000
  EPA HEADER    (YYEPAHDR)
    ATT1  80              JOPT  00              TYPE  02        STYP  01
    NAME  QLIADOPT
    SPATT 00              SPIN  00              SPSZ  0         OSIZ  00000003   PBAU  0040
    VER   2301            TIME  07/25/93  21:26:06              UP0   0003 00020200 0000
    AG0   0000 00000000 0000                    CT0   0003 00023100 0000         OHDR  0003 000DCB00 0100
    RCVY  00000000        PERF  01000000        MDTS  07/01/94  08:13:57         JP0   0000 00000000 0000
    COB0  0000 00000000 0000                    JID   00000000000000000000       OWAU  FF00
    IPL#  0000029D        AL1   00000000000000000
    000DCB00 0000    01010003 00030000   00030000 CB000000     00000000 00000000   00000000 FF000000   *................
    000DCB00 0020    80000201 D8D3C9C1   C4D6D7E3 40404040     40404040 40404040   40404040 40404040   *....QLIADOPT
    000DCB00 0040    40400000 00000000   00000003 00402301     74753EA8 F0C000FA   00030002 02000000   *  ............0......
    000DCB00 0060    00000000 00000000   00030002 31000000     00030000 CB000100   00000000 01000000   *................
    000DCB00 0080    76214998 62400033   00000000 00000000     00000000 00000000   00000000 00000000   *................
    000DCB00 00A0    0000FF00 0000029D   00000000 00000000     00000000 00000000   00000000 00000000   *....  000DCB00 0000
  MI PROGRAM              SUBTYPE:  01     NAME:  QLIADOPT                             ADDRESS:  0003  000DCB00  0000
                                                    START CONSTANTS
    000DCB00 0200    F5F7F3F8 60E2E2F1   404DC35D 40C3D6D7     E8D9C7C8 E8340C9    C2D4400C3 D6D9D74B  *5738.SS1 .C. COPYRIGHT IBM CORP
    000DCB00 0220    40F1F9F8 F06B40F1   F9F9F34B 4040C1D3     D340D9C9 C7C8E3E2   40D9C5E2 C5D9E5C5  * 1980. 1993.   ALL RIGHTS RESERV
    000DCB00 0240    C440D3C9 C3C5D5E2   C5C440D4 C1E3C5D9     C9C1D3E2 406040D7   D9D6D7C5 D9E3E840  *D LICENSED MATERIALS . PROPERTY
    000DCB00 0260    D6C640C9 C2D48000   20800000 00000000     00000000 00000000   00000000 00000000  *OF IBM..............
    000DCB00 0280    0000FE00 00000000   00000000 00000000     00000000 00000000   00000000 00000000  *................
```

Figure 19.5c Browse the report using the Work with Spooled file (WRKSPLF) command.

If there is one reason for the existence of this book, it is the illumination of the fact that there is no such thing as absolute security, only degrees of acceptable risk. Today's security administrators are faced with the difficult task of guarding corporate information assets from the prying eyes of their competitors, disgruntled employees, and possibly, unwanted and unexpected electronic visitors from around the globe. At the same time, such valuable information must be available to those who require it, quickly and with an unparalleled ease of use. In this time of fierce competition and hunger for knowledge, it is imperative to use the best built-in security means possible within the OS/400 operating system; to fail to do so not only invites trouble, but also demonstrates irresponsible management.

APPENDIX

Sample Programs

The following programs are provided for reference purposes. Their inclusion is intended to illustrate specific points of interest and not to teach programming techniques. Although every effort has been made to verify their functional effectiveness, it is ultimately the readers' responsibility to ensure usefulness and accuracy prior to utilizing the programs listed below or on the disk accompanying this book.

Installation instructions:

1. Establish the PC Support router connection with the AS/400.
2. Assign the QIWSFLR folder to a PC drive. (e.g., I:\QIWSFLR>).
3. Initiate PC installation procedure from the QIWSFLR shared folders drive:

```
I:\QIWSFLR>    A:\INSTALL
```

INACTMSGQ   Inactive Workstation Handling Program

This program may be modified to conditionally terminate or disconnect user jobs based on configuration records kept in a database.

```
/*-*-*-*-*-*-*-*-*-*-*-*-*-*-*-*-*-*-*-*-*-*-*-*-*-*-*-*-*-*/
/*          OBJECT : WORKSTATION ACTIVITIES MONITOR         */
/*                                                          */
/*                 : JP                                     */
/*-*-*-*-*-*-*-*-*-*-*-*-*-*-*-*-*-*-*-*-*-*-*-*-*-*-*-*-*-*/
PGM
DCL        VAR(&JOB#)   TYPE(*CHAR) LEN(6)
DCL        VAR(&USRN)   TYPE(*CHAR) LEN(10)
DCL        VAR(&JOBN)   TYPE(*CHAR) LEN(10)
DCL        VAR(&MSG#ID) TYPE(*CHAR) LEN(7)
DCL        VAR(&MSGTXT) TYPE(*CHAR) LEN(132)
DCL        VAR(&MSGDTA) TYPE(*CHAR) LEN(256)
MONMSG     MSGID(CPF0000)

CHKOBJ     OBJ(QUSRSYS/QINACTMSGQ) OBJTYPE(*MSGQ)
           MONMSG    MSGID(CPF0000) EXEC( +
           CRTMSGQ   MSGQ(QUSRSYS/QINACTMSGQ))

CHGSYSVAL  SYSVAL(QINACTITV)  VALUE('120')
CHGSYSVAL  SYSVAL(QINACTMSGQ) VALUE('QINACTMSGQ QUSRSYS')
CLRMSGQ    MSGQ(QUSRSYS/QINACTMSGQ)

LOOP:      RCVMSG    MSGQ(QUSRSYS/QINACTMSGQ) MSG(&MSGTXT) MSGDTA(&MSGDTA) +
                     MSGID(&MSG#ID)
           IF        COND(&MSG#ID *EQ CPI1126) +
                     THEN(SNDMSG MSG(&MSGTXT) TOMSGQ(*SYSOPR))

/*         Optional conditioning...                                      */
/*         Parse &MSGDTA to individual &JOB#, &USRN, and &JOBN variables.*/
/*         If &MSGDTA contains particular user, job, or job number...    */

/*         SNDMSG    MSG('Job &JOB#/&USRN/&JOBN terminated immediately..') */
/*                   TOMSGQ(*SYSOPR)                                     */
/*         ENDJOB    JOB(&JOB#/&USRN/&JOBN) OPTION(*IMMED) LOGLMT(0)     */

           GOTO      CMDLBL(LOOP)

ENDPGM
/*-*-*-*-*-*-*-*-*-*-*-*-*-*-*-*-*-*-*-*-*-*-*-*-*-*-*-*-*-*/
```

DSPTPGM   Display Station Passthrough User Exit Program

This program may be modified to conditionally allow specific users to pass through to other systems. It may be further customized to automate the sign-on process or to force users to sign on again at a remote AS/400.

```
/*-*-*-*-*-*-*-*-*-*-*-*-*-*-*-*-*-*-*-*-*-*-*-*-*-*-*-*-*-*-*/
/*         OBJECT : DISPLAY STATION PASSTHROUGH USER EXIT      */
/*                                                             */
/*                : JP                                         */
/*-*-*-*-*-*-*-*-*-*-*-*-*-*-*-*-*-*-*-*-*-*-*-*-*-*-*-*-*-*-*/
PGM          PARM(&DATA &RTNC)
DCL          VAR(&RTNC)    TYPE(*CHAR) LEN(1)
DCL          VAR(&USER)    TYPE(*CHAR) LEN(10)
DCL          VAR(&DATA)    TYPE(*CHAR) LEN(128)
MONMSG       MSGID(CPF0000)

CHGVAR       VAR(&RTNC) VALUE('0')
IF           COND(%SST(&DATA 37 1) *EQ '0') THEN(GOTO CMDLBL(RETRN))

CHGVAR       VAR(&USER) VALUE(%SST(&DATA 17 10))

/* Disable passthrough by profile...                           */
IF           COND(&USER *EQ 'QSRV      ') THEN(GOTO CMDLBL(RETRN))
IF           COND(&USER *EQ 'QSECOFR   ') THEN(GOTO CMDLBL(RETRN))
IF           COND(&USER *EQ 'MGUADAGNOL') THEN(GOTO CMDLBL(RETRN))
IF           COND(&USER *EQ 'SRICHARDSN') THEN(GOTO CMDLBL(RETRN))
IF           COND(&USER *EQ 'RPACKHEM  ') THEN(GOTO CMDLBL(RETRN))

/* Allow passthrough...                                        */
CHGVAR       VAR(&RTNC) VALUE('1')

RETRN:
ENDPGM
/*-*-*-*-*-*-*-*-*-*-*-*-*-*-*-*-*-*-*-*-*-*-*-*-*-*-*-*-*-*-*/
```

PCSACC   PC Support Access User Exit Program

This program allows the PC Support transfer function to only a selected group of users.

```
/*-*-*-*-*-*-*-*-*-*-*-*-*-*-*-*-*-*-*-*-*-*-*-*-*-*-*-*-*-*-*/
/*         OBJECT : PC SUPPORT ACCESS USER EXIT                */
/*                                                             */
/*                : JP                                         */
/*-*-*-*-*-*-*-*-*-*-*-*-*-*-*-*-*-*-*-*-*-*-*-*-*-*-*-*-*-*-*/
PGM          PARM(&RTNC &DATA)
DCL          VAR(&RTNC)    TYPE(*CHAR) LEN(1)
DCL          VAR(&USER)    TYPE(*CHAR) LEN(10)
DCL          VAR(&RQST)    TYPE(*CHAR) LEN(10)
DCL          VAR(&DATA)    TYPE(*CHAR) LEN(128)
```

226 APPENDIX

```
MONMSG      MSGID(CPF0000)

CHGVAR      VAR(&RTNC) VALUE('1')
CHGVAR      VAR(&USER) VALUE(%SST(&DATA  1 10))
CHGVAR      VAR(&RQST) VALUE(%SST(&DATA 21 10))

IF          COND(&RQST *NE '*TFRFCL   ') THEN(DO)
            CHGVAR     VAR(&RTNC) VALUE('0')
            GOTO       CMDLBL(RETRN)
            ENDDO

/* Enable by profile...                                          */
IF          COND(&USER *EQ 'QSRV      ' *OR +
                 &USER *EQ 'QSECOFR   ' *OR +
                 &USER *EQ 'MGUADAGNOL' *OR +
                 &USER *EQ 'SRICHARDSN' *OR +
                 &USER *EQ 'RPACKHEM  ') THEN(DO)
            CHGVAR     VAR(&RTNC) VALUE('0')
            GOTO       CMDLBL(RETRN)
            ENDDO

CHGVAR      VAR(&RTNC) VALUE('1')

RETRN:
ENDPGM
/*-*-*-*-*-*-*-*-*-*-*-*-*-*-*-*-*-*-*-*-*-*-*-*-*-*-*-*-*-*-*-*/
```

DDMACC   Distributed Data Management Access User Exit Program

This program allows only a selected group of users to restore objects onto the target DDM system.

```
/*-*-*-*-*-*-*-*-*-*-*-*-*-*-*-*-*-*-*-*-*-*-*-*-*-*-*-*-*-*-*-*/
/*           OBJECT : DDM ACCESS USER EXIT                      */
/*                                                              */
/*                  : JP                                        */
/*-*-*-*-*-*-*-*-*-*-*-*-*-*-*-*-*-*-*-*-*-*-*-*-*-*-*-*-*-*-*-*/
PGM         PARM(&RTNC &DATA)
DCL         VAR(&RTNC)  TYPE(*CHAR) LEN(1)
DCL         VAR(&USER)  TYPE(*CHAR) LEN(10)
DCL         VAR(&RQST)  TYPE(*CHAR) LEN(10)
DCL         VAR(&DATA)  TYPE(*CHAR) LEN(128)
MONMSG      MSGID(CPF0000)

CHGVAR      VAR(&RTNC) VALUE('1')
```

```
CHGVAR       VAR(&USER) VALUE(%SST(&DATA  1 10))
CHGVAR       VAR(&RQST) VALUE(%SST(&DATA 21 10))

IF           COND(&RQST *NE 'RSTLIB    ' *AND +
                  &RQST *NE 'RSTOBJ    ') THEN(DO)   /* SPECIFIC COMMANDS */
             CHGVAR    VAR(&RTNC) VALUE('0')
             GOTO      CMDLBL(RETRN)
             ENDDO

/* Enable by profile...                                                  */
IF           COND(&USER *EQ 'QSRV      ' *OR +
                  &USER *EQ 'QSECOFR   ' *OR +
                  &USER *EQ 'MGUADAGNOL' *OR +
                  &USER *EQ 'SRICHARDSN' *OR +
                  &USER *EQ 'RPACKHEM  ') THEN(DO)
             CHGVAR    VAR(&RTNC) VALUE('0')
             GOTO      CMDLBL(RETRN)
             ENDDO

CHGVAR       VAR(&RTNC) VALUE('1')

RETRN:
ENDPGM
/*-*-*-*-*-*-*-*-*-*-*-*-*-*-*-*-*-*-*-*-*-*-*-*-*-*-*-*-*-*/
```

CHGSECVAL   Change Security Values

This program is used to configure system values to their recommended settings. It will automatically create and initiate both the resource accounting and the security audit journals.

```
/*-*-*-*-*-*-*-*-*-*-*-*-*-*-*-*-*-*-*-*-*-*-*-*-*-*-*-*-*-*/
/*         OBJECT : CHGSECVAL                                */
/*                                                           */
/*                : Change Security Values                   */
/*                                                           */
/*                : JP                                       */
/*-*-*-*-*-*-*-*-*-*-*-*-*-*-*-*-*-*-*-*-*-*-*-*-*-*-*-*-*-*/
CMD     PROMPT('CHANGE SECURITY VALUES')
/*-*-*-*-*-*-*-*-*-*-*-*-*-*-*-*-*-*-*-*-*-*-*-*-*-*-*-*-*-*/
/*-*-*-*-*-*-*-*-*-*-*-*-*-*-*-*-*-*-*-*-*-*-*-*-*-*-*-*-*-*/


/*-*-*-*-*-*-*-*-*-*-*-*-*-*-*-*-*-*-*-*-*-*-*-*-*-*-*-*-*-*/
/*         OBJECT : CHGSECVAL                                */
/*                                                           */
```

```
/*                  : JP                                              */
/*-*-*-*-*-*-*-*-*-*-*-*-*-*-*-*-*-*-*-*-*-*-*-*-*-*-*-*-*-*-*-*/
PGM
       DCL        VAR(&MSGI) TYPE(*CHAR) LEN(7)
       DCL        VAR(&MSGD) TYPE(*CHAR) LEN(132)
       MONMSG     MSGID(CPF0000) EXEC(GOTO CMDLBL(ERROR))

       CHKOBJ     OBJ(QSYS/QACGJRN) OBJTYPE(*JRN)
                  MONMSG     MSGID(CPF0000) EXEC(DO)
                  CRTJRNRCV  JRNRCV(QUSRSYS/QACGJRN001) +
                             TEXT('Resource Accounting Journal Receiver')
                  CRTJRN     JRN(QSYS/QACGJRN) JRNRCV(QUSRSYS/QACGJRN001) +
                             TEXT('Resource Accounting Journal')
                  ENDDO

       CHKOBJ     OBJ(QSYS/QAUDJRN) OBJTYPE(*JRN)
                  MONMSG     MSGID(CPF0000) EXEC(DO)
                  CRTJRNRCV  JRNRCV(QUSRSYS/QAUDJRN001) +
                             TEXT('Security Audit Journal Receiver')
                  CRTJRN     JRN(QSYS/QAUDJRN) JRNRCV(QUSRSYS/QAUDJRN001) +
                             TEXT('Security Audit Journal')
                  ENDDO

       CHGSYSVAL  SYSVAL(QACGLVL)     VALUE('*JOB *PRINT')
/*     CHGSYSVAL  SYSVAL(QALWOBJRST)  VALUE('0')                      */
       CHGSYSVAL  SYSVAL(QALWUSRDMN)  VALUE('*ALL')
       CHGSYSVAL  SYSVAL(QAUDCTL)     VALUE('*AUDLVL')
       CHGSYSVAL  SYSVAL(QAUDENDACN)  VALUE('*NOTIFY')
       CHGSYSVAL  SYSVAL(QAUDFRCLVL)  VALUE('*SYS')
       CHGSYSVAL  SYSVAL(QAUDLVL)     VALUE('*AUTFAIL *OFCSRV *PGMADP +
                                             *PGMFAIL *SAVRST *SERVICE')
       CHGSYSVAL  SYSVAL(QCRTAUT)     VALUE('*CHANGE')
       CHGSYSVAL  SYSVAL(QCRTOBJAUD)  VALUE('*NONE')
       CHGSYSVAL  SYSVAL(QDSCJOBITV)  VALUE('*NONE')
       CHGSYSVAL  SYSVAL(QDSPSGNINF)  VALUE('0')
       CHGSYSVAL  SYSVAL(QINACTITV)   VALUE('30')
       CHGSYSVAL  SYSVAL(QINACTMSGQ)  VALUE('*ENDJOB')
       CHGSYSVAL  SYSVAL(QLMTDEVSSN)  VALUE('1')
       CHGSYSVAL  SYSVAL(QLMTSECOFR)  VALUE('1')
       CHGSYSVAL  SYSVAL(QMAXSIGN)    VALUE('3')
       CHGSYSVAL  SYSVAL(QMAXSGNACN)  VALUE('3')
       CHGSYSVAL  SYSVAL(QPWDEXPITV)  VALUE('30')
       CHGSYSVAL  SYSVAL(QPWDMINLEN)  VALUE(6)
       CHGSYSVAL  SYSVAL(QPWDMAXLEN)  VALUE(10)
       CHGSYSVAL  SYSVAL(QPWDRQDDIF)  VALUE('0')        /* V3R1=YES FOR 4      */
       CHGSYSVAL  SYSVAL(QPWDLMTCHR)  VALUE('*NONE')
```

```
         CHGSYSVAL   SYSVAL(QPWDLMTAJC) VALUE('1')
         CHGSYSVAL   SYSVAL(QPWDLMTREP) VALUE('0')       /* V3R1=YES (Adjacent) */
         CHGSYSVAL   SYSVAL(QPWDPOSDIF) VALUE('1')
         CHGSYSVAL   SYSVAL(QPWDRQDDGT) VALUE('1')
         CHGSYSVAL   SYSVAL(QRMTSIGN)   VALUE('*FRCSIGNON')
         CHGSYSVAL   SYSVAL(QPWDVLDPGM) VALUE('*NONE')
         CHGSYSVAL   SYSVAL(QSECURITY)  VALUE('40')

         /* Normal completion notification...                              */
         SNDPGMMSG   MSGID(CPF9898) MSGF(QCPFMSG) +
                     MSGDTA('CHGSECVAL successfully completed') +
                     TOPGMQ(*EXT) MSGTYPE(*STATUS)
                     GOTO CMDLBL(RETRN)

         /* Standard error notification...                                 */
         ERROR:     RCVMSG     MSGDTA(&MSGD) MSGID(&MSGI)
                    IF         (%SST(&MSGI 1 3) = 'CPC') GOTO ERROR
                    IF         (&MSGI = 'CPF0001') GOTO ERROR
                    IF         (&MSGI = ' ') GOTO ENDER
                    IF         (%SST(&MSGI 1 2) = 'CP') +
                               SNDPGMMSG MSGID(&MSGI) MSGF(QCPFMSG) +
                               MSGDTA(&MSGD) MSGTYPE(*DIAG)
                    ELSE       SNDPGMMSG MSGID(&MSGI) MSGF(('Q' || +
                               %SST(&MSGI 1 3) || 'MSG')) MSGDTA(&MSGD)
                    GOTO       ERROR

         ENDER:     SNDPGMMSG  MSGID(CPF0001) MSGF(QCPFMSG) +
                               MSGDTA('CHGSECVAL') MSGTYPE(*ESCAPE)

         RETRN:     RCLRSC     LVL(*CALLER)

ENDPGM
/*-*-*-*-*-*-*-*-*-*-*-*-*-*-*-*-*-*-*-*-*-*-*-*-*-*-*-*-*-*-*-*/
/*-*-*-*-*-*-*-*-*-*-*-*-*-*-*-*-*-*-*-*-*-*-*-*-*-*-*-*-*-*-*-*/
```

DLTOLDRCV   Delete Old Journal Receivers

This program removes the specified journal receivers that are not currently attached to their respective journals.

```
         /*-*-*-*-*-*-*-*-*-*-*-*-*-*-*-*-*-*-*-*-*-*-*-*-*-*-*-*-*/
         /*         OBJECT : DLTOLDRCV                            */
         /*                                                       */
         /*                : Delete Old Journal Receivers         */
         /*                                                       */
```

```
/*                    : JP                                        */
/*-*-*-*-*-*-*-*-*-*-*-*-*-*-*-*-*-*-*-*-*-*-*-*-*-*-*-*-*-*-*-*-*/
CMD     PROMPT('DELETE OLD JOURNAL RECEIVERS')
        PARM       KWD(JRNRCV) TYPE(*GENERIC) LEN(10) DFT(*ALL) +
                   SPCVAL((*ALL)) PROMPT('Journal Receivers')
        PARM       KWD(LIBRARY) TYPE(*NAME) LEN(10) DFT(*LIBL) +
                   SPCVAL((*LIBL) (*CURLIB) (*ALL) +
                   (*USRLIBL) (*ALLUSR)) +
                   PROMPT('Receiver Library')
/*-*-*-*-*-*-*-*-*-*-*-*-*-*-*-*-*-*-*-*-*-*-*-*-*-*-*-*-*-*-*-*-*/
/*-*-*-*-*-*-*-*-*-*-*-*-*-*-*-*-*-*-*-*-*-*-*-*-*-*-*-*-*-*-*-*-*/

/*-*-*-*-*-*-*-*-*-*-*-*-*-*-*-*-*-*-*-*-*-*-*-*-*-*-*-*-*-*-*-*-*/
/*         OBJECT : DLTOLDRCV0                                   */
/*                                                               */
/*                    : JP                                       */
/*-*-*-*-*-*-*-*-*-*-*-*-*-*-*-*-*-*-*-*-*-*-*-*-*-*-*-*-*-*-*-*-*/
PGM     PARM(&RCVR &LIBN)
        DCL        VAR(&RCVR) TYPE(*CHAR) LEN(10)
        DCL        VAR(&LIBN) TYPE(*CHAR) LEN(10)
        DCL        VAR(&MSGI) TYPE(*CHAR) LEN(7)
        DCL        VAR(&MSGD) TYPE(*CHAR) LEN(132)
        DCLF       FILE(QOBJD)
        MONMSG     MSGID(CPF0000)

        DSPOBJD    OBJ(&LIBN/&RCVR) OBJTYPE(*JRNRCV) +
                   DETAIL(*BASIC) OUTPUT(*OUTFILE) +
                   OUTFILE(QTEMP/QOBJD)

        ADDRPYLE   SEQNBR(7025) MSGID(CPA7025) RPY(I)
        CHGJOB     INQMSGRPY(*SYSRPYL)

        LOOP:      RCVF
                   MONMSG     MSGID(CPF0864) EXEC(GOTO RETRN)
                   DLTJRNRCV  JRNRCV(&ODLBNM/&ODOBNM)
                   GOTO       CMDLBL(LOOP)

        SNDPGMMSG  MSGID(CPF9898) MSGF(QCPFMSG) +
                   MSGDTA('DLTOLDRCV successfully completed') +
                   TOPGMQ(*EXT) MSGTYPE(*STATUS)
                   GOTO CMDLBL(RETRN)

        RETRN:     RMVRPYLE   SEQNBR(7025)
                   RCLRSC     LVL(*CALLER)
                   DLTF       FILE(QTEMP/QOBJD)
ENDPGM
```

VLDUSRPWD   Validate User Passwords

This password validation program ensures that users can only change their passwords once a day. It should be contained in a secure library.

```
/*-*-*-*-*-*-*-*-*-*-*-*-*-*-*-*-*-*-*-*-*-*-*-*-*-*-*-*-*-*-*-*/
/*         OBJECT : VLDUSRPWD                                  */
/*                                                             */
/*                : JP                                         */
/*-*-*-*-*-*-*-*-*-*-*-*-*-*-*-*-*-*-*-*-*-*-*-*-*-*-*-*-*-*-*-*/
PGM     PARM(&NEW &OLD &RTN)
        DCL       VAR(&NEW) TYPE(*CHAR) LEN(10)
        DCL       VAR(&OLD) TYPE(*CHAR) LEN(10)
        DCL       VAR(&RTN) TYPE(*CHAR) LEN(1)
        DCL       VAR(&JOB) TYPE(*CHAR) LEN(6)
        DCL       VAR(&CHG) TYPE(*CHAR) LEN(6)
        DCL       VAR(&EXP) TYPE(*CHAR) LEN(4)

        RTVJOBA   DATE(&JOB)
        CHGVAR    VAR(&RTN) VALUE('1')
        RTVUSRPRF PWDCHGDAT(&CHG) PWDEXP(&EXP)
        CVTDAT    DATE(&JOB) TOVAR(&JOB) TOFMT(*YMD) TOSEP(*NONE)

        IF        COND((&JOB *EQ &CHG) *AND (&EXP *EQ '*NO ')) +
                    THEN(SNDPGMMSG MSGID(CPF9898) MSGF(QCPFMSG) +
                    MSGDTA('Password may be changed only once a day') +
                    MSGTYPE(*ESCAPE))
        ELSE
                  CHGVAR    VAR(&RTN) VALUE('0')

ENDPGM
/*-*-*-*-*-*-*-*-*-*-*-*-*-*-*-*-*-*-*-*-*-*-*-*-*-*-*-*-*-*-*-*/
```

PRTSECJRN   Print Security Journals

This utility may be used to report authority failures (AF), changed profiles (CP), object ownership alterations (OW), and system value modifications (SV). It may also be modified to host a variety of new functions with relative ease. The PRTSECJRN command initiates the PRTSECJRN0 program, which in turn

APPENDIX

calls PRTSECJRN1 and PRTSECJRN2 programs. The PRTSECJRN2 program utilizes the PSECJRN printer file to print the requested security report.

```
/*-*-*-*-*-*-*-*-*-*-*-*-*-*-*-*-*-*-*-*-*-*-*-*-*-*-*-*-*-*-*-*/
/*           OBJECT : PRTSECJRN                                 */
/*                                                              */
/*                  : JP                                        */
/*-*-*-*-*-*-*-*-*-*-*-*-*-*-*-*-*-*-*-*-*-*-*-*-*-*-*-*-*-*-*-*/
 CMD         PROMPT('SECURITY JOURNAL ANALYSIS')
             PARM      KWD(ENTTYP) TYPE(*CHAR) LEN(4) RSTD(*YES) +
                         DFT(AF) VALUES(AF CP OW SV) +
                         SPCVAL((*ALL)) MIN(0) ALWUNPRT(*YES) +
                         PROMPT('Journal Entry Type . . . .( 2)')
             PARM      KWD(SORT) TYPE(*CHAR) LEN(5) RSTD(*YES) +
                         DFT(*OBJ) VALUES(*OBJ *JOB *PGM *ALL) +
                         MIN(0) ALWUNPRT(*YES) PROMPT('Report Sort +
                         Order')
/*-*-*-*-*-*-*-*-*-*-*-*-*-*-*-*-*-*-*-*-*-*-*-*-*-*-*-*-*-*-*-*/
/*-*-*-*-*-*-*-*-*-*-*-*-*-*-*-*-*-*-*-*-*-*-*-*-*-*-*-*-*-*-*-*/


/*-*-*-*-*-*-*-*-*-*-*-*-*-*-*-*-*-*-*-*-*-*-*-*-*-*-*-*-*-*-*-*/
/*           OBJECT : PRTSECJRN0                                */
/*                                                              */
/*                  : JP                                        */
/*-*-*-*-*-*-*-*-*-*-*-*-*-*-*-*-*-*-*-*-*-*-*-*-*-*-*-*-*-*-*-*/
 PGM         PARM(&ENTT &SORT)

             DCL       VAR(&ENTT) TYPE(*CHAR) LEN( 4)
             DCL       VAR(&SORT) TYPE(*CHAR) LEN( 5)
             DCL       VAR(&RTRN) TYPE(*CHAR) LEN( 1)
             DCL       VAR(&JOBT) TYPE(*CHAR) LEN(1)
             MONMSG    MSGID(CPF0000)

             RTVJOBA   TYPE(&JOBT)
             IF        COND(&JOBT *EQ '1') THEN(DO)
                SBMJOB    CMD(PRTSECJRN ENTTYP(&ENTT) SORT(&SORT)) +
                            JOB(PRTSECJRN)
                GOTO      CMDLBL(RETRN)
             ENDDO

             DSPJRN    JRN(QSYS/QAUDJRN) OUTPUT(*OUTFILE) +
                         OUTFILFMT(*TYPE2) OUTFILE(SMDAJ) +
                         OUTMBR(*FIRST *ADD)

             CHGJRN    JRN(QSYS/QAUDJRN) JRNRCV(*GEN) SEQOPT(*RESET)
```

```
            IF         COND(&ENTT *EQ '*ALL') THEN(DO)
                       CALL       PGM(PRTSECJRN1) PARM('AF' &SORT &RTRN)
                       CALL       PGM(PRTSECJRN1) PARM('CP' &SORT &RTRN)
                       CALL       PGM(PRTSECJRN1) PARM('OW' &SORT &RTRN)
                       CALL       PGM(PRTSECJRN1) PARM('SV' &SORT &RTRN)
                       GOTO       CMDLBL(RETRN)
            ENDDO
            CALL       PGM(PRTSECJRN1) PARM(&ENTT &SORT &RTRN)

            RETRN:     RCLRSC     LVL(*CALLER)
ENDPGM
/*-*-*-*-*-*-*-*-*-*-*-*-*-*-*-*-*-*-*-*-*-*-*-*-*-*-*-*-*-*-*-*-*/
/*-*-*-*-*-*-*-*-*-*-*-*-*-*-*-*-*-*-*-*-*-*-*-*-*-*-*-*-*-*-*-*-*/


          **-*-*-*-*-*-*-*-*-*-*-*-*-*-*-*-*-*-*-*-*-*-*-*-*-*-*-*-*
          **        OBJECT : PRTSECJRN1
          **
          **                : JP
          **-*-*-*-*-*-*-*-*-*-*-*-*-*-*-*-*-*-*-*-*-*-*-*-*-*-*-*-*
          FSMDAJ    IF  E          K        DISK
          FQSJRN    O   E                   DISK                          UC
          **-*-*-*-*-*-*-*-*-*-*-*-*-*-*-*-*-*-*-*-*-*-*-*-*-*-*-*-*
          E                   CMD    1   2 80
          E                   FIL    1   5 10
          **-*-*-*-*-*-*-*-*-*-*-*-*-*-*-*-*-*-*-*-*-*-*-*-*-*-*-*-*
          IAF#DTA      DS                    256
          I                                   1   1 AF#VT
          I                                   2  11 AF#ON
          I                                  12  21 AF#OL
          I                                  22  29 AF#OT
          I                                  30  30 AF#VV
          I                                  31  40 AF#JN
          I                                  41  50 AF#JU
          I                                  51  56 AF#J#
          I                                  57  66 AF#PN
          I                                  67  76 AF#PL
          I                                  77  86 AF#PU
          I                                  87  96 AF#WS
          **-*-*-*-*-*
          ICP#DTA      DS                    256
          I                                   2  10 CP#CP
          I                                  30  32 CP#CT
          I                                  33  33 CP#PC
          I                                  34  34 CP#PN
          I                                  35  35 CP#PE
```

```
I                                      36  36 CP#AO
I                                      37  37 CP#JC
I                                      38  38 CP#SS
I                                      39  39 CP#SA
I                                      40  40 CP#SC
I                                      41  41 CP#SV
**-*-*-*-*-*
IOW#DTA       DS                          256
I                                       1   1 OW#ET
I                                       2  11 OW#ON
I                                      12  21 OW#OL
I                                      22  29 OW#OT
I                                      30  39 OW#OO
I                                      40  49 OW#NO
**-*-*-*-*-*
ISV#DTA       DS                          512
I                                       1   1 SV#ET
I                                       2  11 SV#VN
I                                      12  61 SV#VB
I                                     261 310 SV#VA
**-*-*-*-*-*
ICONSTN       DS                           10
I I              'PRTSECJRN2'           1  10 REPORT
**-*-*-*-*-*-*-*-*-*-*-*-*-*-*-*-*-*-*-*-*-*-*-*-*
C             *ENTRY    PLIST
C                       PARM            ENTTYP  2
C                       PARM            #SORT   4
C                       PARM            RTNCDE  1
**-*-*-*-*-*-*-*-*-*-*-*-*-*-*-*-*-*-*-*-*-*-*-*-*
C             PRTLST    PLIST
C                       PARM            ENTTYP
C                       PARM            #SORT
C                       PARM            RTNCDE
**-*-*-*-*-*-*-*-*-*-*-*-*-*-*-*-*-*-*-*-*-*-*-*-*
C                       EXSR INITZE
**
C             #SORT     IFEQ '*ALL'
C                       EXSR #ALL
C                       ELSE
C                       EXSR #DOIT
C                       END
**
C                       MOVE '1'        *INLR
C                       RETRN
**-*-*-*-*-*-*-*-*-*-*-*-*-*-*-*-*-*-*-*-*-*-*-*-*
C             #ALL      BEGSR
```

```
 **
C                   MOVE '*OBJ'      #SORT
C                   EXSR #DOIT
 **
C                   CLOSEQSJRN                   99
C                   MOVELCMD,2       C#CMD
C                   CALL 'QCMDEXC'               99
C                   PARM             C#CMD
C                   PARM 80          C#LNTH
C                   MOVE '*JOB'      #SORT
C                   OPEN QSJRN                   99
C         *IN99     IFEQ '1'
C                   MOVE '1'         RTNCDE
C                   RETRN
C                   END
C                   EXSR #DOIT
 **
C                   MOVELCMD,2       C#CMD
C                   CALL 'QCMDEXC'               99
C                   PARM             C#CMD
C                   PARM 80          C#LNTH
C                   MOVE '*PGM'      #SORT
C                   OPEN QSJRN                   99
C         *IN99     IFEQ '1'
C                   MOVE '1'         RTNCDE
C                   RETRN
C                   END
C                   EXSR #DOIT
 **
C                   MOVE '*ALL'      #SORT
 **
C                   ENDSR
 **-*-*-*-*-*-*-*-*-*-*-*-*-*-*-*-*-*-*-*-*-*-*-*-*-*
C         #DOIT     BEGSR
 **
C         ENTTYP    CASEQ'AF'        AF           OK
C         ENTTYP    CASEQ'CP'        CP           OK
C         ENTTYP    CASEQ'OW'        OW           OK
C         ENTTYP    CASEQ'PA'        PA
C         ENTTYP    CASEQ'RP'        RP
C         ENTTYP    CASEQ'SV'        SV           OK
C                   CAS              DFT
C                   END
 **
C                   CLOSEQSJRN                   99
C                   CALL REPORT      PRTLST      99
```

```
 **
 C                   ENDSR
 **-*-*-*-*-*-*-*-*-*-*-*-*-*-*-*-*-*-*-*-*-*-*-*-*-*-*-*-*-*
 **-*-*-*-*-*-*-*-*-*-*-*-*-*-*-*-*-*-*-*-*-*-*-*-*-*-*-*-*-*
 C          AF       BEGSR
 C          ENTTYP   SETLLQJORDJE2
 C          ENTTYP   READEQJORDJE2                    99
 C          *IN99    DOWEQ'0'
 C                   MOVELJOESD     AF#DTA
 **
 C          #SORT    IFEQ '*OBJ'
 C                   MOVE AF#ON     SMKEY1
 C          AF#OL    IFLE *BLANK
 C                   MOVELFIL,1     AF#OL
 C                   END
 C                   MOVE AF#OL     SMKEY2
 C                   MOVE AF#OT     SMKEY3
 C                   ELSE
 C          #SORT    IFEQ '*JOB'
 C                   MOVE AF#JN     SMKEY1
 C                   MOVE AF#JU     SMKEY2
 C                   MOVE *BLANK    SMKEY3
 C                   MOVE AF#J#     SMKEY3
 C                   ELSE
 C          #SORT    IFEQ '*PGM'
 C                   MOVE JOPGM     SMKEY1
 C                   MOVE JOLIB     SMKEY2
 C                   MOVE AF#PU     SMKEY3
 C                   ELSE
 C                   MOVE JOPGM     SMKEY1
 C                   MOVE JOUSER    SMKEY2
 C                   MOVE JOJOB     SMKEY3
 C                   END
 C                   END
 C                   END
 **
 C                   MOVELAF#DTA    SMESD
 C                   EXSR #SPIT#
 C          ENTTYP   READEQJORDJE2                    99
 C                   END
 **
 C                   ENDSR
 **-*-*-*-*-*-*-*-*-*-*-*-*-*-*-*-*-*-*-*-*-*-*-*-*-*-*-*-*-*
 **-*-*-*-*-*-*-*-*-*-*-*-*-*-*-*-*-*-*-*-*-*-*-*-*-*-*-*-*-*
 C          CP       BEGSR
 C          ENTTYP   SETLLQJORDJE2
```

```
C           ENTTYP    READEQJORDJE2              99
C           *IN99     DOWEQ'0'
C                     MOVELJOESD     CP#DTA
 **
C           #SORT     IFEQ '*OBJ'
C                     MOVE CP#CP     SMKEY1
C                     MOVE JOJOB     SMKEY2
C                     MOVE JOUSER    SMKEY3
C                     ELSE
C           #SORT     IFEQ '*JOB'
C                     MOVE JOJOB     SMKEY1
C                     MOVE JOUSER    SMKEY2
C                     MOVE JOPGM     SMKEY3
C                     ELSE
C           #SORT     IFEQ '*PGM'
C                     MOVE JOPGM     SMKEY1
C                     MOVE JOUSER    SMKEY2
C                     MOVE JOJOB     SMKEY3
C                     ELSE
C                     MOVE JOPGM     SMKEY1
C                     MOVE JOUSER    SMKEY2
C                     MOVE JOJOB     SMKEY3
C                     END
C                     END
C                     END
 **
C                     MOVELCP#DTA    SMESD
C                     EXSR #SPIT#
C           ENTTYP    READEQJORDJE2              99
C                     END
 **
C                     ENDSR
 **-*-*-*-*-*-*-*-*-*-*-*-*-*-*-*-*-*-*-*-*-*-*-*-*-*-*-*-*-*
 **-*-*-*-*-*-*-*-*-*-*-*-*-*-*-*-*-*-*-*-*-*-*-*-*-*-*-*-*-*
C           OW        BEGSR
C           ENTTYP    SETLLQJORDJE2
C           ENTTYP    READEQJORDJE2              99
C           *IN99     DOWEQ'0'
C                     MOVELJOESD     OW#DTA
 **
C           #SORT     IFEQ '*OBJ'
C                     MOVE OW#ON     SMKEY1
C                     MOVE JOJOB     SMKEY2
C                     MOVE JOUSER    SMKEY3
C                     ELSE
C           #SORT     IFEQ '*JOB'
```

```
C                    MOVE JOJOB     SMKEY1
C                    MOVE JOUSER    SMKEY2
C                    MOVE JOPGM     SMKEY3
C                    ELSE
C          #SORT     IFEQ '*PGM'
C                    MOVE JOPGM     SMKEY1
C                    MOVE JOUSER    SMKEY2
C                    MOVE JOJOB     SMKEY3
C                    ELSE
C                    MOVE JOPGM     SMKEY1
C                    MOVE JOUSER    SMKEY2
C                    MOVE JOJOB     SMKEY3
C                    END
C                    END
C                    END
 **
C                    MOVELOW#DTA    SMESD
C                    EXSR #SPIT#
C          ENTTYP    READEQJORDJE2              99
C                    END
 **
C                    ENDSR
 **-*-*-*-*-*-*-*-*-*-*-*-*-*-*-*-*-*-*-*-*-*-*-*-*-*-*-*-*
 **-*-*-*-*-*-*-*-*-*-*-*-*-*-*-*-*-*-*-*-*-*-*-*-*-*-*-*-*
C          PA        BEGSR
C                    ENDSR
 **-*-*-*-*-*-*-*-*-*-*-*-*-*-*-*-*-*-*-*-*-*-*-*-*-*-*-*-*
 **-*-*-*-*-*-*-*-*-*-*-*-*-*-*-*-*-*-*-*-*-*-*-*-*-*-*-*-*
C          RP        BEGSR
C                    ENDSR
 **-*-*-*-*-*-*-*-*-*-*-*-*-*-*-*-*-*-*-*-*-*-*-*-*-*-*-*-*
 **-*-*-*-*-*-*-*-*-*-*-*-*-*-*-*-*-*-*-*-*-*-*-*-*-*-*-*-*
C          SV        BEGSR
C          ENTTYP    SETLLQJORDJE2
C          ENTTYP    READEQJORDJE2              99
C          *IN99     DOWEQ'0'
C                    MOVELJOESD     SV#DTA
 **
C          #SORT     IFEQ '*OBJ'
C                    MOVE SV#VN     SMKEY1
C                    MOVE JOJOB     SMKEY2
C                    MOVE JOUSER    SMKEY3
C                    ELSE
C          #SORT     IFEQ '*JOB'
C                    MOVE JOJOB     SMKEY1
C                    MOVE JOUSER    SMKEY2
```

```
C                    MOVE JOPGM      SMKEY3
C                    ELSE
C          #SORT     IFEQ '*PGM'
C                    MOVE JOPGM      SMKEY1
C                    MOVE JOUSER     SMKEY2
C                    MOVE JOJOB      SMKEY3
C                    ELSE
C                    MOVE JOPGM      SMKEY1
C                    MOVE JOUSER     SMKEY2
C                    MOVE JOJOB      SMKEY3
C                    END
C                    END
C                    END
**
C                    MOVELSV#DTA     SMESD
C                    EXSR #SPIT#
C          ENTTYP    READEQJORDJE2                  99
C                    END
**
C                    ENDSR
**-*-*-*-*-*-*-*-*-*-*-*-*-*-*-*-*-*-*-*-*-*-*-*-*-*-*
**-*-*-*-*-*-*-*-*-*-*-*-*-*-*-*-*-*-*-*-*-*-*-*-*-*-*
C          DFT       BEGSR
C                    ENDSR
**-*-*-*-*-*-*-*-*-*-*-*-*-*-*-*-*-*-*-*-*-*-*-*-*-*-*
**-*-*-*-*-*-*-*-*-*-*-*-*-*-*-*-*-*-*-*-*-*-*-*-*-*-*
C          #SPIT#    BEGSR
C                    MOVE JOSEQN     SMSEQN
C                    MOVE JOENTT     SMENTT
C                    MOVE JODATE     SMDATE
C                    MOVE JOTIME     SMTIME
C                    MOVE JOJOB      SMJOB
C                    MOVE JOUSER     SMUSER
C                    MOVE JONBR      SMNBR
C                    MOVE JOPGM      SMPGM
C                    WRITESMRAI
C                    ENDSR
**-*-*-*-*-*-*-*-*-*-*-*-*-*-*-*-*-*-*-*-*-*-*-*-*-*-*
**-*-*-*-*-*-*-*-*-*-*-*-*-*-*-*-*-*-*-*-*-*-*-*-*-*-*
C          INITZE    BEGSR
**
C                    MOVELCMD,1      C#CMD   80
C                    CALL 'QCMDEXC'                 99
C                    PARM            C#CMD
C                    PARM 80         C#LNTH  155
**
```

```
     C                   MOVE *BLANK    C#CMD
     C                   MOVELCMD,2     C#CMD
     C                   CALL 'QCMDEXC'                99
     C                   PARM           C#CMD
     C                   PARM 80        C#LNTH
    **
     C                   OPEN QSJRN                    99
     C         *IN99     IFEQ '1'
     C                   MOVE '1'       RTNCDE
     C                   RETRN
     C                   END
    **
     C                   ENDSR
    **-*-*-*-*-*-*-*-*-*-*-*-*-*-*-*-*-*-*-*-*-*-*-*-*-*-*-*
    **-*-*-*-*-*-*-*-*-*-*-*-*-*-*-*-*-*-*-*-*-*-*-*-*-*-*-*
** CMD
CPYF FROMFILE(SMDAI) TOFILE(QTEMP/QSJRN) CRTFILE(*YES) MBROPT(*REPLACE)
CLRPFM FILE(QTEMP/QSJRN)
** FIL
*NONE




           **-*-*-*-*-*-*-*-*-*-*-*-*-*-*-*-*-*-*-*-*-*-*-*-*-*-*-*
           **         OBJECT : PRTSECJRN2
           **
           **                : JP
           **-*-*-*-*-*-*-*-*-*-*-*-*-*-*-*-*-*-*-*-*-*-*-*-*-*-*-*
           FPSECJRN O   E              PRINTER     KINFDS PRT#DS
           FQSJRN   IF  E       K      DISK                       UC
           **-*-*-*-*-*-*-*-*-*-*-*-*-*-*-*-*-*-*-*-*-*-*-*-*-*-*-*
           E                   TT     1  21  2
           E                   SO     1   3 10
           E                   MG     1  22 50
           E                   VT     1   9 50
           E                   VV     1   5 50
           **-*-*-*-*-*-*-*-*-*-*-*-*-*-*-*-*-*-*-*-*-*-*-*-*-*-*-*
           IPRT#DS       DS
           I                              *FILE    FIL#01
           I                              *RECORD  FMT#01
           I                                93 102 STLBF1
           I                              B 152 1530ST#LP#
           I                              B 154 1550STCOLS
           I                              B 188 1890ST#OVF
           I                              B 367 3680STLINE
           I                              B 369 3720STPAGE
           **-*-*-*-*-*
```

SAMPLE PROGRAMS 241

```
IPGM#DS      SDS
I                              *PROGRAM ST#PRG
I                               40   42 STEXTP
I                               43   46 ST#EX#
I                               81   90 ST#LIB
I                               91  170 ST#MSG
I                              244  253 ST#JOB
I                              254  263 ST#USR
I                              264 2690STJOB#
**-*-*-*-*-*
ISMDATE      DS                       6
I                                1    2 SM#DD
I                                3    4 SM#MM
I                                5    6 SM#YY
**-*-*-*-*-*
IAF#DTA      DS                     256
I                                1    1 AF#VT
I                                2   11 AF#ON
I                               12   21 AF#OL
I                               22   29 AF#OT
I                               30   30 AF#VV
I                               31   40 AF#JN
I                               41   50 AF#JU
I                               51   56 AF#J#
I                               57   66 AF#PN
I                               67   76 AF#PL
I                               77   86 AF#PU
I                               87   96 AF#WS
**-*-*-*-*-*
ICP#DTA      DS                     256
I                                2   10 CP#CP
I                               30   32 CP#CT
I                               33   33 CP#PC
I                               34   34 CP#PN
I                               35   35 CP#PE
I                               36   36 CP#AO
I                               37   37 CP#JC
I                               38   38 CP#SS
I                               39   39 CP#SA
I                               40   40 CP#SC
I                               41   41 CP#SV
**-*-*-*-*-*
IOW#DTA      DS                     256
I                                1    1 OW#ET
I                                2   11 OW#ON
I                               12   21 OW#OL
```

```
I                                      22  29 OW#OT
I                                      30  39 OW#OO
I                                      40  49 OW#NO
**-*-*-*-*-*
ISV#DTA     DS                           512
I                                       1   1 SV#ET
I                                       2  11 SV#VN
I                                      12  61 SV#VA
I                                     261 310 SV#VB
**-*-*-*-*-*
ICP#FLD     DS                           120
I I            'Password Canged= '      1  17 F1
I I            'Password *NONE = '     19  35 F2
I I            'Pswrd Expired  = '     37  53 F3
I I            '*ALLOBJ = '            55  64 F4
I I            '*JOBCTL = '            66  75 F5
I I            '*SAVSYS = '            77  86 F6
I I            '*SECADM = '            88  97 F7
I I            '*SPLCTL = '            99 108 F8
I I            '*SERVICE= '           110 119 F9
I                                       1 120 CP#ETC
**-*-*-*-*-*-*-*-*-*-*-*-*-*-*-*-*-*-*-*-*-*-*-*-*-*
C           *ENTRY    PLIST
C                     PARM      ENTTYP  2
C                     PARM      #SORT   4
C                     PARM      #RTRN   1
**-*-*-*-*-*-*-*-*-*-*-*-*-*-*-*-*-*-*-*-*-*-*-*-*-*
C           AJ#K02    KLIST
C                     KFLD      SMKEY1
**-*-*-*-*-*
C           AJ#K03    KLIST
C                     KFLD      SMKEY1
C                     KFLD      SMKEY2
**-*-*-*-*-*-*-*-*-*-*-*-*-*-*-*-*-*-*-*-*-*-*-*-*-*
C                     EXSR INITZE
**
C           *LOVAL    SETLLSMRAI
C                     READ SMRAI                       01
C           *IN01     DOWEQ'0'
C           *IN02     DOWEQ'0'
C           *IN03     DOWEQ'0'
**
C                     ADD  1    ITEMS
C           ENTTYP    CASEQ'AF' AF               OK
C           ENTTYP    CASEQ'CP' CP               OK
C           ENTTYP    CASEQ'OW' OW               OK
```

SAMPLE PROGRAMS 243

```
C           ENTTYP    CASEQ'PA'     PA
C           ENTTYP    CASEQ'RP'     RP
C           ENTTYP    CASEQ'SV'     SV              OK
C                     CAS           DFT
C                     END
 **
C           AJ#K03    READESMRAI                    03
C                     END
C           AJ#K03    SETGTSMRAI
C                     MOVE '0'      *IN03
 **
C           AJ#K02    READESMRAI                    02
C                     END
C           AJ#K02    SETGTSMRAI
C                     MOVE '1'      *IN52
C                     MOVE '0'      *IN02
 **
C                     READ SMRAI                    01
C                     END
 **
C           *IN98     IFEQ '1'
C                     WRITETTL#01                   51
C                     WRITEBTM#01                   51
C                     END
 **
C*                    MOVE '1'      *INLR
C                     CLOSEQSJRN
C                     RETRN
 **-*-*-*-*-*-*-*-*-*-*-*-*-*-*-*-*-*-*-*-*-*-*-*-*-*
C           AF        BEGSR
 **
C                     MOVELSMESD    AF#DTA
C                     SELEC
C           AF#VT     WHEQ 'A'
C                     MOVE VT,1     VTDSC
C           AF#VT     WHEQ 'B'
C                     MOVE VT,2     VTDSC
C           AF#VT     WHEQ 'C'
C                     MOVE VT,3     VTDSC
C           AF#VT     WHEQ 'D'
C                     MOVE VT,4     VTDSC
C           AF#VT     WHEQ 'J'
C                     MOVE VT,5     VTDSC
C           AF#VT     WHEQ 'S'
C                     MOVE VT,6     VTDSC
C           AF#VT     WHEQ 'R'
```

```
C                       MOVE VT,7      VTDSC
C           AF#VT       WHEQ 'P'
C                       MOVE VT,8      VTDSC
C                       OTHER
C                       MOVE VT,9      VTDSC
C                       END
**
**
C           AF#VT       IFEQ 'C'
**
C                       SELEC
C           AF#VV       WHEQ ' '
C                       MOVE *BLANK    VVDSC
C           AF#VV       WHEQ 'A'
C                       MOVE VV,1      VVDSC
C           AF#VV       WHEQ 'C'
C                       MOVE VV,3      VVDSC
C           AF#VV       WHEQ 'D'
C                       MOVE VV,4      VVDSC
C           AF#VV       WHEQ 'J'
C                       MOVE VV,5      VVDSC
C                       OTHER
C                       MOVE *BLANK    VVDSC
C                       END
**
C                       ELSE                           VT='C' (Restore)
**
C                       SELEC
C           #SORT       WHEQ '*OBJ'
C                       MOVE '1'       *IN13
C           #SORT       WHEQ '*JOB'
C                       MOVE '1'       *IN14
C                       OTHER
C                       MOVE '1'       *IN15
C                       END
**
C                       END
**
**
C           *IN51       IFEQ '1'
C           STLINE      ORGT DET#CK
C                       WRITEHDR#01              51
C                       WRITEHDR#AF              51
C                       END
C           *IN52       IFEQ '1'
C                       WRITEJUNK                51
```

```
C                     MOVE '0'       *IN52
C                     END
C                     WRITEDTL#AF              51
C                     MOVE '1'       *IN98
C                     ENDSR
**-*-*-*-*-*-*-*-*-*-*-*-*-*-*-*-*-*-*-*-*-*-*-*-*-*-*-*-*-*
**-*-*-*-*-*-*-*-*-*-*-*-*-*-*-*-*-*-*-*-*-*-*-*-*-*-*-*-*-*
C           CP        BEGSR
**
C                     MOVELSMESD     CP#DTA
**
C                     MOVE *BLANK    CTD
C           CP#CT     IFEQ 'CRT'
C                     MOVEL'Created 'CTD
C                     ELSE
C           CP#CT     IFEQ 'CHG'
C                     MOVEL'Changed 'CTD
C                     ELSE
C           CP#CT     IFEQ 'RST'
C                     MOVEL'Restored'CTD
C                     ELSE
C           CP#CT     IFEQ 'DST'
C                     MOVEL'CHGDST'  CTD
C                     MOVE 'PWD '    CTD
C                     ELSE
C                     MOVELCP#CT     CTD
C                     END
C                     END
C                     END
C                     END
**
C                     MOVE CP#PC     F1
C                     MOVE CP#PN     F2
C                     MOVE CP#PE     F3
C                     MOVE CP#AO     F4
C                     MOVE CP#JC     F5
C                     MOVE CP#SS     F6
C                     MOVE CP#SA     F7
C                     MOVE CP#SC     F8
C                     MOVE CP#SV     F9
**
C           *IN51     IFEQ '1'
C           STLINE    ORGT DET#CK
C                     WRITEHDR#01              51
C                     WRITEHDR#CP              51
C                     END
```

```
C                    *IN52     IFEQ '1'
C                              WRITEJUNK                    51
C                              MOVE '0'       *IN52
C                              END
C                              WRITEDTL#CP                  51
C                              MOVE '1'       *IN98
 **
C                              ENDSR
 **-*-*-*-*-*-*-*-*-*-*-*-*-*-*-*-*-*-*-*-*-*-*-*-*-*-*-*-*-*
 **-*-*-*-*-*-*-*-*-*-*-*-*-*-*-*-*-*-*-*-*-*-*-*-*-*-*-*-*-*
C           OW       BEGSR
 **
C                              MOVELSMESD     OW#DTA
 **
C           *IN51    IFEQ '1'
C           STLINE   ORGT DET#CK
C                              WRITEHDR#01                  51
C                              WRITEHDR#OW                  51
C                              END
C           *IN52    IFEQ '1'
C                              WRITEJUNK                    51
C                              MOVE '0'       *IN52
C                              END
C                              WRITEDTL#OW                  51
C                              MOVE '1'       *IN98
 **
C                              ENDSR
 **-*-*-*-*-*-*-*-*-*-*-*-*-*-*-*-*-*-*-*-*-*-*-*-*-*-*-*-*-*
 **-*-*-*-*-*-*-*-*-*-*-*-*-*-*-*-*-*-*-*-*-*-*-*-*-*-*-*-*-*
C           PA       BEGSR
C                    ENDSR
 **-*-*-*-*-*-*-*-*-*-*-*-*-*-*-*-*-*-*-*-*-*-*-*-*-*-*-*-*-*
 **-*-*-*-*-*-*-*-*-*-*-*-*-*-*-*-*-*-*-*-*-*-*-*-*-*-*-*-*-*
C           RP       BEGSR
C                    ENDSR
 **-*-*-*-*-*-*-*-*-*-*-*-*-*-*-*-*-*-*-*-*-*-*-*-*-*-*-*-*-*
 **-*-*-*-*-*-*-*-*-*-*-*-*-*-*-*-*-*-*-*-*-*-*-*-*-*-*-*-*-*
C           SV       BEGSR
 **
C                              MOVELSMESD     SV#DTA
 **
C           *IN51    IFEQ '1'
C           STLINE   ORGT DET#CK
C                              WRITEHDR#01                  51
C                              WRITEHDR#SV                  51
C                              END
```

SAMPLE PROGRAMS 247

```
C           *IN52       IFEQ '1'
C                       WRITEJUNK                       51
C                       MOVE '0'        *IN52
C                       END
C                       WRITEDTL#SV                     51
C                       MOVE '1'        *IN98
 **
C                       ENDSR
 **-*-*-*-*-*-*-*-*-*-*-*-*-*-*-*-*-*-*-*-*-*-*-*-*-*-*-*-*
 **-*-*-*-*-*-*-*-*-*-*-*-*-*-*-*-*-*-*-*-*-*-*-*-*-*-*-*-*
C           DFT         BEGSR
C                       ENDSR
 **-*-*-*-*-*-*-*-*-*-*-*-*-*-*-*-*-*-*-*-*-*-*-*-*-*-*-*-*
 **-*-*-*-*-*-*-*-*-*-*-*-*-*-*-*-*-*-*-*-*-*-*-*-*-*-*-*-*
C           INITZE      BEGSR
 **
C                       MOVE *BLANK     RPTTYP 50
C                       Z-ADD1          I      30
C           ENTTYP      LOKUPTT,I                       99
C           *IN99       IFEQ '1'
C                       MOVELMG,I       RPTTYP
C                       ELSE
C                       MOVELMG,22      RPTTYP
C                       END
 **
C                       Z-ADD0          ITEMS
C           ST#OVF      SUB  3          DET#CK 50
C                       MOVE '1'        *IN51
C                       MOVE '0'        *IN10              +
C                       MOVE '0'        *IN11              Sort Order
C                       MOVE '0'        *IN12              +
C                       MOVE '0'        *IN13              +
C                       MOVE '0'        *IN14              For 'AF' header
C                       MOVE '0'        *IN15              +
C                       MOVE '0'        *IN98
 **
C                       MOVE *BLANK     SRTODR 10
C                       SELEC
C           #SORT       WHEQ '*OBJ'
C                       MOVELSO,1       SRTODR
C                       MOVE '1'        *IN10
C           #SORT       WHEQ '*JOB'
C                       MOVELSO,2       SRTODR
C                       MOVE '1'        *IN11
C                       OTHER
C                       MOVELSO,3       SRTODR
```

APPENDIX

```
C                       MOVE '1'      *IN12
C                       END
**
C                       OPEN QSJRN                  99
C          *IN99        IFEQ '1'
C                       MOVE '1'      #RTRN
C                       RETRN
C                       END
**
C                       ENDSR
**-*-*-*-*-*-*-*-*-*-*-*-*-*-*-*-*-*-*-*-*-*-*-*-*-*-*-*-*-*
**-*-*-*-*-*-*-*-*-*-*-*-*-*-*-*-*-*-*-*-*-*-*-*-*-*-*-*-*-*
```
** TT Transaction Type
AF
CP
OW
PA
RP
SV
PW
CO
DO
OM
OR
RA
RJ
RO
RU
CA
DS
JD
NA
PS
SE
** SO (Sort Order)
Object
Job
Program
** MG (Message)
AF (Authority Failure)
CP (Create/Change/Restore User Profile)
OW (Changes to Object Ownership)
PA (Changes to Programs: Adopt)
RP (Restore of Programs: Adopt)
SV (Changes to System Values)
PW (Password Invalid)

```
    CO (Create Object)
    DO (Delete Object)
    OM (Object Move or Rename)
    OR (Object Restore)
    RA (Authority Change during Restore)
    RJ (Restoring Job Desc with User specified)
    RO (Change Object Owner during Restore)
    RU (Restoring User Profile Authority)
    CA (Authority Changes)
    DS (DST Security Password Reset)
    JD (Change of USER parameter on JOBD)
    NA (Network Attribute Changed)
    PS (Profile Swap)
    SE (Subsystem Reouting Entry Changed)
    ?? (Unknown Type)
 ** VT (Violation Type)                                      |
    A: User not authorized to operation or object.
    B: Program ran a restricted MI instruction
    C: Validation Failure (See Validation Value)
    D: Use of unsupported interface: Domain Failure.
    J: Attempt to submit job with unauthorised USRPRF.
    S: Attempt to signon without user ID or password.
    R: Hardware Protection Error.
    P: Profile swap error: not valid on QWTSETP
     : Unknown violation type.
 ** VV (Violation Value)                                     |
    A: Changed object restored that violates security.
    B: Object restore and all authority revoked.
    C: PGM validation failure: Translated PGM Restored
    D: Changed object restored by security officer.
    E: System install time error detected.
```

GPHRSCDTA   Graph Resource Data

This program prints a bar chart illustration that reflects resource usage by individuals or departments. Users may request to view processor (CPU), database (IO), or report (SPL) utilization information.

```
/*-*-*-*-*-*-*-*-*-*-*-*-*-*-*-*-*-*-*-*-*-*-*-*-*-*-*-*/
/*     OBJECT NAME : GPHRSCDTA                        */
/*                                                    */
/*                 : JP                               */
/*-*-*-*-*-*-*-*-*-*-*-*-*-*-*-*-*-*-*-*-*-*-*-*-*-*-*-*/
   CMD   PROMPT('GRAPH RESOURCE ACCOUNTING DATA')
         PARM KWD(NAME) TYPE(*CHAR) LEN(15) DFT(*ALL) +
```

```
                    PROMPT('Department or User name')
            PARM   KWD(TYPE) TYPE(*CHAR) LEN(10) RSTD(*YES) +
                    DFT(*USER) SPCVAL((*USER) (*DEPT)) +
                    PROMPT('Type of Inquiry')
            PARM   KWD(PERIOD) TYPE(*CHAR) LEN(10) RSTD(*YES) +
                    DFT(*DAILY) SPCVAL((*DAILY) +
                    (*MONTHLY) (*YEARLY)) PROMPT('Inquiry by +
                    Period')
            PARM   KWD(DATA) TYPE(*CHAR) LEN(10) RSTD(*YES) +
                    DFT(*CPU) SPCVAL((*CPU) (*IO) (*SPL)) +
                    PROMPT('Data to Graph')
            PARM   KWD(SKIP) TYPE(*CHAR) LEN(4) RSTD(*YES) +
                    DFT(*NO) SPCVAL((*YES) (*NO)) PMTCTL(P1) +
                    PROMPT('Skip Weekends')

  P1:      PMTCTL CTL(PERIOD) COND((*EQ *DAILY))
/*-*-*-*-*-*-*-*-*-*-*-*-*-*-*-*-*-*-*-*-*-*-*-*-*-*-*-*-*-*/
/*-*-*-*-*-*-*-*-*-*-*-*-*-*-*-*-*-*-*-*-*-*-*-*-*-*-*-*-*-*/



/*-*-*-*-*-*-*-*-*-*-*-*-*-*-*-*-*-*-*-*-*-*-*-*-*-*-*-*-*-*-*/
/*           OBJECT : GPHRSCDTA0                              */
/*                                                            */
/*                  : JP                                      */
/*-*-*-*-*-*-*-*-*-*-*-*-*-*-*-*-*-*-*-*-*-*-*-*-*-*-*-*-*-*-*/
PGM     PARM(&NAME &TYPE &MTHD &DATA &SKIP)
        DCL    VAR(&NAME) TYPE(*CHAR) LEN(15)
        DCL    VAR(&TYPE) TYPE(*CHAR) LEN(10)
        DCL    VAR(&MTHD) TYPE(*CHAR) LEN(10)
        DCL    VAR(&DATA) TYPE(*CHAR) LEN(10)
        DCL    VAR(&SKIP) TYPE(*CHAR) LEN(4)
        DCL    VAR(&JOBT) TYPE(*CHAR) LEN(1)
        MONMSG MSGID(CPF0000)

        RTVJOBA TYPE(&JOBT)
        IF     COND(&JOBT *EQ '1') THEN(DO)
               SBMJOB  CMD(GPHRSCDTA NAME(&NAME) TYPE(&TYPE) +
                           PERIOD(&MTHD) DATA(&DATA) SKIP(&SKIP)) +
                           JOB(GPHRSCDTA)
               GOTO    CMDLBL(RETRN)
        ENDDO

        DSPJRN JRN(QACGJRN) JRNCDE(A) ENTTYP(JB) OUTPUT(*OUTFILE) +
                OUTFILE(SMDR1) OUTMBR(*FIRST *ADD)
        CHGJRN JRN(QACGJRN) JRNRCV(*GEN) SEQOPT(*RESET)
        CALL   PGM(GPHRSCDTA5)
```

```
            RGZPFM       FILE(SMDR1)

            TFRCTL       PGM(GPHRSCDTA1) PARM(&NAME &TYPE &MTHD &DATA &SKIP)
            RETRN:       RCLRSC     LVL(*CALLER)
 ENDPGM
 /*-*-*-*-*-*-*-*-*-*-*-*-*-*-*-*-*-*-*-*-*-*-*-*-*-*-*-*-*-*-*-*-*-*/
 /*-*-*-*-*-*-*-*-*-*-*-*-*-*-*-*-*-*-*-*-*-*-*-*-*-*-*-*-*-*-*-*-*-*/


            **-*-*-*-*-*-*-*-*-*-*-*-*-*-*-*-*-*-*-*-*-*-*-*-*-*-*-*-*
            **      OBJECT NAME : GPHRSCDTA1
            **
            **                 : JP
            **-*-*-*-*-*-*-*-*-*-*-*-*-*-*-*-*-*-*-*-*-*-*-*-*-*-*-*-*
            FGPHRSCD20   E                   PRINTER     KINFDS PRT#DS
            FSMDR1   IF  E          K        DISK
            F            QWTJAJBE                        KRENAMESMRR1
            FSMDR11  IF  E          K        DISK
            F            QWTJAJBE                        KRENAMESMRR11
            **-*-*-*-*-*-*-*-*-*-*-*-*-*-*-*-*-*-*-*-*-*-*-*-*-*-*-*-*
            E                   A00         198  1
            E                   BAR         50198
            **
            E                   SYS         45 15 0
            E                   OBJ         45 15 0
            E                   PCT         45  5 2
            E                   PRD         45  6
            E                   DAY         45  6
            **
            E                   TXT          1  1 20
            **-*-*-*-*-*-*-*-*-*-*-*-*-*-*-*-*-*-*-*-*-*-*-*-*-*-*-*-*
            IPRT#DS      DS
            I                                  *FILE    FIL#01
            I                                  *RECORD  FMT#01
            I                                      93 102 STLBF1
            I                                    B 152 1530ST#LP#
            I                                    B 154 1550STCOLS
            I                                    B 188 1890ST#OVF
            I                                    B 367 3680STLINE
            I                                    B 369 3720STPAGE
            **-*-*-*-*-*
            IPGM#DS      SDS
            I                                  *PROGRAM ST#PRG
            I                                       40  42 STEXTP
            I                                       43  46 ST#EX#
            I                                       91 170 ST#MSG
```

252 *APPENDIX*

```
I                                    244 253 ST#JOB
I                                    254 263 ST#USR
I                                    264 2690STJOB#
**-*-*-*-*-*
ISCREEN       DS                        9900
I                                      19900 BAR
I                                       1 198 LINE01
I                                     199 396 LINE02
I                                     397 594 LINE03
I                                     595 792 LINE04
I                                     793 990 LINE05
I                                     9911188 LINE06
I                                    11891386 LINE07
I                                    13871584 LINE08
I                                    15851782 LINE09
I                                    17831980 LINE10
I                                    19812178 LINE11
I                                    21792376 LINE12
I                                    23772574 LINE13
I                                    25752772 LINE14
I                                    27732970 LINE15
I                                    29713168 LINE16
I                                    31693366 LINE17
I                                    33673564 LINE18
I                                    35653762 LINE19
I                                    37633960 LINE20
I                                    39614158 LINE21
I                                    41594356 LINE22
I                                    43574554 LINE23
I                                    45554752 LINE24
I                                    47534950 LINE25
I                                    49515148 LINE26
I                                    51495346 LINE27
I                                    53475544 LINE28
I                                    55455742 LINE29
I                                    57435940 LINE30
I                                    59416138 LINE31
I                                    61396336 LINE32
I                                    63376534 LINE33
I                                    65356732 LINE34
I                                    67336930 LINE35
I                                    69317128 LINE36
I                                    71297326 LINE37
I                                    73277524 LINE38
I                                    75257722 LINE39
I                                    77237920 LINE40
```

SAMPLE PROGRAMS   253

```
I                                          79218118 LINE41
I                                          81198316 LINE42
I                                          83178514 LINE43
I                                          85158712 LINE44
I                                          87138910 LINE45
I                                          89119108 LINE46
I                                          91099306 LINE47
I                                          93079504 LINE48
I                                          95059702 LINE49
I                                          97039900 LINE50
**-*-*-*-*-*
ICONSTN       DS                               10
I I              'GPHRSCDTA3'           1    10 CALCIT
**-*-*-*-*-*-*-*-*-*-*-*-*-*-*-*-*-*-*-*-*-*-*-*-*-*-*
C            *ENTRY     PLIST
C                       PARM           $NAME$ 15
C                       PARM           #TYPE# 10
C                       PARM           #MTHD# 10
C                       PARM           #DATA# 10
C                       PARM           #SKIP#  4
**-*-*-*-*-*-*-*-*-*-*-*-*-*-*-*-*-*-*-*-*-*-*-*-*-*-*
C            J12LST     PLIST
C                       PARM           #NAME# 15
C                       PARM           #TYPE#
C                       PARM           #MTHD#
C                       PARM           #DATA#
C                       PARM           #SKIP#
C                       PARM           SYS
C                       PARM           OBJ
C                       PARM           PCT
C                       PARM           PRD
C                       PARM           DAY
**-*-*-*-*-*-*-*-*-*-*-*-*-*-*-*-*-*-*-*-*-*-*-*-*-*-*
C                       MOVEL'#####'   ###### 5
C                       MOVEL'     '   BLANKS 5
C                       MOVEL$NAME$    @NAME@ 10
C                       Z-ADD2         #SCALE 30
**
C            #TYPE#     IFEQ '*DEPT'
C            $NAME$     SETLLSMRR11
C            $NAME$     IFNE '*ALL'
C            $NAME$     READESMRR11                01
C                       ELSE
C                       READ SMRR11                01
C                       END
C            *IN01      DOWEQ'0'
```

```
C                    MOVE *BLANK    #NAME#
C                    MOVELJACDE     #NAME#
C                    EXSR PGRAPH
C          JACDE     SETGTSMRR11
C          $NAME$    IFNE '*ALL'
C          $NAME$    READESMRR11                    01
C                    ELSE
C                    READ SMRR11                    01
C                    END
C                    END
C                    ELSE
**
C          @NAME@    SETLLSMRR1
C          @NAME@    IFNE '*ALL'
C          @NAME@    READESMRR1                     01
C                    ELSE
C                    READ SMRR1                     01
C                    END
C          *IN01     DOWEQ'0'
C                    MOVE *BLANK    #NAME#
C                    MOVELJAUSER    #NAME#
C                    EXSR PGRAPH
C          JAUSER    SETGTSMRR1
C          @NAME@    IFNE '*ALL'
C          @NAME@    READESMRR1                     01
C                    ELSE
C                    READ SMRR1                     01
C                    END
C                    END
C                    END
**
C                    CALL 'QCMDEXC'                 99
C                    PARM 'RCLRSC'  C#CMND 80
C                    PARM 80        C#LNTH 155
**
C                    MOVE '1'       *INLR
C                    RETRN
**-*-*-*-*-*-*-*-*-*-*-*-*-*-*-*-*-*-*-*-*-*-*-*-*-*-*-*-
C          PGRAPH    BEGSR
C                    CALL CALCIT    J12LST          99
C          #SCALE    MULT 50        @SCALE 52
C          #SCALE    DIV  2         @ROUND 52
C                    MOVEAPRD,1     LEDGND
C                    MOVEADAY,1     FOOTER
C                    MOVEA*BLANK    BAR
C                    EXSR PRTFLD
```

SAMPLE PROGRAMS   255

```
 **
 C                       Z-ADD1         T0        50
 C           T0          DOWLE50
 C                       Z-ADD1         T1        50
 C                       Z-ADD1         T2        50
 C                       Z-ADD1         T3        50
 C                       MOVEA*BLANK    A00
 **
 C           T2          DOWLE31
 C           PCT,T1      ADD   @ROUND   #ROUND    52
 C           #ROUND      IFGE  @SCALE
 C                       MOVEA######    A00,T3
 C                       ELSE
 C                       MOVEABLANKS    A00,T3
 C                       END
 C                       ADD   1        T1
 C                       ADD   1        T2
 C                       ADD   6        T3
 C                       END
 **
 C                       MOVEAA00       BAR,T0
 C                       SUB   #SCALE   @SCALE
 C                       ADD   1        T0
 C                       END
 **
 C                       Z-ADD1         T0
 C                       MOVEA*BLANK    A00
 C                       MOVEA#MTHD#    A00,1
 C           ' '         LOKUPA00,T0                99
 C           *IN99       IFEQ  '1'
 C                       ADD   1        T0
 C                       MOVEATXT,1     A00,T0
 C                       ADD   18       T0
 C                       MOVEA#NAME#    A00,T0
 C                       MOVEAA00,1     LINE00
 C                       END
 **
 C                       WRITEPAGE#1              51
 C                       WRITEPAGE#2              51
 C                       ENDSR
 **-*-*-*-*-*-*-*-*-*-*-*-*-*-*-*-*-*-*-*-*-*-*-*-*-*-*
 C           PRTFLD      BEGSR
 C                       Z-ADDPCT,1     P01
 C                       Z-ADDPCT,2     P02
 C                       Z-ADDPCT,3     P03
 C                       Z-ADDPCT,4     P04
```

```
C                       Z-ADDPCT,5      P05
C                       Z-ADDPCT,6      P06
C                       Z-ADDPCT,7      P07
C                       Z-ADDPCT,8      P08
C                       Z-ADDPCT,9      P09
C                       Z-ADDPCT,10     P10
C                       Z-ADDPCT,11     P11
C                       Z-ADDPCT,12     P12
C                       Z-ADDPCT,13     P13
C                       Z-ADDPCT,14     P14
C                       Z-ADDPCT,15     P15
C                       Z-ADDPCT,16     P16
C                       Z-ADDPCT,17     P17
C                       Z-ADDPCT,18     P18
C                       Z-ADDPCT,19     P19
C                       Z-ADDPCT,20     P20
C                       Z-ADDPCT,21     P21
C                       Z-ADDPCT,22     P22
C                       Z-ADDPCT,23     P23
C                       Z-ADDPCT,24     P24
C                       Z-ADDPCT,25     P25
C                       Z-ADDPCT,26     P26
C                       Z-ADDPCT,27     P27
C                       Z-ADDPCT,28     P28
C                       Z-ADDPCT,29     P29
C                       Z-ADDPCT,30     P30
C                       Z-ADDPCT,31     P31
 **
C                       Z-ADD@SCALE     HGHT01
C            HGHT01     SUB   #SCALE    HGHT02
C            HGHT02     SUB   #SCALE    HGHT03
C            HGHT03     SUB   #SCALE    HGHT04
C            HGHT04     SUB   #SCALE    HGHT05
C            HGHT05     SUB   #SCALE    HGHT06
C            HGHT06     SUB   #SCALE    HGHT07
C            HGHT07     SUB   #SCALE    HGHT08
C            HGHT08     SUB   #SCALE    HGHT09
C            HGHT09     SUB   #SCALE    HGHT10
C            HGHT10     SUB   #SCALE    HGHT11
C            HGHT11     SUB   #SCALE    HGHT12
C            HGHT12     SUB   #SCALE    HGHT13
C            HGHT13     SUB   #SCALE    HGHT14
C            HGHT14     SUB   #SCALE    HGHT15
C            HGHT15     SUB   #SCALE    HGHT16
C            HGHT16     SUB   #SCALE    HGHT17
C            HGHT17     SUB   #SCALE    HGHT18
```

```
C                HGHT18   SUB   #SCALE   HGHT19
C                HGHT19   SUB   #SCALE   HGHT20
C                HGHT20   SUB   #SCALE   HGHT21
C                HGHT21   SUB   #SCALE   HGHT22
C                HGHT22   SUB   #SCALE   HGHT23
C                HGHT23   SUB   #SCALE   HGHT24
C                HGHT24   SUB   #SCALE   HGHT25
C                HGHT25   SUB   #SCALE   HGHT26
C                HGHT26   SUB   #SCALE   HGHT27
C                HGHT27   SUB   #SCALE   HGHT28
C                HGHT28   SUB   #SCALE   HGHT29
C                HGHT29   SUB   #SCALE   HGHT30
C                HGHT30   SUB   #SCALE   HGHT31
C                HGHT31   SUB   #SCALE   HGHT32
C                HGHT32   SUB   #SCALE   HGHT33
C                HGHT33   SUB   #SCALE   HGHT34
C                HGHT34   SUB   #SCALE   HGHT35
C                HGHT35   SUB   #SCALE   HGHT36
C                HGHT36   SUB   #SCALE   HGHT37
C                HGHT37   SUB   #SCALE   HGHT38
C                HGHT38   SUB   #SCALE   HGHT39
C                HGHT39   SUB   #SCALE   HGHT40
C                HGHT40   SUB   #SCALE   HGHT41
C                HGHT41   SUB   #SCALE   HGHT42
C                HGHT42   SUB   #SCALE   HGHT43
C                HGHT43   SUB   #SCALE   HGHT44
C                HGHT44   SUB   #SCALE   HGHT45
C                HGHT45   SUB   #SCALE   HGHT46
C                HGHT46   SUB   #SCALE   HGHT47
C                HGHT47   SUB   #SCALE   HGHT48
C                HGHT48   SUB   #SCALE   HGHT49
C                HGHT49   SUB   #SCALE   HGHT50
C                         ENDSR
 **-*-*-*-*-*-*-*-*-*-*-*-*-*-*-*-*-*-*-*-*-*-*-*-*-*-*-*-*-*
**
computer usage by


            **-*-*-*-*-*-*-*-*-*-*-*-*-*-*-*-*-*-*-*-*-*-*-*-*-*-*-*-*-*
            **         OBJECT : GPHRSCDTA3
            **
            **                : JP
            **-*-*-*-*-*-*-*-*-*-*-*-*-*-*-*-*-*-*-*-*-*-*-*-*-*-*-*-*-*
            FSMDR16   IF   E              K        DISK
            F              QWTJAJBE                                  KRENAMESMRR16
            FSMDR17   IF   E              K        DISK
```

APPENDIX

```
         F          QWTJAJBE                        KRENAMESMRR17
         **-*-*-*-*-*-*-*-*-*-*-*-*-*-*-*-*-*-*-*-*-*-*-*-*-*-*-*
         E                     SYS           45 15 0
         E                     OBJ           45 15 0
         E                     PCT           45  5 2
         E                     PRD           45  6
         E                     DAY           45  6
         **
         E                     MTH            1 12 5
         **-*-*-*-*-*-*-*-*-*-*-*-*-*-*-*-*-*-*-*-*-*-*-*-*-*-*-*
         IJASDTE    DS                         6
         I                                     1  2 MNTH
         I                                     3  4 DATE
         I                                     5  6 YEAR
         **-*-*-*-*-*
         IPERIOD    DS                         6
         I                                     1  2 PFX
         I                                     3  3 SEP
         I                                     4  5 SFX
         **-*-*-*-*-*
         I#PDAY#    DS                         5
         I                                     1  4 #PDAY
         **-*-*-*-*-*
         ICONSTN    DS                        10
         I I       'GPHRSCDTA4'                1 10 TOTALS
         **-*-*-*-*-*-*-*-*-*-*-*-*-*-*-*-*-*-*-*-*-*-*-*-*-*-*-*
         C          *ENTRY     PLIST
         C                     PARM     #NAME# 15
         C                     PARM     #TYPE# 10     *USER *DEPT
         C                     PARM     #MTHD# 10     *YR *MN *WK *DY
         C                     PARM     #DATA# 10     *CPU *IO *SPL
         C                     PARM     #SKIP#  4     *YES *NO
         C                     PARM       SYS
         C                     PARM       OBJ
         C                     PARM       PCT
         C                     PARM       PRD
         C                     PARM       DAY
         **-*-*-*-*-*-*-*-*-*-*-*-*-*-*-*-*-*-*-*-*-*-*-*-*-*-*-*
         C          J1SLST     PLIST
         C                     PARM     S#DEPT  15
         C                     PARM     S#USER  10
         C                     PARM     S#CPU# 150
         C                     PARM     S#DIO# 150
         C                     PARM     S#SPL# 150
         C                     PARM     F#DATE  50
         C                     PARM     T#DATE  50
```

```
       **-*-*-*-*-*
     C          DTELST    PLIST
     C                    PARM            INDATE 10
     C                    PARM 'C'        DT#FMT  1
     C                    PARM 'MDY'      CODFMT  3
     C                    PARM            #PERRC  1
     C                    PARM            #P8DTE 80
     C                    PARM            #P6DTE 60
     C                    PARM            #PHDTE 50
     C                    PARM            #PEDTE 10
     C                    PARM            #PYR   40
     C                    PARM            #PCMON 20
     C                    PARM            #PCMTH  4
     C                    PARM            #PCDAY 20
     C                    PARM            #PDAY   4
     C                    PARM            #PMEND 20
     C                    PARM            #PLEAP 10
     C                    PARM            #EDITC  1
     C                    PARM            #PCDTE 12
     C                    PARM            #PFDTE 20
       **-*-*-*-*-*-*-*-*-*-*-*-*-*-*-*-*-*-*-*-*-*-*-*-*
     C          USR#YR    KLIST
     C                    KFLD            JAUSER
     C                    KFLD            JAYEAR
       **-*-*-*-*-*
     C          USR#MM    KLIST
     C                    KFLD            JAUSER
     C                    KFLD            JAYEAR
     C                    KFLD            JAMNTH
       **-*-*-*-*-*
     C          USR#DD    KLIST
     C                    KFLD            JAUSER
     C                    KFLD            JAYEAR
     C                    KFLD            JAMNTH
     C                    KFLD            JADAYS
       **-*-*-*-*-*
       **-*-*-*-*-*
     C          DPT#YR    KLIST
     C                    KFLD            JACDE
     C                    KFLD            JAYEAR
       **-*-*-*-*-*
     C          DPT#MM    KLIST
     C                    KFLD            JACDE
     C                    KFLD            JAYEAR
     C                    KFLD            JAMNTH
       **-*-*-*-*-*
```

```
C           DPT#DD      KLIST
C                       KFLD            JACDE
C                       KFLD            JAYEAR
C                       KFLD            JAMNTH
C                       KFLD            JADAYS
 **-*-*-*-*-*-*-*-*-*-*-*-*-*-*-*-*-*-*-*-*-*-*-*-*-*-*-*-*
C                       Z-ADD*ZEROS     SYS
C                       Z-ADD*ZEROS     OBJ
C                       Z-ADD*ZEROS     PCT
C                       MOVEA*BLANK     PRD
C                       MOVEA*BLANK     DAY
C                       MOVE '/'        SEP
C                       Z-ADD1          P1      50
C                       Z-ADD1          T1      50
 **
C                       MOVEL#NAME#     JACDE
C                       MOVEL#NAME#     JAUSER
C           #MTHD#      IFEQ '*DAILY'
C                       MOVE '01'       JADAYS
C                       MOVE UMONTH     JAMNTH
C                       MOVE UYEAR      JAYEAR
C                       END
C           #MTHD#      IFEQ '*MONTHLY'
C                       MOVE '01'       JADAYS
C                       MOVE '01'       JAMNTH
C                       MOVE UYEAR      JAYEAR
C                       END
C           #MTHD#      IFEQ '*YEARLY'
C                       MOVE '01'       JADAYS
C                       MOVE '01'       JAMNTH
C                       MOVE '91'       JAYEAR
C                       END
 **
C           #TYPE#      CASEQ'*USER'    #USER#
C           #TYPE#      CASEQ'*DEPT'    #DEPT#
C                       END
 **
C                       MOVE '1'        *INLR
C                       RETRN
 **-*-*-*-*-*-*-*-*-*-*-*-*-*-*-*-*-*-*-*-*-*-*-*-*-*-*-*-*
C           #USER#      BEGSR
 **
C           #MTHD#      CASEQ'*DAILY'   DD#USR
C           #MTHD#      CASEQ'*MONTHLY' MM#USR
C           #MTHD#      CASEQ'*YEARLY'  YY#USR
C                       END
```

```
 **
C                   ENDSR
 **-*-*-*-*-*-*-*-*-*-*-*-*-*-*-*-*-*-*-*-*-*-*-*-*-*
C         DD#USR    BEGSR
C         USR#MM    SETLLSMRR16
C         USR#MM    READESMRR16                    01
C         *IN01     DOWEQ'0'
C                   Z-ADDJARTGS   F#DATE
 **
C         *IN02     DOWEQ'0'
C         #DATA#    CASEQ'*CPU'   #CPU#S
C         #DATA#    CASEQ'*IO'    #DIO#S
C         #DATA#    CASEQ'*SPL'   #SPL#S
C                   END
C         USR#DD    READESMRR16                    02
C                   END
 **
C                   Z-ADD0        S#CPU#
C                   Z-ADD0        S#DIO#
C                   Z-ADD0        S#SPL#
C                   Z-ADDJARTGS   T#DATE
C                   CALL TOTALS   J1SLST         99
C         #DATA#    CASEQ'*CPU'   #CPU#T
C         #DATA#    CASEQ'*IO'    #DIO#T
C         #DATA#    CASEQ'*SPL'   #SPL#T
C                   END
 **
C                   MOVE MNTH     PFX
C                   MOVE DATE     SFX
C                   MOVEAPERIOD   PRD,P1
 **
C                   MOVE *BLANK   INDATE
C                   MOVE JASDTE   INDATE
C                   CALL 'MCPRTVDT'DTELST
 **
C         #SKIP#    IFEQ '*NO'
C                   MOVE #PDAY#   DAY,P1
C                   ADD  1        P1
C                   ELSE
C         #PDAY     IFNE 'SAT.'
C         #PDAY     ANDNE'SUN.'
C                   MOVE #PDAY#   DAY,P1
C                   ADD  1        P1
C                   ELSE
C                   Z-ADD0        SYS,P1
C                   Z-ADD0        OBJ,P1
```

```
C                       Z-ADD0          PCT,P1
C                       MOVE *BLANK     PRD,P1
C                       MOVE *BLANK     DAY,P1
C                       END
C                       END
**
C                       MOVE '0'        *IN02
C         USR#DD        SETGTSMRR16
C         USR#MM        READESMRR16                   01
C                       END
C                       ENDSR
**-*-*-*-*-*-*-*-*-*-*-*-*-*-*-*-*-*-*-*-*-*-*-*-*-*-*-*
C         MM#USR        BEGSR
C         USR#YR        SETLLSMRR16
C         USR#YR        READESMRR16                   01
C         *IN01         DOWEQ'0'
C                       Z-ADDJARTGS     F#DATE
**
C         *IN02         DOWEQ'0'
C         #DATA#        CASEQ'*CPU'     #CPU#S
C         #DATA#        CASEQ'*IO'      #DIO#S
C         #DATA#        CASEQ'*SPL'     #SPL#S
C                       END
C         USR#MM        READESMRR16                   02
C                       END
**
C                       Z-ADD0          S#CPU#
C                       Z-ADD0          S#DIO#
C                       Z-ADD0          S#SPL#
C                       Z-ADDJARTGS     T#DATE
C                       CALL TOTALS     J1SLST        99
C         #DATA#        CASEQ'*CPU'     #CPU#T
C         #DATA#        CASEQ'*IO'      #DIO#T
C         #DATA#        CASEQ'*SPL'     #SPL#T
C                       END
**
C                       MOVE MNTH       PFX
C                       MOVE YEAR       SFX
C                       MOVEAPERIOD     PRD,P1
**
C                       MOVE MNTH       T1
C                       MOVE MTH,T1     DAY,P1
**
C                       ADD  1          P1
C                       MOVE '0'        *IN02
C         USR#MM        SETGTSMRR16
```

```
C           USR#YR      READESMRR16                 01
C                       END
C                       ENDSR
**-*-*-*-*-*-*-*-*-*-*-*-*-*-*-*-*-*-*-*-*-*-*-*-*-*-*-*-*
C           YY#USR      BEGSR
C           JAUSER      SETLLSMRR16
C           JAUSER      READESMRR16                 01
C           *IN01       DOWEQ'0'
C                       Z-ADDJARTGS   F#DATE
**
C           *IN02       DOWEQ'0'
C           #DATA#      CASEQ'*CPU'   #CPU#S
C           #DATA#      CASEQ'*IO'    #DIO#S
C           #DATA#      CASEQ'*SPL'   #SPL#S
C                       END
C           USR#YR      READESMRR16                 02
C                       END
**
C                       Z-ADD0        S#CPU#
C                       Z-ADD0        S#DIO#
C                       Z-ADD0        S#SPL#
C                       Z-ADDJARTGS   T#DATE
C                       CALL TOTALS   J1SLST      99
C           #DATA#      CASEQ'*CPU'   #CPU#T
C           #DATA#      CASEQ'*IO'    #DIO#T
C           #DATA#      CASEQ'*SPL'   #SPL#T
C                       END
**
C                       MOVE YEAR     SFX
C                       MOVEAPERIOD   PRD,P1
**
C                       ADD  1        P1
C                       MOVE '0'      *IN02
C           USR#YR      SETGTSMRR16
C           JAUSER      READESMRR16                 01
C                       END
C                       ENDSR
**-*-*-*-*-*-*-*-*-*-*-*-*-*-*-*-*-*-*-*-*-*-*-*-*-*-*-*-*
C           #DEPT#      BEGSR
**
C           #MTHD#      CASEQ'*DAILY'   DD#DPT
C           #MTHD#      CASEQ'*MONTHLY' MM#DPT
C           #MTHD#      CASEQ'*YEARLY'  YY#DPT
C                       END
**
C                       ENDSR
```

APPENDIX

```
     **-*-*-*-*-*-*-*-*-*-*-*-*-*-*-*-*-*-*-*-*-*-*-*-*-*-*-*-*
C          DD#DPT    BEGSR
C          DPT#MM    SETLLSMRR17
C          DPT#MM    READESMRR17                      01
C          *IN01     DOWEQ'0'
C                    Z-ADDJARTGS    F#DATE
 **
C          *IN02     DOWEQ'0'
C          #DATA#    CASEQ'*CPU'    #CPU#S
C          #DATA#    CASEQ'*IO'     #DIO#S
C          #DATA#    CASEQ'*SPL'    #SPL#S
C                    END
C          DPT#DD    READESMRR17                      02
C                    END
 **
C                    Z-ADD0         S#CPU#
C                    Z-ADD0         S#DIO#
C                    Z-ADD0         S#SPL#
C                    Z-ADDJARTGS    T#DATE
C                    CALL TOTALS    J1SLST           99
C          #DATA#    CASEQ'*CPU'    #CPU#T
C          #DATA#    CASEQ'*IO'     #DIO#T
C          #DATA#    CASEQ'*SPL'    #SPL#T
C                    END
 **
C                    MOVE MNTH      PFX
C                    MOVE DATE      SFX
C                    MOVEAPERIOD    PRD,P1
 **
C                    MOVE *BLANK    INDATE
C                    MOVE JASDTE    INDATE
C                    CALL 'MCPRTVDT'DTELST
 **
C          #SKIP#    IFEQ '*NO'
C                    MOVE #PDAY#    DAY,P1
C                    ADD  1         P1
C                    ELSE
C          #PDAY     IFNE 'SAT.'
C          #PDAY     ANDNE'SUN.'
C                    MOVE #PDAY#    DAY,P1
C                    ADD  1         P1
C                    ELSE
C                    Z-ADD0         SYS,P1
C                    Z-ADD0         OBJ,P1
C                    Z-ADD0         PCT,P1
C                    MOVE *BLANK    PRD,P1
```

```
C                       MOVE *BLANK    DAY,P1
C                       END
C                       END
**
C                       MOVE '0'       *IN02
C          DPT#DD       SETGTSMRR17
C          DPT#MM       READESMRR17                  01
C                       END
C                       ENDSR
**-*-*-*-*-*-*-*-*-*-*-*-*-*-*-*-*-*-*-*-*-*-*-*-*-*-*-*
C          MM#DPT       BEGSR
C          DPT#YR       SETLLSMRR17
C          DPT#YR       READESMRR17                  01
C          *IN01        DOWEQ'0'
C                       Z-ADDJARTGS    F#DATE
**
C          *IN02        DOWEQ'0'
C          #DATA#       CASEQ'*CPU'    #CPU#S
C          #DATA#       CASEQ'*IO'     #DIO#S
C          #DATA#       CASEQ'*SPL'    #SPL#S
C                       END
C          DPT#MM       READESMRR17                  02
C                       END
**
C                       Z-ADD0         S#CPU#
C                       Z-ADD0         S#DIO#
C                       Z-ADD0         S#SPL#
C                       Z-ADDJARTGS    T#DATE
C                       CALL TOTALS    J1SLST        99
C          #DATA#       CASEQ'*CPU'    #CPU#T
C          #DATA#       CASEQ'*IO'     #DIO#T
C          #DATA#       CASEQ'*SPL'    #SPL#T
C                       END
**
C                       MOVE MNTH      PFX
C                       MOVE YEAR      SFX
C                       MOVEAPERIOD    PRD,P1
**
C                       MOVE MNTH      T1
C                       MOVE MTH,T1    DAY,P1
**
C                       ADD  1         P1
C                       MOVE '0'       *IN02
C          DPT#MM       SETGTSMRR17
C          DPT#YR       READESMRR17                  01
C                       END
```

```
C                    ENDSR
**-*-*-*-*-*-*-*-*-*-*-*-*-*-*-*-*-*-*-*-*-*-*-*-*-*-*-*-*
C           YY#DPT   BEGSR
C           JACDE    SETLLSMRR17
C           JACDE    READESMRR17                    01
C           *IN01    DOWEQ'0'
C                    Z-ADDJARTGS    F#DATE
**
C           *IN02    DOWEQ'0'
C           #DATA#   CASEQ'*CPU'    #CPU#S
C           #DATA#   CASEQ'*IO'     #DIO#S
C           #DATA#   CASEQ'*SPL'    #SPL#S
C                    END
C           DPT#YR   READESMRR17                    02
C                    END
**
C                    Z-ADD0         S#CPU#
C                    Z-ADD0         S#DIO#
C                    Z-ADD0         S#SPL#
C                    Z-ADDJARTGS    T#DATE
C                    CALL TOTALS    J1SLST          99
C           #DATA#   CASEQ'*CPU'    #CPU#T
C           #DATA#   CASEQ'*IO'     #DIO#T
C           #DATA#   CASEQ'*SPL'    #SPL#T
C                    END
**
C                    MOVE YEAR      SFX
C                    MOVEAPERIOD    PRD,P1
**
C                    ADD  1         P1
C                    MOVE '0'       *IN02
C           DPT#YR   SETGTSMRR17
C           JACDE    READESMRR17                    01
C                    END
C                    ENDSR
**-*-*-*-*-*-*-*-*-*-*-*-*-*-*-*-*-*-*-*-*-*-*-*-*-*-*-*-*
C           #CPU#S   BEGSR
C                    ADD  JACPU     OBJ,P1
C                    ENDSR
**-*-*-*-*-*-*-*-*-*-*-*-*-*-*-*-*-*-*-*-*-*-*-*-*-*-*-*-*
C           #DIO#S   BEGSR
C                    ADD  JAAUX     OBJ,P1
C                    ADD  JADBPT    OBJ,P1
C                    ADD  JADBGT    OBJ,P1
C                    ADD  JADBUP    OBJ,P1
C                    ENDSR
```

```
**-*-*-*-*-*-*-*-*-*-*-*-*-*-*-*-*-*-*-*-*-*-*-*-*-*-*-*-*-*
C              #SPL#S     BEGSR
C                         ADD  JAPAGE    OBJ,P1
C                         ENDSR
**-*-*-*-*-*-*-*-*-*-*-*-*-*-*-*-*-*-*-*-*-*-*-*-*-*-*-*-*-*
C              #CPU#T     BEGSR
C                         ADD  S#CPU#    SYS,P1
**
C              SYS,P1     IFGT 0
C              OBJ,P1     ANDGT0
C              OBJ,P1     MULT 100       N###15 150
C              N###15     DIV  SYS,P1    PCT,P1     H
C                         END
C                         ENDSR
**-*-*-*-*-*-*-*-*-*-*-*-*-*-*-*-*-*-*-*-*-*-*-*-*-*-*-*-*-*
C              #DIO#T     BEGSR
C                         ADD  S#DIO#    SYS,P1
**
C              SYS,P1     IFGT 0
C              OBJ,P1     ANDGT0
C              OBJ,P1     MULT 100       N###15
C              N###15     DIV  SYS,P1    PCT,P1     H
C                         END
C                         ENDSR
**-*-*-*-*-*-*-*-*-*-*-*-*-*-*-*-*-*-*-*-*-*-*-*-*-*-*-*-*-*
C              #SPL#T     BEGSR
C                         ADD  S#SPL#    SYS,P1
**
C              SYS,P1     IFGT 0
C              OBJ,P1     ANDGT0
C              OBJ,P1     MULT 100       N###15
C              N###15     DIV  SYS,P1    PCT,P1     H
C                         END
C                         ENDSR
**-*-*-*-*-*-*-*-*-*-*-*-*-*-*-*-*-*-*-*-*-*-*-*-*-*-*-*-*-*
**
JAN.
FEB.
MAR.
APR.
MAY.
JUN.
JUL.
AUG.
SEP.
OCT.
```

268 APPENDIX

NOV.
DEC.

```
**-*-*-*-*-*-*-*-*-*-*-*-*-*-*-*-*-*-*-*-*-*-*-*-*-*-*-*
**           OBJECT : GPHRSCDTA4
**
**                  : COPYRIGHT  SOFTWARE ARCHITECTS INTERNATIONAL
**
**                  : JP
**-*-*-*-*-*-*-*-*-*-*-*-*-*-*-*-*-*-*-*-*-*-*-*-*-*-*-*
FSMDR13  IF  E         K         DISK
**-*-*-*-*-*-*-*-*-*-*-*-*-*-*-*-*-*-*-*-*-*-*-*-*-*-*-*
C           *ENTRY    PLIST
C                     PARM           S#DEPT  15
C                     PARM           S#USER  10
C                     PARM           #CPU    150
C                     PARM           #DIO    150
C                     PARM           #SPL    150
C                     PARM           F#DATE  50
C                     PARM           T#DATE  50
**-*-*-*-*-*-*-*-*-*-*-*-*-*-*-*-*-*-*-*-*-*-*-*-*-*-*-*
C                     Z-ADD0         #CPU    150
C                     Z-ADD0         #DIO    150
C                     Z-ADD0         #SPL    150
**
**
C           F#DATE    SETLLQWTJAJBE
C                     READ QWTJAJBE                  01
C           *IN01     DOWEQ'0'
C           JARTGS    ANDLET#DATE
C                     MOVE '0'       *IN98
**
C           S#DEPT    IFNE *BLANK
C           S#DEPT    ANDNEJACDE
C                     MOVE '1'       *IN98
C                     END
**
C           S#USER    IFNE *BLANK
C           S#USER    ANDNEJAUSER
C                     MOVE '1'       *IN98
C                     END
**
C           *IN98     IFEQ '0'
C                     ADD  JACPU     #CPU
C                     ADD  JAPAGE    #SPL
```

```
C                   ADD  JAAUX     #DIO
C                   ADD  JADBPT    #DIO
C                   ADD  JADBGT    #DIO
C                   ADD  JADBUP    #DIO
C                   END
**
C                   READ QWTJAJBE                01
C                   END
**
**
C                   RETRN
**-*-*-*-*-*-*-*-*-*-*-*-*-*-*-*-*-*-*-*-*-*-*-*-*-*-*-*-*-*


**-*-*-*-*-*-*-*-*-*-*-*-*-*-*-*-*-*-*-*-*-*-*-*-*-*-*-*-*-*
**         OBJECT : GPHRSCDTA5
**
**                : COPYRIGHT   SOFTWARE ARCHITECTS INTERNATIONAL
**
**                : JP
**-*-*-*-*-*-*-*-*-*-*-*-*-*-*-*-*-*-*-*-*-*-*-*-*-*-*-*-*-*
FSMDR1   UF  E           K        DISK                         A
**-*-*-*-*-*-*-*-*-*-*-*-*-*-*-*-*-*-*-*-*-*-*-*-*-*-*-*-*-*
C           DTELST  PLIST
C                   PARM           INDATE 10
C                   PARM 'C'       DT#FMT  1
C                   PARM 'MDY'     CODFMT  3
C                   PARM           #PERRC  1
C                   PARM           #P8DTE 80
C                   PARM           #P6DTE 60
C                   PARM           #PHDTE 50
C                   PARM           #PEDTE 10
C                   PARM           #PYR   40
C                   PARM           #PCMON 20
C                   PARM           #PCMTH  4
C                   PARM           #PCDAY 20
C                   PARM           #PDAY   4
C                   PARM           #PMEND 20
C                   PARM           #PLEAP 10
C                   PARM           #EDITC  1
C                   PARM           #PCDTE 12
C                   PARM           #PFDTE 20
**-*-*-*-*-*-*-*-*-*-*-*-*-*-*-*-*-*-*-*-*-*-*-*-*-*-*-*-*-*
C           KEY003  KLIST
C                   KFLD           JAUSER
C                   KFLD           JASDTE
```

```
**-*-*-*-*-*-*-*-*-*-*-*-*-*-*-*-*-*-*-*-*-*-*-*-*-*
C           *LOVAL     SETLLQWTJAJBE
C                      READ  QWTJAJBE                       01
C           *IN01      DOWEQ'0'
C                      MOVE  *BLANK    INDATE
C                      MOVE  JASDTE    INDATE
C                      CALL  'MCPRTVDT'DTELST              99
C                      Z-ADD#PHDTE     JARTGS
C                      UPDATQWTJAJBE
C                      READ  QWTJAJBE                       01
C                      END
**
C           *LOVAL     SETLLQWTJAJBE
C                      READ  QWTJAJBE                       01
C           *IN01      DOWEQ'0'
C           *IN02      DOWEQ'0'
C           *IN03      DOWEQ'0'
C                      ADD   JACPU     CPU     150
C                      ADD   JAPAGE    SPL     150
C                      ADD   JAAUX     AUX     150
C                      ADD   JADBPT    DPT     150
C                      ADD   JADBGT    DGT     150
C                      ADD   JADBUP    DUP     150
C                      DELETQWTJAJBE
C           KEY003     READEQWTJAJBE                        03
C                      END
**
C                      Z-ADDCPU        JACPU
C                      Z-ADDSPL        JAPAGE
C                      Z-ADDAUX        JAAUX
C                      Z-ADDDPT        JADBPT
C                      Z-ADDDGT        JADBGT
C                      Z-ADDDUP        JADBUP
C                      WRITEQWTJAJBE
C                      Z-ADD0          CPU
C                      Z-ADD0          SPL
C                      Z-ADD0          AUX
C                      Z-ADD0          DPT
C                      Z-ADD0          DGT
C                      Z-ADD0          DUP
C                      MOVE  '0'       *IN03
C           KEY003     SETGTQWTJAJBE
C           JAUSER     READEQWTJAJBE                        02
C                      END
**
C                      MOVE  '0'       *IN02
```

```
C           JAUSER      SETGTQWTJAJBE
C                       READ QWTJAJBE                01
C                       END
**
C                       MOVE '1'        *INLR
C                       RETRN
**-*-*-*-*-*-*-*-*-*-*-*-*-*-*-*-*-*-*-*-*-*-*-*-*-*-*-*
```

PRTPRFMGT   Print Profile Management

This utility generates several reports, each of which focuses on a specific security-related issue, from indefinite password expiration duration to patched user profiles identification.

```
/*-*-*-*-*-*-*-*-*-*-*-*-*-*-*-*-*-*-*-*-*-*-*-*-*-*-*-*/
/*         OBJECT : PRTPRFMGT                          */
/*                                                     */
/*                : JP                                 */
/*-*-*-*-*-*-*-*-*-*-*-*-*-*-*-*-*-*-*-*-*-*-*-*-*-*-*-*/
CMD        PROMPT('PROFILE MANAGEMENT ANALYSIS')
/*-*-*-*-*-*-*-*-*-*-*-*-*-*-*-*-*-*-*-*-*-*-*-*-*-*-*-*/
/*-*-*-*-*-*-*-*-*-*-*-*-*-*-*-*-*-*-*-*-*-*-*-*-*-*-*-*/


/*-*-*-*-*-*-*-*-*-*-*-*-*-*-*-*-*-*-*-*-*-*-*-*-*-*-*-*/
/*         OBJECT : PRTPRFMGTO                         */
/*                                                     */
/*                : JP                                 */
/*-*-*-*-*-*-*-*-*-*-*-*-*-*-*-*-*-*-*-*-*-*-*-*-*-*-*-*/
PGM
    DCL       VAR(&JOBT) TYPE(*CHAR) LEN(1)
    DCLF      FILE(QUSER)
    MONMSG    MSGID(CPF0000)

    RTVJOBA   TYPE(&JOBT)
    IF        COND(&JOBT *EQ '1') THEN(DO)
      SBMJOB    CMD(PRTPRFMGT) JOB(PRTPRFMGT)
      GOTO      CMDLBL(RETRN)
    ENDDO

    WRKSYSVAL OUTPUT(*PRINT)

    DSPUSRPRF USRPRF(*ALL) TYPE(*BASIC) OUTPUT(*OUTFILE) +
                OUTFILE(QTEMP/QUSER) OUTMBR(*FIRST *REPLACE)
```

272   APPENDIX

```
RUNQRY      QRY(PRTPRFMGT1)     /* NoMax Password Duration                */
RUNQRY      QRY(PRTPRFMGT2)     /* Invalid signon attempts                */
RUNQRY      QRY(PRTPRFMGT3)     /* System Profiles with passwords         */
RUNQRY      QRY(PRTPRFMGT4)     /* Priviliged users with unlimited signons */
RUNQRY      QRY(PRTPRFMGT5)     /* Group profile authority adoption       */
RUNQRY      QRY(PRTPRFMGT6)     /* Patched User Profiles                  */

READF:      RCVF
            MONMSG    MSGID(CPF0864) EXEC(GOTO RETRN)
            IF        COND((&UPUPRF *EQ 'QSRV      ') *OR +
                            (&UPUPRF *EQ 'QSRVBAS   ') *OR +
                            (&UPUPRF *EQ 'QSYS      ') *OR +
                            (&UPUPRF *EQ 'QSPL      ') *OR +
                            (&UPUPRF *EQ 'QSPLJOB   ') *OR +
                            (&UPUPRF *EQ 'QRJE      ') *OR +
                            (&UPUPRF *EQ 'QDOC      ') *OR +
                            (&UPUPRF *EQ 'QFNC      ') *OR +
                            (&UPUPRF *EQ 'QSNADS    ') *OR +
                            (&UPUPRF *EQ 'QGATE     ') *OR +
                            (&UPUPRF *EQ 'QDFTOWN   ') *OR +
                            (&UPUPRF *EQ 'QTSTRQS   ') *OR +
                            (&UPUPRF *EQ 'QDSNX     ') *OR +
                            (&UPUPRF *EQ 'QLPAUTO   ') *OR +
                            (&UPUPRF *EQ 'QLPINSTALL') *OR +
                            (&UPUPRF *EQ 'QDBSHR    ')) +
                      THEN(GOTO CMDLBL(READF))

            IF        COND(&UPGRPF *NE '*NONE') +
                      THEN(GOTO CMDLBL(READF))

            IF        COND((&UPUSCL *EQ '*SECOFR   ') *OR +
                            (&UPUSCL *EQ '*SECADM   ')) +
                      THEN(DSPUSRPRF  USRPRF(&UPUPRF) +
                      TYPE(*ALL) OUTPUT(*PRINT))
            ELSE      CMD(DO)
            IF        COND((%SST(&UPSPAU  1 10) *EQ '*ALLOBJ   ') *OR +
                            (%SST(&UPSPAU 11 10) *EQ '*ALLOBJ   ') *OR +
                            (%SST(&UPSPAU 21 10) *EQ '*ALLOBJ   ') *OR +
                            (%SST(&UPSPAU 31 10) *EQ '*ALLOBJ   ') *OR +
                            (%SST(&UPSPAU 41 10) *EQ '*ALLOBJ   ') *OR +
                            (%SST(&UPSPAU 51 10) *EQ '*ALLOBJ   ') *OR +
                            (%SST(&UPSPAU 61 10) *EQ '*ALLOBJ   ')) THEN(DO)
                      DSPUSRPRF  USRPRF(&UPUPRF) +
                      TYPE(*ALL) OUTPUT(*PRINT)
                      GOTO    CMDLBL(READF)
                      ENDDO
```

```
                IF          COND((%SST(&UPSPAU  1 10) *EQ '*SECADM    ') *OR +
                                  (%SST(&UPSPAU 11 10) *EQ '*SECADM    ') *OR +
                                  (%SST(&UPSPAU 21 10) *EQ '*SECADM    ') *OR +
                                  (%SST(&UPSPAU 31 10) *EQ '*SECADM    ') *OR +
                                  (%SST(&UPSPAU 41 10) *EQ '*SECADM    ') *OR +
                                  (%SST(&UPSPAU 51 10) *EQ '*SECADM    ') *OR +
                                  (%SST(&UPSPAU 61 10) *EQ '*SECADM    ')) THEN(DO)
                            DSPUSRPRF  USRPRF(&UPUPRF) +
                            TYPE(*ALL) OUTPUT(*PRINT)
                            GOTO    CMDLBL(READF)
                            ENDDO

                IF          COND((%SST(&UPSPAU  1 10) *EQ '*AUDIT     ') *OR +
                                  (%SST(&UPSPAU 11 10) *EQ '*AUDIT     ') *OR +
                                  (%SST(&UPSPAU 21 10) *EQ '*AUDIT     ') *OR +
                                  (%SST(&UPSPAU 31 10) *EQ '*AUDIT     ') *OR +
                                  (%SST(&UPSPAU 41 10) *EQ '*AUDIT     ') *OR +
                                  (%SST(&UPSPAU 51 10) *EQ '*AUDIT     ') *OR +
                                  (%SST(&UPSPAU 61 10) *EQ '*AUDIT     ')) THEN(DO)
                            DSPUSRPRF  USRPRF(&UPUPRF) +
                            TYPE(*ALL) OUTPUT(*PRINT)
                            GOTO    CMDLBL(READF)
                            ENDDO

                IF          COND((%SST(&UPSPAU  1 10) *EQ '*SERVICE   ') *OR +
                                  (%SST(&UPSPAU 11 10) *EQ '*SERVICE   ') *OR +
                                  (%SST(&UPSPAU 21 10) *EQ '*SERVICE   ') *OR +
                                  (%SST(&UPSPAU 31 10) *EQ '*SERVICE   ') *OR +
                                  (%SST(&UPSPAU 41 10) *EQ '*SERVICE   ') *OR +
                                  (%SST(&UPSPAU 51 10) *EQ '*SERVICE   ') *OR +
                                  (%SST(&UPSPAU 61 10) *EQ '*SERVICE   ')) THEN(DO)
                            DSPUSRPRF  USRPRF(&UPUPRF) +
                            TYPE(*ALL) OUTPUT(*PRINT)
                            GOTO    CMDLBL(READF)
                            ENDDO
                ENDDO
                GOTO        CMDLBL(READF)
      RETRN:    DLTF        FILE(QTEMP/QUSER)

ENDPGM
/*-*-*-*-*-*-*-*-*-*-*-*-*-*-*-*-*-*-*-*-*-*-*-*-*-*-*-*-*-*/
/*-*-*-*-*-*-*-*-*-*-*-*-*-*-*-*-*-*-*-*-*-*-*-*-*-*-*-*-*-*/
```

DBF2SAVF   Database File to Save File Transfer

This is a simple installation program that assumes the source drive is A: and the current drive contains programs RMTCMD and RFROMPCB. This installation process requires the use of QIWSFLR shared folders. It also requires a connection to an AS/400 via an IBM PC Support router. Although the I: drive usually contains PC Support–related programs, if the programs found in the QIWSFLR shared folders have been downloaded to a local drive, the installation procedure may be executed from the local C:\PCS directory with much better performance results.

This installation procedure creates a temporary database file, save file, and a source file in the QUSRSYS library. A REXX procedure source member is uploaded into the QUSRSYS/QSAISRC(DBF2SAVF) source file and is subsequently changed to reflect the correct source type of REXX. The process continues with uploading of the actual product into the database file QUSRSYS/QSAI(QSAI). Once the product is transferred to the AS/400, the REXX procedure is activated to copy the database records into the savefile. The savefile is then restored into a product-specific library. The procedure terminates after it deletes all unnecessary objects.

```
/*-*-*-*-*-*-*-*-*-*-*-*-*-*-*-*-*-*-*-*-*-*-*-*-*-*-*-*-*-*/
/*          OBJECT : DBF2SAVF.REXX                          */
/*                                                          */
/*                 : JP                                     */
/*-*-*-*-*-*-*-*-*-*-*-*-*-*-*-*-*-*-*-*-*-*-*-*-*-*-*-*-*-*/
'OVRDBF FILE(STDIN) TOFILE(QUSRSYS/QSAI) MBR(QSAI)'
'OVRDBF FILE(STDOUT) TOFILE(QUSRSYS/QSAVF)'

Do forever
   Parse Linein Record
   If Record == '' then Leave
      Say Record
End

/*-*-*-*-*-*-*-*-*-*-*-*-*-*-*-*-*-*-*-*-*-*-*-*-*-*-*-*-*-*/
/*-*-*-*-*-*-*-*-*-*-*-*-*-*-*-*-*-*-*-*-*-*-*-*-*-*-*-*-*-*/
/*          OBJECT : INSTALL.BAT                            */
/*                                                          */
/*                 : JP                                     */
/*-*-*-*-*-*-*-*-*-*-*-*-*-*-*-*-*-*-*-*-*-*-*-*-*-*-*-*-*-*/
@echo off
rfrompcb a:\dbf2savf.tfr
rmtcmd "chgpfm file(qusrsys/qsaisrc) mbr(dbf2savf) srctype(rexx)" /z
```

```
          rmtcmd "crtpf file(qusrsys/qsai) rcdlen(528) size(*nomax)" /z
          rfrompcb a:\qsai.tfr
          rmtcmd "crtsavf file(qusrsys/qsavf)" /z
          rmtcmd "strrexprc srcmbr(dbf2savf) srcfile(qusrsys/qsaisrc)" /z
          rmtcmd "rstlib savlib(cau) dev(*savf) savf(qusrsys/qsavf)" /z
          rmtcmd "dltf file(qusrsys/qsaisrc)" /z
          rmtcmd "dltf file(qusrsys/qsai)" /z
          rmtcmd "dltf file(qusrsys/qsavf)" /z
          cls
          echo   Software has been installed.
          echo   Activate the utility by using the LICENSE command.
          echo   .
          echo   .  CAU/LICENSE (F4)
          echo   .
          echo   *** END ***
          /*-*-*-*-*-*-*-*-*-*-*-*-*-*-*-*-*-*-*-*-*-*-*-*-*-*-*-*-*-*-*/
```

LEMPLEZIV   IBM LZ1 Compression Technique

This program compresses data using the LZ1 compression technique indigenous to the AS/400 operating system. The program is written using Machine Interface language for best overall performance.

```
; /*-*-*-*-*-*-*-*-*-*-*-*-*-*-*-*-*-*-*-*-*-*-*-*-*-*-*-*-*-*-*-*/
; /*          OBJECT : LEMPLEZIV-1                                */
; /*                                                              */
; /*                 : IBM LZ1 Compression Technique              */
; /*                                                              */
; /*                 : Parameters                                 */
; /*                   SrcSiz      pkd(15,0)                      */
; /*                               Input - Source byte count to compress  */
; /*                               output- Actual compressed byte count   */
; /*                                                              */
; /*                   SnkSiz      pkd(15,0)  Target Space Size   */
; /*                               Input - Target space byte count available */
; /*                                                              */
; /*                   SrcSpcNam   char(20)                       */
; /*                               Input - LIBRARY/SPACENAME      */
; /*                                                              */
; /*                   SnkSpcNam   char(20)                       */
; /*                               Input - LIBRARY/SPACENAME      */
; /*                                                              */
; /*                 : If source size is > 0                      */
; /*                      compress source space contents to target. */
; /*                      output.: compressed byte count=SrcSiz   */
```

```
;   /*                      Else                                       */
;   /*                          decompress source space contents to target.  */
;   /*                          output.: decompressed byte count=SrcSiz   */
;   /*                      End                                        */
;   /*                                                                 */
;   /*                  To compress                                    */
;   /*                  ===========                                    */
;   /*                  : Create two user spaces, Source and Sink using the  */
;   /*                    QUSCRTUS API.                                */
;   /*                  : Insert the desired text to compress into the Source  */
;   /*                    user space using QUSCHGUS API.               */
;   /*                  : Calculate and specify the source text size in bytes  */
;   /*                    to compress. SrcSiz                          */
;   /*                  : Call LEMPLEZIV to compress.                  */
;   /*                  : Retrive the compressed data from the target space  */
;   /*                    using QUSRTVUS API.                          */
;   /*                  : Store the retrieved data to a permanent storage.  */
;   /*                                                                 */
;   /*                  To decompress                                  */
;   /*                  =============                                  */
;   /*                  : Create two user spaces, Source and Sink using the  */
;   /*                    QUSCRTUS API.                                */
;   /*                  : Insert the desired text to decompress into the Source  */
;   /*                    user space using QUSCHGUS API.               */
;   /*                  : Specify 0 in SrcSiz parameter to decompress data.  */
;   /*                  : Call LEMPLEZIV to decompress.                */
;   /*                  : Retrive the decompressed data from the target space  */
;   /*                    using QUSRTVUS API.                          */
;   /*                  : Store the retrieved data to a permanent storage.  */
;   /*                                                                 */
;   /*                                                                 */
;   /*                  : JP    6.3.93                                 */
;   /*-*-*-*-*-*-*-*-*-*-*-*-*-*-*-*-*-*-*-*-*-*-*-*-*-*-*-*-*-*-*-*-*/
;   ENTRY * (*ENTRY)   EXT
;           DCL SPCPTR P01 PARM
;           DCL SPCPTR P02 PARM
;           DCL SPCPTR P03 PARM
;           DCL SPCPTR P04 PARM
;           DCL OL     *ENTRY (P01, P02, P03, P04) EXT PARM MIN(4)
;
;           DCL DD     SRCSIZ    PKD(15,0)    BAS(P01)
;           DCL DD     SNKSIZ    PKD(15,0)    BAS(P02)
;           DCL DD     SPCNAM    CHAR(20)     BAS(P03)
;           DCL DD     SPCOBJ    CHAR(10)     DEF(SPCNAM) POS(1)
;           DCL DD     SPCLIB    CHAR(10)     DEF(SPCNAM) POS(11)
;           DCL DD     SNKNAM    CHAR(20)     BAS(P04)
```

```
;           DCL DD      SNKOBJ  CHAR(10)    DEF(SNKNAM) POS(1)
;           DCL DD      SNKLIB  CHAR(10)    DEF(SNKNAM) POS(11)
;
;           DCL SYSPTR  P_SRCPTR
;           DCL SYSPTR  P_SNKPTR
;           DCL SYSPTR  QCTX_PTR
;           DCL SPCPTR  WCB_TEMP BASPCO     POS(65)
;           DCL DD      RSLV_PTR CHAR(34)   AUTO
;           DCL DD      TST     CHAR(2)     DEF(RSLV_PTR) POS(1)
;           DCL DD      OBJ     CHAR(30)    DEF(RSLV_PTR) POS(3)
;           DCL DD      AUT     CHAR(2)     DEF(RSLV_PTR) POS(33)
;
;           DCL DD      TEMPLATE CHAR(64)   BDRY(16)
;           DCL DD      T_SRCSIZ BIN(4)     DEF(TEMPLATE) POS(1)
;           DCL DD      T_SNKSIZ BIN(4)     DEF(TEMPLATE) POS(5)
;           DCL DD      T_RTNSIZ BIN(4)     DEF(TEMPLATE) POS(9)
;           DCL DD      T_ALGTHM BIN(2)     DEF(TEMPLATE) POS(13)
;           DCL SPCPTR  T_SRCPTR            DEF(TEMPLATE) POS(33)
;           DCL SPCPTR  T_SNKPTR            DEF(TEMPLATE) POS(49)
;           DCL SPCPTR  T_POINTR            INIT(TEMPLATE)
;
;           DCL EXCM    * EXCID(H'0000')  BP(ENDPGM) IGN CV('CPF')
;           DCL EXCM    * EXCID(H'2201')  BP(ENDPGM) IMD CV(X'00000000')
; /*-*-*-*-*-*-*-*-*-*-*-*-*-*-*-*-*-*-*-*-*-*-*-*-*-*-*-*-*-*-*-*-*-*/
; /*-*-*-*-*-*-*-*-*-*-*-*-*-*-*-*-*-*-*-*-*-*-*-*-*-*-*-*-*-*-*-*-*-*/
; LIB_01:
;           CMPBLA(B)   SPCLIB, 'QTEMP     '          /EQ(SPC_L1)
;           CMPBLA(B)   SPCLIB, '*LIBL     '          /EQ(SPC_L2)
;           CMPBLA(B)   SPCLIB, '          '          /EQ(SPC_L2)
; SPC_L0:
;           CPYBLA      TST,    X'0401'
;           CPYBLAP     OBJ,    SPCLIB,     ' '
;           RSLVSP      QCTX_PTR, RSLV_PTR, *,        X'0000'
;           CPYBLA      TST,    X'1934'
;           CPYBLAP     OBJ,    SPCOBJ,     ' '
;           RSLVSP      P_SRCPTR, RSLV_PTR, QCTX_PTR, X'0000'
;           B           LIB_02
; SPC_L1:
;           CPYBWP      QCTX_PTR, WCB_TEMP
;           CPYBLA      TST,    X'1934'
;           CPYBLAP     OBJ,    SPCOBJ,     ' '
;           RSLVSP      P_SRCPTR, RSLV_PTR, QCTX_PTR, X'0000'
;           B           LIB_02
; SPC_L2:
;           CPYBLA      TST,    X'1934'
;           CPYBLAP     OBJ,    SPCOBJ,     ' '
```

```
;          RSLVSP      P_SRCPTR, RSLV_PTR, *,          X'0000'
; LIB_02:
;          CMPBLA(B)   SNKLIB,   'QTEMP     '          /EQ(SNK_L1)
;          CMPBLA(B)   SNKLIB,   '*LIBL     '          /EQ(SNK_L2)
;          CMPBLA(B)   SNKLIB,   '          '          /EQ(SNK_L2)
; SNK_L0:
;          CPYBLA      TST,      X'0401'
;          CPYBLAP     OBJ,      SNKLIB,    ' '
;          RSLVSP      QCTX_PTR, RSLV_PTR, *,          X'0000'
;          CPYBLA      TST,      X'1934'
;          CPYBLAP     OBJ,      SNKOBJ,    ' '
;          RSLVSP      P_SNKPTR, RSLV_PTR, QCTX_PTR,   X'0000'
;          B           LIB_03
; SNK_L1:
;          CPYBWP      QCTX_PTR, WCB_TEMP
;          CPYBLA      TST,      X'1934'
;          CPYBLAP     OBJ,      SNKOBJ,    ' '
;          RSLVSP      P_SNKPTR, RSLV_PTR, QCTX_PTR,   X'0000'
;          B           LIB_03
; SNK_L2:
;          CPYBLA      TST,      X'1934'
;          CPYBLAP     OBJ,      SNKOBJ,    ' '
;          RSLVSP      P_SNKPTR, RSLV_PTR, *,          X'0000'
; LIB_03:
;          SETSPPFP    T_SRCPTR, P_SRCPTR
;          SETSPPFP    T_SNKPTR, P_SNKPTR
; CRUNCH :
;          CMPNV(B)    SRCSIZ, 0 /EQ(EXPAND)
;          CPYNV       T_SRCSIZ, SRCSIZ
;          CPYNV       T_SNKSIZ, SNKSIZ
;          CPYNV       T_RTNSIZ, 0
;          CPYNV       T_ALGTHM, 2
;          CPRDATA     T_POINTR
;          CPYNV       SRCSIZ,   T_RTNSIZ
;          B           ENDPGM
; EXPAND :
;          CPYNV       T_SNKSIZ, SNKSIZ
;          DCPDATA     T_POINTR
;          CPYNV       SRCSIZ,   T_RTNSIZ
; ENDPGM :
;          DEACTPG     *
;          RTX         *
; /*"/*'/* */PEND;;;
; /*-*-*-*-*-*-*-*-*-*-*-*-*-*-*-*-*-*-*-*-*-*-*-*-*-*-*-*-*-*-*-*/
; /*-*-*-*-*-*-*-*-*-*-*-*-*-*-*-*-*-*-*-*-*-*-*-*-*-*-*-*-*-*-*-*/
```

Bibliography

Books/Manuals

AS/400 Audit and Security Enhancements in OS/400 Release 3, First Edition, IBM GG24-3639, Feb. 1991.

AS/400 Basic Security Guide, Second Edition, IBM SC41-0047, Nov. 1993.

AS/400 Guide to Enabling C2 Security, First Edition, IBM SC41-0103, Nov. 1993.

AS/400 Machine Interface Functional Reference, Third Edition, IBM SC41-8226, Sept. 1993.

AS/400 Security Reference, Third Edition, IBM SC41-8083, Nov. 1993.

AS/400 System Programmer's Interface Reference, Third Edition, IBM SC41-8223, Nov. 1993.

AS/400 System Support: Diagnostic Aids, Second Edition, IBM LY21-0597, Sept. 1989.

AS/400 Work Management Guide, Third Edition, IBM SC41-8078, Nov. 1993.

Cooperative Processing and Graphical User Interfaces in an AS/400 Environment, First Edition, IBM GG24-3877-00, Nov. 1993.

Custer, Helen. *Inside Windows NT*, Microsoft Press, 1993.

IBM System/38 Control Program Facility Concepts Manual, Fourth Edition, IBM GC21-7729-3, Sept. 1984.

IBM System/38 Control Program Facility Logic Overviews and Component Description, Eighth Edition, IBM LY21-0571-7, Oct. 1986.

IBM System/38 Vertical Microcode Logic Overviews and Component Descriptions Manual, Seventh Edition, IBM SY21-0889-6, Oct. 1986.

Jennings, Karla. The Devouring Fungus: Tales of Computer Age, W. W. Norton & Company, 1990.

Managing Multiple AS/400s in a Peer Network, Third Edition, IBM GG24-3614, Mar. 1994.

PC Support/400 Application Program Interface Reference, First Edition, IBM SC41-8254, May 1991.

PC Support/400: DOS and OS/2 Technical Reference, First Edition, IBM SC41-8091, May 1991.

Articles

Abraham, Dolan, and Steven Double. *Transaction Security System*, IBM Systems Journal, v. 30, n. 2 (1991).

Anderson, Robert E. *A Network by Any Other Name...*, NEWS 3X/400, Jan. 1991.

Beckman, Mel. *Data Encryption*, NEWS 3X/400, Aug. 1994.

Conte, Paul. *OS/400 Level 30 Security Exposures*, NEWS 3X/400, Jan. 1990.

———*A Principled Approach to Computer Security*, NEWS 3X/400, Jan. 1990.

———*38/400 Authorization Implementation*, NEWS 3X/400, Jan. 1990.

Conn, Sandra. *A Client/Server View of Sales and Marketing*, AS/400, Oct. 1994.

Dawson, Mike. *Making Distributed Databases a Reality*, 3X/400 Systems Management, Sept. 1994.

Enck, John. *Asynch and Synch Without a Modem*, NEWS 3X/400, Jan. 1994.

Evans, Wayne O. *Security Patrol*, Midrange Computing, Sep. 1994.

Faubion, Trish. *Openness APIs: An Inside Look*, NEWS 3X/400, Mar. 1991.

Heidelberg, Jelan, and Carol Woodbury. *Using V3R1 Security Enhancements*, NEWS 3X/400, Aug. 1994.

Johnson, Steve. *S/370: An AS/400 Perspective*, NEWS 3X/400, Sept. 1991.

Jones, Ron. *Build a Client/Server Application*, NEWS 3X/400, Jan. 1994.

Kelley, Ken. *APIs: Gateways to System Function*, NEWS 3X/400, Mar. 1991.

Kelly, John. *Security Level 50: A Better Choice*, NEWS 3X/400, Jun. 1990.

Madden, Wayne. *The Evolution of Client "Serving,"* NEWS 3X/400, Jan. 1994.

———*Plan for Security*, NEWS 3X/400, Jan. 1990.

———*Implementing Field-Level Security*, NEWS 3X/400, Mar. 1994.

Meyers, Bryan. *Fluffing Up Your Security Blanket*, NEWS 3X/400, Dec. 1992.

Mueller, Bob. *Making It Tougher on the Bad Guys*, 3X/400 Systems Management, Aug. 1994.

Neely, Kris. *Client/Server Spotlight*, Midrange Computing, Aug. 1994.

Park, Joseph S. *A Reality Check for AS/400 Security*, NEWS 3X/400, Aug. 1994.

Rhodes, Wayne. *Strategies for Client/Server Development*, 3X/400 Systems Management, May 1994.

Russell, Michael. *Distributing Data with DDM++*, NEWS 3X/400, May 1992.

Soltise, Frank G. *The AS/400's Declaration of Independence*, NEWS 3X/400, May 1993.

———*Parallel Computing and the AS/400*, NEWS 3X/400, Jul. 1992.

Stansbury, Darry. *Network Security*, NEWS 3X/400, Feb. 1990.

Tipton, Bob. *How Hacker-Proof Is Your AS/400*, NEWS 3X/400, Aug. 1994.

Wandling, George. *Growing Mobile*, AS/400, Oct. 1994.

Wong, Ignatius. *Creating Client/Server Application with ODBC*, Midrange Computing, Aug. 1994.

Index

Accounting Code parameter, 39–40
advanced program-to-program communications (APPC), 58–59
altered objects, 103–116. *See also* patches
APIs (Application Program Interfaces), 99
    and object state rule, 20
    and security level 40, 100
    user domain/system state objects, 29
APPC (advanced program-to-program communications), 58–59
application
    developers, profiles, 168–169
    groups, 157
    object security, 77–78
Application Program Interfaces. *See* APIs
Application System/400. *See* AS/400
AS/400
    announced, 8
    design, 7–8
    history of, 8–9
    internal documentation, 8
    introduced, 96
    number of, 6
associated spaces, 44–45
auditing, 189–194
    audit controls, 28–31
    insulate systems auditing, 13
    resource usage audit, 201–208
    soul of a hacker, 209–221
    system values, 191–194
    user profiles, 195–200
authentication rules, and level 50, 22
authority, 173–181
    adoption, 49–52
    authorization lists, 47–48
    default propagation, 26
    exception management, 163–165
    Failure report, 192–193
    holders, 48–49
    job descriptions, 176–178
    libraries, 175–176
    management, 173–181
    object authorities, 173–175
    ownership, 45–46
    primary group, 52–54
    private, 46–47
    public, 12, 46
    resource, 58
    restored objects, 178–179
    saved objects, 178
    system objects, 179–181
    validation procedure, 52–53, 161
    verification process, 36
AUTOANS parameter, 68

B

backup and recovery, 183–187
    recovering security data, 184–185
    restoring objects, 185–186
    restoring programs, 186–187
    saving security data, 183–184
Bertrum, Jack, 7
BIND, 58–59
    validation, 59
"blue box", 133

C

Captain Crunch, phone phreak, 132–133
Cary, Frank, 7
Change Journal (CHGJRN), 203
Change Object Primary Group (CHGOBJPGP), 160
Change Password (CHGPWD), 142
Change Program (CHGPGM), 51
Change Security Values (CHGSECVAL), 139–141
    disadvantage of, 140
    establish security journals, 202
    print security journal function, 192
    sample program, 227–229
Change User Audit (CHGUSRAUD), 203
Change User Profiles (CHGUSRPRF), 109
    password validation, 143
Check Object Integrity (CHKOBJITG), 215–216
client/server computing, 69–85
    application object concept, 76
    application object security, 77–78
    automated synchronization of security information, 77
    client platforms, 72–73
    concept, 70–72
    connections, 60–62

client/server computing (*continued*)
   data security, 83
   dataset object security, 79
   defined, 69
   environment security, 74–75
   field object security, 81–83
   folder object security, 75–77
   function object security, 80–81
   portable clients, 83–85
   role topology, 73–74
code names, 35
cold calls, 210–211
commands
   CHGDSTPWD, 37
   CHGJRN, 203
   CHGOBJPGP, 160
   CHGPGM, 51
   CHGPWD, 142
   CHGSECVAL, 139–141, 192, 202
      sample program, 227–229
   CHGUSRAUD, 203
   CHGUSRPRF, 109, 143
   CHKOBJITG, 215–216
   CRTAUTHDR, 49
   CRTUSRPRF, 158
   DLTAUTHLR, 49
   DLTOLDRCV, 141–142, 204
      sample program, 229–231
   DMPSYSOBJ, 111, 214, 215
   DMPTAP, 178
   DSPAUDLOG, 204
   DSPAUTUSR, 167, 197
   DSPOBJAUT, 49, 201
   DSPSYSVAL, 191
   EDTOBJAUT, 47, 49, 141, 174
   GRTOBJAUT, 49
   LODRUN, 114
   PRTPRFMGT, 195
      sample program, 271–273
   PRTSECJRN, 192, 204
      sample program, 231–249
   RSTAUT, 184
   RSTCFG, 184
   RSTLIB, 184
   RSTOBJ, 184, 186, 187
   RSTUSRPRF, 184
   RVKOBJAUT, 49
   SBMNETJOB, 60
   WRKOBJOWN, 47
   WRKSYSVAL, 139–140, 191
communication management, 55–68
   client/server connections, 60–62
   data encryption, 66–67
   device configuration, 67–68
   fundamental concepts, 57–59
   integrated file system, 63–65
   location passwords, 58
   PC workstations, 65–66
   shared folders, 62–63
   user exits, 59–60
company group security, 83
compilation process, 90–91
compression, 67
configuration, 67–68
Conte, Paul, 20, 98
controls
   audit, 28–31
   password, 23–24
   security, 25–27
cooperative processing, 71
CPF operating system
   as foundation, 87
   CPF3848 violation, 113, 114
   security, 88
Create Authority Holder (CRTAUTHDR), 49
Create User Profiles (CRTUSRPRF), 158
C2 security guidelines, 13, 21–23
   compliant software, 22
   QAUDENDACN, 30
   QTEMP library, 25
curiosity, and hacking, 211–212
customer support profiles, 171
cyberpunks, 209

D

data
   Database File to Save File transfer, 274–275
   encryption, 66–67
   recovering security data, 184–185
   saving security data, 183–184
   security, 83
Data Processing Operations, profiles, 167–168
dataset object security, 79
DDM (Distributed Data Management), 70–71
   vs. client/server access, 70
   what it provides, 70
DDMACC (Distributed Data Management Access), 60
   sample program, 226–227
Delete Authority Holder (DLTAUTHLR), 49
Delete Old Journal Receivers (DLTOLDRCV), 141–142, 204
   sample program, 229–231
device configuration, 67–68
Display Audit Logs (DSPAUDLOG), 204
Display Authorized User (DSPAUTUSR), 167, 197
Display Object Authority (DSPOBJAUT), 49, 201
Display System Values (DSPSYSVAL), 191
distributed data management (DDM), 70–71
   vs. client/server access, 70
   what it provides, 70
Distributed Data Management Access (DDMACC), 60
   sample program, 226–227
distributed processing concept, 70–71
DLL (Dynamic Link Library), 81
domain/state processing, 29
Draper, John, phone phreak, 132–133
Dump System Object (DMPSYSOBJ), 111, 214, 215
Dump Tape (DMPTAP), 178
Dynamic Link Library (DLL), 81

INDEX 285

E

Edit Object Authority
(EDTOBJAUT), 47, 49, 174
  sample, 141
eminent domain, 112–113
encapsulation, 10
  Encapsulate Program
    Architecture (EPA), 44
  program validation, 117
  what it ensures, 43
encryption
  APPC applications, 59
  data encryption, 66–67
  devices, 137–138
  passwords, 37, 59
EPA (Encapsulate Program
  Architecture), 44
exception management, 163–165
exits, user, 59–60

F

Fido, program, 209
5250 emulation software, 61
field object security, 81–83
file-driven operating system, 11
files, 11–12
folders
  object security, 75–77
  shared, 62–63
Foreign Corrupt Practices Act of
  1977 (FCPA), 14
FS project, 7–9
function object security, 80–81
functional spaces, 44–45
Future Systems project, 7–9

G

gift horses, virus, 213–221
Grant Object Authority
  (GRTOBJAUT), 49
GRiD Compass computers, 66
group owner concept, 160
group profiles
  audit report, 199–200
  creating, 157–158
  and passwords, 158
  special authorities, 35–37
  status, 158

H

hackers, 209–221
  assigning passwords, 37–38
  cold calls, 210–211
  and defaults, 34
  and Machine Interface layer, 9
  need to capture, 41
  password validation
    programs, 24
  social engineering, 34, 56, 209
  staff curiosity, 211–212
  System Entry Point table, 214
  tricks, 212–213
  virus, gift horses, 213–221
Hierarchial File System (HFS), 64
HMC (Horizontal Licensed
  Internal Code), 98
Horizontal Licensed Internal
  Code (HMC), 98

I

IBM
  Advanced Systems
    Development Division
    (ASDD), 7–8
  Future Systems project, 7–9
  and security level value 40,
    20–21
ICB (Invocation Control Block),
  118
IFS (integrated file system), 63–65
image integration feature, 62
image objects, 62–63
IMPI (Internal Micro-Program
  Instructions), 111, 115
Implementation, 129
  authority management,
    173–181
  backup and recovery, 183–187
  designing profiles, 155–171
  physical security, 131–138
  system values, 139–154
Information Resource
  Accounting program, 40
installation, of sample programs,
  223
integrated file system (IFS), 63–65
Intermediate Representation of
  Program (IRP), 90
internal intruders, 25–27
Internal Micro-Program
  Instructions (IMPI), 111, 115
Invocation Control Block (ICB),
  118
IRP (Intermediate Representation
  of Program), 90

J

J. Edgar Hoover, program,
  209–210
Job Action (JOBACN), 60
job description
  authority management,
    176–178
  patch, 104
journals
  delete journal receivers,
    141–142
  list of journal entries, 205–206
  Print Security Journal, 192,
    204, 231–249
  program failure journals, 206
  resource accounting journals,
    193–194
  security audit journals,
    192–193
  system security audit journals,
    202–206

K

Kerberos network security
  system, 56
KY-12 scramblers, 66

L

layered architecture, 9–11
Lemple Ziv 1 (LZ1) algorithm, 67
  sample program, 275–278
libraries
  authority management,
    175–176

libraries (*continued*)
    provide default authority to, 25
    security 50, 22
Layered Operating System
    concept, 9–10
lineman's set, 134
Load Run (LODRUN), 114

M

Machine Context, 63–64
Machine Interface. *See* MI
management, 1–16
    the assault, 3–16
    authority management, 173–181
    client/server issues, 69–85
    communication management, 55–68
    dream team, 13–14
    exception management, 163–165
    impact of altered objects, 103–116
    object management, 43–54
    object states and domains, 87–102
    program validation values, 117–126
    system values, 17–31
    user profiles, 33–41
message queue break handler, 40
MI (Machine Interface)
    compiler, 19
    exploitation of MI layer, 9
    IBM-supplied MI compiler, 96–97
    instructions, and System/38, 19
    introduction of AS/400, 96–97
    MI purpose, 93–95
    object types, 44
    program compilation process, 90–91
    secured access, 101–102
    security risks, 95
    VMC translator, 91–93
    what IBM considered hazardous, 96

Monolithic Operating System model, 9–10
Morris, Robert Tappan, 15

N

network
    administration, group profile, 170
    weakest link, 57
NEWS 3X/400, 20, 98

O

object design concept, 8
object domain rule, 20
    eminent domain, 112–113
    what it does, 20
objects
    altered, 103–116
    anatomy, 43–45
    associated spaces, 44–45
    authorities, 173–174
    authority adoption, 49–52
    authority holders, 48–49
    authorization lists, 47–48
    default authority, 25
    default owner, 185
    definition, 43
    encapsulation, 10
    and files, 11–12
    functional spaces, 44–45
    Machine Interface object types, 44
    management, 43–54
    name, 44
    object-oriented approach, 11–12
    object security, 18
    ownership authority, 45–46
    parts, 44–45
    primary group authority, 52–54
    private authority, 46–47
    public authority, 46
    restored, 178–179
    restoring, 185–186
    saved, 178
    system objects, 179–181

object states and domains, 20, 87–102
    background, 88–90
    concept, 20
    illustration, 99
    introduced, 87
    MI purpose, 93–95
    object domain attribute, 111–112
    object state attribute, 113–116
    object state rule, 20
    overcome object state/domain boundary, 111–112
    program compilation process, 90–91
    road less traveled, 91–93
Open Database Connectivity (ODBC) driver, 73
OS/400
    and EPA header information, 44
    MI instructions, removal of, 19
    object encapsulation, 10
    OS/400 layer, 9
    program validation value, 9
    predetermined attributes, 11
    version 1 release 3, 9, 100
    version 2 release 1, 9
    version 2 release 3, 21
    version 3, 9

P

passwords
    adjacent digits, 24
    changing, 142–143
    check for default passwords, 167
    CHGDSTPWD command, 37
    CHGPWD command, 142
    CHGUSRPRF command, 143
    cold calls, 210–222
    controls, 23–24
    default location password, 58
    encrypted passwords, 37
    expiration interval, 24, 37
    group profiles, 158

INDEX 287

hackers, assign passwords, 37–38
indefinite password duration, 195–196
insert into QSYS profile, 109
location passwords, 58, 68
minimum length, 24
operating system profiles, 38–39
"piping in", 74
privileged users, 198–199
repeating characters, 24
repeating passwords, 24
reports, 195–199
secret passwords, 37–39
security level value 20, 18
security level value 30, 21
security level value 40, 21
signon attempts, invalid, 196–197
system profiles with passwords report, 197
and user profile, 159
validation program, 24, 142–143, 231
patches
   Change User Profiles command, 109
   duplicate operating system program, 113
   Internal Micro-program Instructions, 111
   insert password into QSYS profile, 109
   job description patch, 104
   object domain attribute, 111–112, 114
   program example, 120–126
   program state attribute, 114
   and program validation values, 120–126
   report of altered profiles, 199
   screen swapping, 108–109
   System Entry Point Table, 106–108
   system work control block table, 104–106

turn user programs into system state programs, 113–115
PC Support Access (PCSACC), 60
   sample program, 225–226
PC workstations, 65–66
performance, and security level 50, 22
phone phreaks, 132–133, 134
   protocol analyzers, 134–137
physical security, 57–58, 131–138
   encryption devices, 137–138
   list of recommendations, 138
   local switches, 133–134
   phone phreaks, 132–134
   protocol analyzers, 134–137
   recommendations, 138
platforms, client/server, 72–73
portable clients, 83–85
POSIX-compliant QOpenSys file system, 63
PowerPC chips, 9
primary groups, 159–163
   authority, 52–54
Print Profile Management (PRTPRFMGT), 195–200
   group profile audit, 199–200
   indefinite password duration, 195–196
   invalid signon attempts, 196–197
   patched user profiles, 199
   privileged users, 198–199
   sample program, 271–273
   system profiles with passwords, 197–198
print program object, 216–220
Print Security Journal (PRTSECJRN), 192, 204
   sample program, 231–249
private authority, 46–47
privileged users report, 198–199
PRM (Program Resolution Monitor)
   access to in System 38, 8
   entry program, 93, 97
   and program compilation, 10, 90–91

profiles. *See also* group profiles; profiles, designing; reports; system profiles; user profiles
   auditing, 195–200
   creator's profile pointer, 45
   names, 34–35
   primary group authority, 52–54
   Print Profile Management, 195, 271–273
   security levels, 18, 21
profiles, designing, 155–171
   application development, 168–169
   application groups, 157
   customer support, 171
   data processing operations, 167–168
   exception management, 163–165
   group profiles, 157–158
   network administration, 170
   primary groups, 159–163
   security management, 170–171
   technical profiles, 165–167
   user profiles, 158–159
   work groups, 156–158
Program Resolution Monitor (PRM)
   access to in System 38, 8
   entry program, 93, 97
   and program compilation, 10, 90–91
programs. *See also* sample programs
   compilation process, 10, 90–91
   gift horses, 213–221
   object state and domain concept, 20
   OS/400 programs, 9
   print program objects, 216–220
   program failure journals, 206
   restoring, 186–187
   state/domain boundaries, 28–29
   user state programs, 29
program state attribute, 113–114

INDEX

program validation value, 100, 117–126
  how it is derived, 118
  patched program example, 120–126
  purpose of, 9, 20
  restoring programs, 186–187
  runtime verification, 118
  verification of, 28
program status flags, 9
Program Status Word, 9
protocol analyzers, 134–137
  and encryption devices, 137–138
public authority, 12, 46
  authority propagation, 26
  defaults, 46

Q

QACGJRN, 140
QACGLVL, 140, 146
  recommended value, 143
QALWOBJRST, 25, 146
  recommended value, 143
QALWUSRDMN, 25, 146
  recommended value, 144
QAUDCTL, 30, 146
  recommended value, 144
QAUDENDACN, 30, 146–147
  recommended value, 144
QAUDFRCLVL, 147
  recommended value, 144
QAUDLVL, 30, 147–148
  recommended value, 144
QAUTOVRT, 27, 68, 148–149
  recommended value, 144
QCRTAUT, 25, 149
  recommended value, 144
QCRTOBJAUD, 149
  recommended value, 144
QDDDUPDF program, 82
QDFTOWN, 52
QDLS file system, 64
QDSCJOBITV, 149–150
  recommended value, 144
QDSPSGNINF, 150
  recommended value, 144
QINACTITV, 25, 27, 150

recommended value, 144
QINACTMSGQ, 25, 150
  recommended value, 144
QINSEPT, 106–108
QLMTDEVSSN, 150
  recommended value, 144
QLMTSECOFR, 141, 150–151
  recommended value, 144
QMAXSGNACN, 68, 151
  recommended value, 145
QMAXSIGN, 151
  recommended value, 145
QPROCT table, 97, 98
QPRODT table, 97, 98
QPRROOTP, 19, 93, 97
QPWDEXPITV, 151
  recommended value, 145
QPWDLMTAJC, 151
  recommended value, 145
QPWDLMTCHR, 151–152
  recommended value, 145
QPWDLMTREP, 152
  recommended value, 145
QPWDMAXLEN, 152
  recommended value, 145
QPWDMINLEN, 152
  recommended value, 145
QPWDPOSDIF, 152
  recommended value, 145
QPWDRQDDGT, 152
  recommended value, 145
QPWDRQDDIF, 152
  recommended value, 145
QPWDVLDPGM, 142, 153
  recommended value, 145
QPWXCWN, 63
QRMTSIGN, 27, 153
  recommended value, 145
QRMTSIGNON, 59–60
QSECURITY, 18, 154
  recommended value, 145
QSYS, 19
  eminent domain, 112–113
  introduce as group profile, 39
  passwords, 38, 106, 109
  shared folders, 63
QTEMP library
  C2 guidelines, 25

duplicate display files, 82
QT3REQIO program, 132
QWCBT, 104, 106

R

recovery. *See* backup and recovery
reports, 195
  group profile audit, 199–200
  indefinite password duration, 195–196
  invalid signon attempts, 196–197
  patched user profiles, 199
  privileged users with unlimited access, 198–199
  system profiles with passwords, 197–198
resource accounting journals, 193–194
resource authority, 58
resource usage audit, 201–208
  program failure journals, 206–208
  system security journals, 202–206
Restore
  Authorities (RSTAUT), 184
  Configuration (RSTCFG), 184
  Library (RSTLIB), 184
  Object (RSTOBJ), 184, 186, 187
  verification of validation value, 28
  User Profiles (RSTUSRPRF), 184
Revoke Object Authority (RVKOBJAUT), 49
REXX, 60, 109, 179
RPG, 90, 93–94
root compiler program (QPRROOTP), 19

S

sample programs, 223–278
  Change Security Values, 227–229
  CHGSECVAL, 227–229

INDEX 289

Database File to Save File Transfer, 274–275
DBF2SAVF, 274–275
DDMACC, 226–227
Delete Old Journal Receivers, 229–231
Display Station Passthrough User Exit Program, 224–225
Distributed Data Management Access User Exit Program, 226–227
DLTOLDRCV, 229–231
DSPTPGM, 224–225
GPHRSCDTA, 249–271
Graph Resource Data, 249–271
IBM LZ1 Compression Technique, 275–278
Inactive Workstation Handling Program, 223–224
INACTMSGQ, 27, 223–224
installation of, 223
LEMPLEZIV, 275–278
PC Support Access User Exit Program, 225–226
PCSACC, 225–226
Print Security Journals, 231–249
Print Profile Management, 271–273
PRTPRFMGT, 271–273
PRTSECJRN, 231–249
Validate User Passwords, 231
VLDUSRPWD, 231
saved objects, 178
Save Security Data (SAVSECDTA), 184
SAVSCDTA, 184
scramblers, 66
screen swapping, 108–109
SDLC communications adapter, 61
SECURELOC parameter, 58
security
   audit journals, 192–193
   controls, 25–27
   fundamental concepts, 57–59
   levels, 17–23

main responsibility, 13–14
management, profile, 170–171
objective, 15–16
QSECURITY parameter, 18, 145, 154
scope of, 12–13
worst threat to, 110–112
security administrators
   backup and recovery, 183
   list of authorized users, 38–39
   privileged users report, 198–199
security journal entries, 205–206
security levels, 17–23
   BIND, 58
   CPF3848 message, 113, 114
   QSECURITY parameter, 18, 145, 154
SEPTWorm, 5–6
server. *See also* client/server computing
   function, 69
service tools, 134–137
shared folders, 62–63
sign-on
   invalid signon attempts report, 196–197
   QMAXSGNACN system value, 68
   QRMTSIGN parameter, 27
"Silver Lake" project, 96
social engineering, 34, 56, 209
software vendors
   MI language programs, 101
   security level 40, 20, 100
Spy, program, 209–210
state and domain concept. *See also* object states and domains
   audit controls, 28–29
   System/370, 20
   security level value 40, 20
status, group profiles', 158
Stoll, Clifford, 210
Submit Network Job (SBMNETJOB), 60

Synchronous Data Link Control communications adapter, 61
syntax check, 97
system auditing controls, 28–31. *See also* auditing
   identify anomaly, 30
   questionable items, 30–31
system configuration information, 191
system domain, 29
System Entry Point Table. *See* QINSEPT
system integrity problems, 9
   Authority Failure report, 192–193
   background, 88
   security level 30, 18
system objects, 179–181
system profiles
   compromised, 38–39
   default profiles, 37
   with passwords report, 197
System Service Tools (SST), 110, 111
system state attributes, 28
System/36
   authority holders, 48–49
   migrate to AS/400, 8
System/38
   debuted, 8
   high-level compilers, 8
   migrate to AS/400, 8
   MI technology, 95–98
   need for security level 40, 18–19
   object-oriented architecture, 8
   similarity to AS/400, 87
System/370, 8, 20
system values, 17–31, 139–154
   adjustments, 139–142
   audit controls, 28–31
   auditing, 191–194
   implementation, 139–154
   management, 17–31
   password controls, 23–24
   password validation, 142–143
   primary purpose, 17

290   INDEX

system values (*continued*)
    QACGLVL, 143, 146
    QALWOBJRST, 143, 146
    QALWUSRDMN, 144, 146
    QAUDCTL, 144, 146
    QAUDENDACN, 144, 146–147
    QAUDFRCLVL, 144, 147
    QAUDLVL, 144, 147–148
    QAUTOVRT, 144, 148–149
    QCRTAUT, 144, 149
    QCRTOBJAUD, 144, 149
    QDSCJOBITV, 144, 149–150
    QDSPSGNINF, 144, 150
    QINACTITV, 144, 150
    QINACTMSGQ, 144, 150
    QLMTDEVSSN, 144, 150
    QLMTSECOFR, 144, 150–151
    QMAXSGNACN, 145, 151
    QMAXSIGN, 145, 151
    QPWDEXPITV, 145, 151
    QPWDLMTAJC, 145, 151
    QPWDLMTCHR, 145, 151–152
    QPWDLMTREP, 145, 152
    QPWDMAXLEN, 145, 152
    QPWDMINLEN, 145, 152
    QPWDPOSDIF, 145, 152
    QPWDRQDDGT, 145, 152
    QPWDRQDDIF, 145, 152
    QPWDVLDPGM, 145, 153
    QRMTSIGN, 145, 153
    QSECURITY, 145, 154
    recommended values, 143–145
    resource accounting journals, 193–194
    security audit journals, 192–193
    security controls, 25–27
    security levels, 17–23
system work control block table. *See* QWCBT

T

technical profiles, 165–167

telephone
    lineman's set, 134
    local switches, 133–134
    phone phreaks, 132–133
    protocol analyzers, 134–137
Terse algorithm, 67
tricks, 212–213
Trojan horses, 14–15
    preventive measure, 215–216
Trusted Computer Evaluation Criteria, 21

U

United States Department of Defense, 21
UNIX group owner concept, 160
user domain, 29
    object domain attribute, 112
user exits, 59–60
user profiles, 33, 195–200
    Accounting Code parameter, 39–40
    application groups, 157
    auditing, 195–200
    authorization lists, 47–48
    Change User Profiles, 109, 143
    creating profiles, 158–159
    CRTUSRPRF, 158
    designing, 155–156
    management, 33–41
    password, 159
    patched user profiles report, 199
    pointer, 19
    profiles and portraits, 34–35
    random profile designations, 34
    reason for, 33
    secret passwords, 37–39
    what it provides, 33
    work groups, 35–37, 156–157
user state programs, 29

V

validation
    application authority validation, 78
    authority validation procedure, 52–53, 161
    BIND, 58–59
    password validation program, 24, 142–143, 231
    program validation values, 117–126
    security level 50
Vertical Licensed Internal Code (VLIC), 98
viruses, 14–15
    damage example, 3–6
    gift horses, 213–221
    probability of having, 6–7
    technical skills needed, 6
    viral signatures, 214
    what it is, 15
VLIC (Vertical Licensed Internal code), 98
VMC translator, 91–93, 97, 111
VT100, 61

W

work groups, 35–37
    create group profiles, 157–158
    identification of, 156–157
workstations, 65–66
    unattended, 25–27
Work with Objects by Owner (WRKOBJDWN), 47
Work with System Values (WRKSYSVAL), 139–140, 191
worms, 14
    SEPTWorm, 5–6
    what it is, 15

X

X.25 networks, 58